Michał P. Garapich

London's Polish Borders

Transnationalizing Class and Ethnicity
among Polish Migrants in London

Michał P. Garapich

LONDON'S POLISH BORDERS

Transnationalizing Class and Ethnicity among Polish Migrants in London

ibidem-Verlag
Stuttgart

Bibliographic information published by the Deutsche Nationalbibliothek
Die Deutsche Nationalbibliothek lists this publication in the Deutsche Nationalbibliografie;
detailed bibliographic data are available in the Internet at http://dnb.d-nb.de.

Bibliografische Information der Deutschen Nationalbibliothek
Die Deutsche Nationalbibliothek verzeichnet diese Publikation in der Deutschen
Nationalbibliografie; detaillierte bibliografische Daten sind im Internet über http://dnb.d-nb.de
abrufbar.

Cover design: Katarzyna Depta-Garapich

ISBN-13: 978-3-8382-0877-0

© *ibidem*-Verlag / *ibidem* Press
Stuttgart, Germany 2016

Printed in the United States of America

To Dorota and Marek — my parents

Table of Contents

Acknowledgements

This book would not have been possible without the financial support of various funding bodies and institutions. Specifically, I would like to thank the Economic and Social Research Council for funding one of the studies this book is based on (RES-000-22-1294). I wish to thank the Grabowski Memorial Fund, Polish Aid Foundation Trust, and Mr Erazm Pruszyński for their assistance in completing the task of writing this book. I am also very grateful for the support generously provided by the Southlands Methodists Trust at University of Roehampton. I want to thank my colleagues at the Department of Social Sciences at University of Roehampton who supported me throughout these years, in particular Dr Stephen Driver, Dr Michele Lamb, and Prof. Steven Groarke. Prof. John Eade from the same department has been far more than a colleague throughout these years, and his friendship was crucial for my own development. Thank you, John.

The assistance, advice, and patience from the *ibidem-Verlag* editors, Max Jakob Horstmann and Valerie Lange also deserve my gratitude.

I wish to also thank my wife, Katarzyna Depta-Garapich, who endured with great resolve and understanding the sometimes annoying fact of having an anthropologist as a husband.

Last but not the least, I want to thank the hundreds of migrants I spoke to for their time and patience.

Dr Michał P. Garapich

Preface

In the early morning of the 6th of June 2003, a long queue began to form in front of the Polish Embassy on Great Portland Street in central London. In the course of the day, this queue grew larger and larger forcing people to wait up to three hours to be let into the building. In total, that day and the following 7th of June, nearly 7,000 Polish citizens turned up. These people, from various generations and cohorts of Poles who made London their home, came to central London to decide on one of the most important historical turning points their country was about to make. They were casting their votes in a referendum over the accession of Poland into the European Union (EU). In many ways, the result of that small-scale ballot among Poles living in London at that time was predictable—around 90% voted 'yes'. In Poland, over 77% of the voters endorsed entry into the EU.

The clear enthusiasm, which the London-based Poles showed over the future of Poland in Europe, was a sign of things to come. The then Labour government's decision—made in early 2003—to open the British labour market to Polish nationals was well known and widely discussed among Poles—both in Poland and in their various communities abroad. In fact, during the propaganda war before the referendum, the right to freedom of movement and employment was presented by the Polish EU-enthusiasts as the biggest benefit for Polish citizens from joining the EU. For Poles living in London, many of whom were working in breach of the immigration law, overstaying their visas or simply working in grey economy, it was a matter of deciding over their future as residents of the UK, it was an affirmation of their right to live, work, and settle in the UK. For many of these migrants, turning out to cast a vote was a political act that would enable them to regularise their immigration status. If anyone is looking for an example of how individuals in their modest way shape the grand schemes of international politics, one needs to look no further.

Many Poles casting the vote that day 'voted themselves in' thereby legitimising flows and subsequent settlement into the UK.

As we now know, the results of the referendum came to have profound consequences for Europe, but especially for Britain, triggering a massive migration wave and changing its demographics, neighbourhoods, and debates about immigration, society, the economy, and Britain's place in Europe. It has prepared the ground for what the British press has called the biggest migration wave since the arrival of the French Huguenots in the late 17th century. Almost exactly a decade later, the British national census showed that the number of Poles has increased tenfold ever since—from a little above 50,000 to over half a million. However, the sensationalist headlines, so cherished by the media, mask some deeper layers of meanings and unanswered questions. Who are we exactly talking about? Who are these Poles who, among other Eastern and Central Europeans, populate London and other towns and villages of the UK and, despite the economic downturn and recession of the last couple of years defy simplistic economic formulas, do not go back to Poland but remain in Britain? Were these migrations so new or were they simply another chapter in a long history of transnational connections woven between Poland and the UK for decades? And how do these people think, act, and negotiate their place, belonging, and life in an increasingly interconnected, interdependent world? How do they articulate their migration experience, their interaction with the British population, and what, in general, do they make of their new home? It is clear that these questions are ultimately questions about the future of Britain itself, since these people will become or already are friends, workmates, relatives, clients, costumers, neighbours, and passers-by in numerous British cities.

This book seeks to answer some of these questions from a classical anthropological perspective by looking from a bottom-up perspective of the everyday meaning-making of various social actors and look at what people do, why they do it, how they interpret the social world around them, and how their actions are embedded in the complex interplay between culture, economy, power, dominant narratives of the states, and ultimately, citizenship in an increasingly fluid, interconnected world. As social anthropologist (as Clifford Geertz famously observed), I see human beings as constructing and being constructed by webs of meanings, actions, and structures they have spun themselves and that relationship constituting social life. In that way, the 7,000 people who turned out to vote that June morning in 2003 in London could be regarded as a symbolic *avant-garde* of today's migrant population, a taste of things to come, and confirmation of the individual's power. They established the foundations for the massive influx of Polish migrants into Britain after Poland joined the EU in 2004. These foundations were not just created by the economic environment, labour market gaps, or migratory networks so crucial in assisting further flows — they were also shaped by a particular migration culture into which Poles are socialised, a specific domain of notions, symbols, and narratives that refer to human mobility in Polish society. In a *grande duree* perspective, then, how Poles act, make meaning of, and position themselves in the new Europe, and especially in such a global city as London, rest to a large extent on their own cultural resources and traditions, which were marked by huge past migratory movements, becoming an essential part of their grand dominant narratives, as well as local stories of resilience, survival, and resistance in the face of historic turmoil, economic calamities, wars, or shifting geographies of power in the post-Cold War world.

The main core of this book's argument is that it is impossible to understand Polish migration to the UK and, in particular, London, without digging deeper into these meaning-making practices, which are also crucial for our understanding of particular features of London's current multicultural politics. This isn't simply to restate the banal that in order to understand the present we need to look at the past, but also how past is being reproduced, selectively revived, and embedded in social practice. To illustrate this, let's look at another small ethnographic detail in the life of

London's Poles: four years after that summer in 2003, many of those Poles who were queuing to cast their votes in the above-mentioned referendum were present at a special reception for 'the Polish community' hosted by the Mayor of London, Ken Livingstone. The reception was viewed widely as an attempt by the Mayor to secure votes from that ethnic group, for his reelection the year after. During the reception, a second-generation Polish community leader made a speech in which he highlighted the continuity of Polish presence in the UK dating from the Second World War. He spoke about the role of Polish pilots in the Battle for Britain and linked this to the role of Poles in contemporary multicultural Britain. As he said, Poles were a 'model for other ethnic minorities' in terms of integration and successful peaceful cohabitation.

At face value, there is nothing special about the speech; in general, a theme probably similar to other statements by ethnic leaders of other minorities of London. But the speech can be also read as an attempt to boost one's group standing in front of political power sources by alluding to other 'ethnic minorities', which for some reason are constructed as more problematic for the establishment. The symbol of the pilot, the defender, is very important here, as it falls against the backdrop of London still in a trauma after the 2005 terrorist attacks and the ongoing debates over fundamentalist Islam and perceived lack of integration some British Muslims demonstrate. Yet, on the other hand, the most fascinating thing was that this person was creating a uniform and homogeneous notion of a Polish 'community' that is, in fact, composed of very diverse groups, networks, and individuals. Between these two democratic rituals—voting for EU enlargement in 2003 by a vast number of, among others, undocumented migrant workers and for the Mayor of London in 2008 as EU citizens—lies a fascinating story of the interaction between cultural traditions, narratives, and agents operating in a transnational social field where crucial aspects of social identities, such as class and ethnicity, are being reconstructed in 21st-century London. Polish migrants, as

EU citizens, have the right to vote in local elections, and their rapid rise from a marginal, secondary, largely undocumented, illegal labour force into a group of potential political actors shaping London politics is a reminder of how quickly things change institutionally in response to both political events as well as human agency. The 2011 census shows that there are almost 600,000 Poles in England and Wales, with over 100,000 registered to vote in London alone. Things do change fast in today's Europe.

These experiences are metaphorically captured by the notion of London's Polish borders which are, in fact, social and cultural boundaries stretching to other localities, states, and regions. The human experience that connects rural families in north-east Poland, the mountaineers of the Tatras, the middle-class youth of Krakow with affluent migrants cashing in on London's property boom, or Polish war veterans is a complex and contingent set of social relations that are transnational in nature and dynamic in their development. I do not know what the long-term outcomes of these migrations will be in 10 or 20 years' time. By bringing together data from research carried out between 2003 and 2014, I seek to explain human behaviour, actions, and meaning-making practices involved in transnational mobility across the EU. By bringing human experience to the forefront, I will challenge some common misconceptions about such prominent notions as social class, ethnicity, nation, and community. Migrating Poles do offer quite a few surprises for scholars, and this book will share them.

Chapter 1

Setting the conceptual scene: migrations, nation-states, and anthropology of class and ethnicity

More than a decade ago, in 2004, Poland and seven other Central and East European former Communist bloc countries joined the EU, symbolically ending the period of division brought to the continent by the Cold War. Among numerous consequences of this great historical moment has been the unprecedented increase in migration flows between the Eastern and Central Europe and the West. Heldback by the emigration- and immigration-restrictive regimes for over half a century, societies of the eastern part of Europe seemed to indulge in this newly gained freedom — freedom to move and settle anywhere in the Union. Polish nationals make up the vast majority of these flows, and Britain became the main destination country — the 2011 Census confirming that Polish-born make up the second largest minority in the UK.[1]

Freedom of movement was something for which Polish politicians fought for during pre-accession negotiations and which the general Polish public regarded as the main benefit in joining the EU. The implementation of one of the EU's fundamental freedoms and rights — the right to move, work, and settle in any of the Member States — was seen as the ultimate unification of the once divided continent. But the principle of solidarity clashed with national egoism and the continental division reemerged in the form of labour market access restrictions for citizens of the new accession states. Although the EU encouraged the Member States to open their labour markets without any limits to newcomers, in

---

[1]   Office for National Statistics. Polish in the UK. Migration Statistics Quartelry Report, ONS, Newport, August 2011.

2004 only Britain, Ireland, and Sweden agreed to do so. Other countries were more concerned about the rapid and massive influx of migrant workers and its impact on their welfare states and economies — highlighting the uneasy position of the nation-states in the face of globalisation and increased freedom of movement. The 'Polish plumber' became a key symbolic figure during the French referendum on the European constitution in 2004, which involved anxious deliberations about globalisation and the extent to which national economic and social structures should change, adapt, and negotiate the dominant forces of modernity. Although the restrictions were temporary and by 2011 all Member States had lifted barriers to the labour market, the initial constraints had important consequences for migration processes as the refusal of most Member States to allow free entry to these new EU citizens diverted migration flows to the few states which did not impose any limits. As scholars today agree, this state of affairs was largely responsible for the waves of migrants from accession states, mainly Poland,[2] heading towards the UK. And by all means, this influx was substantial. In 2011, the Office of National Statistics put the figure of Polish nationals residing in England and Wales at 570,000,[3] an almost tenfold increase from the last census in the UK in 2001 which put the figure of Polish born at 60,000. If we combine seasonal and temporary migrants, who moved between Poland and Britain between 2004 and 2012, some estimates put the numbers of Poles working at some point in the UK at well over a million. Although there is some indication that the flow has slowed down during the economic downturn,[4] in 2014, it rose again. In result, it is widely agreed that EU enlargement created

---

[2]   See, for instance: C. Dustmann. 2005. Immigrants in the British labour market. *Fiscal Studies* 26:423–470; Gilpin N., et al. 2006. The impact of free movement of workers from Central and Eastern Europe on the UK labour market. London: Department of Work and Pensions Working Paper No. 29; S. Drinkwater, J. Eade, M. Garapich. 2009. Poles Apart? EU Enlargement and the Labour Market Outcomes of Immigrants in the UK. *International Migration* 47(1):161–190.

[3]   Office for National Statistics. Polish in the UK. Migration Statistics Quarterly Report, ONS, Newport, August 2011.

[4]   Home Office. 2010. *Control of Immigration: Quarterly Statistical Summary.*

the biggest demographic change in Europe since the devastation and flux at the end of the Second World War,[5] and Britain has been at the centre of that movement.[6] Within few years, this movement created one of the largest minorities in the UK–Polish nationals. The impact on the economy, welfare, and society in general has been positive, but it is clear that the pace of these flows, lead some sections of British society to rethink the whole idea of membership in the EU. It can be said that, indirectly and partially, the massive movement from Poland to the UK resulted in the rise of anti-immigrant parties like the United Kingdom Independence Party and in increased pressure on British political class to call for an in–out EU referendum. After the conservative win in 2015 parliamentary elections, David Cameron's majority conservative government voted for a referendum on EU membership as early as in 2016. Although migration from Poland was not the sole reason, it is clear that it contributed to this huge historical decision.

This book is about people behind this process.

Although many features of this recent influx are similar to previous chapters in Britain's long history of migration, there are striking differences. First, the favourable legal status warrants new forms of mobility: thus, many are circular, short-term migrants taking advantage of the freedom of movement within the EU, cheap travel, and new communication opportunities. They are able to come and go between Poland and Britain, and many have become long-distance commuters rather than typical migrants with the intention of staying for a long time. These storks—as I call them—are a fascinating example of a successful combination of both particular migration culture that developed in Poland throughout generations of mobility and the use of modern means of communication, transport, and networks creation. Secondly,

---

[5]   A. Favell. 2008. The New Face of East-West Migration in Europe. *Journal of Ethnic and Migration Studies* 34(5):701.

[6]   P. Kaczmarczyk, M. Okólski. 2008. Demographic and labour market impacts of migration on Poland. *Oxford Review of Economic Policy* 24(3):600.

they are more widely dispersed across the country. Although in this book I will focus on London, the highest number of Polish migrants is found in East Anglia, and London accounts for only around 20% of post-accession flows. But the focus on numbers of migrants involved seems to miss the role played by individual actors in developing and constructing various transnational fields between two societies and how they find their way through the two social and cultural settings they chose to operate in. In other words, the policy-oriented overemphasis on numbers omits the complex process of migrants' agency shaped by their understandings of the changing world around them— in terms of making sense of their own lives and migration trajectory as well as understanding wider socio-economic constraints—modernity, capitalist labour market, ethnic pluralism, and globalisation.

This book seeks to identify and unpack the complex interplay between Polish migrants' social and cultural resources, which they employ to pursue their individual and family goals— meaning-making, symbols, narratives, myth creation, and agency—and different nation-state ideologies, hegemonies of control, structures, and cultures of representation—both in the UK as well in Poland. Drawing on structuration theory[7] and also on an actor-centred anthropological analysis proposed by Anthony P. Cohen,[8] I argue that people are far from being passive actors in the social world and the sum of individual actions and culturally meaningful practices has an impact on the structures around them. This book is a detailed account about how this happens on the ground and how transnational social fields merge two societies together and in what ways social class and ethnic boundaries emerging between Poland and London are in this new context reformulated, negotiated, and contested.

---

[7]   A. Giddens. 1986. *Constitution of Society. Outline of the Theory of Structuration.* California: University of California Press.

[8]   A.P. Cohen. 1994. *Self-Consciousness. An Alternative Anthropology of Identity.* London: Routledge.

My theoretical position followed here is based on the classical notion of an anthropological enquiry as a search for the meaning of people's actions, practices, discursive performances, and agency. As Nicholas notes, anthropology seeks to find 'order in the chaos of many people, doing many things with many meanings',[9] and so the analysis that follows will go beyond mere numbers and economic forces. This approach views collective categories, such as culture, society, ethnicity, group, symbols, and discourse, as part of the process of socially constructing reality,[10] in which individuals are active and conscious creators rather than passive receivers and reproducers of culture, which means culture, and here I focus on particular migration culture, is in constant shift, change, and adaptation. Here, meaning-making refers to the ways in which people make sense of the world simultaneously being shaped by constraining cultural meanings and reproducing them by action, performance, and negotiation. As Anthony P. Cohen points out:

> Society may well be greater than the sum of its parts, the excess including the means by which to compel the actions of its members. But as an intelligible entity, it cannot be conceptualised apart from individuals who compose it, alone and in their relationships. So far as they are concerned, it is what they perceive it to be, and their actions are motivated by their perceptions of it. Theories of society which ignore these perceptions would therefore seem to be partial at best, vacuous at worst.[11]

Keeping with Clifford Geertz's famous definition of culture as a 'web of meanings' spun by humans themselves,[12] the purpose of this book is to explore and explain individuals' perceptions, attitudes, and meaning-making practices, which are contingent on their own social and cultural backgrounds, conceptualisation of

9   R. Nicholas. 1966. Segmentary factional political systems. [in]: M. Swartz, V. Turner, A. Tuden (ed.) *Political Anthropology*. Chicago: Aldine.

10   P. Berger, T. Luckman. 1967. *The Social Construction of Reality. A Treatise in the Sociology of Knowledge*. Harmondsworth: Penguin Books.

11   A.P. Cohen. 1994. *Self-Consciousness. An Alternative Anthropology of Identity*. London: Routledge. p. 166.

12   C. Geertz. 1973. *The Interpretation of Culture*. New York: Basic Books. Chapter 1. p. 5.

history and modernity, as well as the realities of 21st-century London. Thus, writing about Polish migrants in London needs to incorporate both what people bring with them and what local conditions allow for certain meanings, norms, actions to emerge, and be socially significant in a new setting. In other words, migrants arrive equipped with particular cultural resources constructed collectively but which ones will prove to be useful and will be used depends on a multiple factors in the country of destination. The combination of both sets of conditions results in unique types of social and cultural outcomes.

Globalisation, transnationalism, and nation-states

The central question of modernisation theory has focused on the ways in which global flows of not only people but also capital, goods, information, and images escaped nation-state controls. The collapse of the Iron Curtain in Europe and socialist regimes appeared to herald the victory of Western capitalism, leading some to hail the 'end of history'[13] and welcome the onset of a borderless world. Globalisation was used as a term by this 'hyperglobalist' interpretation to describe this process of postnationalism.[14]

Yet, it is also evident to many commentators that national boundaries and state institutions still remained key actors in the global migration process. Saskia Sassen,[15] for example, pointed out that globalisation developed through opaque dealings that both weaken and strengthen the national idea. In this complex interaction, financial markets played a crucial role through their promotion of global economic flows in both the 'global cities' where they were located and the networks that linked them. The concentration of economic resources and power in particular cities (London, New York, Tokyo, etc.) was accompanied by the exploitation of

---

[13]   F. Fukuyama. 1992. *The End of History and the Last Man*. London: Penguin.
[14]   Y. Soysal. 1994. *The Limits of Citizenship*. Chicago: University of Chicago Press.
[15]   D. Held, A. McGrew, D. Goldblatt, J. Perraton. 1999. *Global Transformations*. Stanford: Stanford University Press.

those at the lower end of the labour market, turning centres of economic power into central nodes of transnational flows — whether these will be globetrotting highly paid bankers, traders, and executives or cleaners, domestic workers, and low-paid clerks who most often are migrants themselves.

But as critics of 'hyperglobalism' pointed out, it was far too soon to celebrate the 'end of history' and the demise of the nation-state. The idea of 'post-nationalism' has been widely criticised both by political scientists[16] and anthropologists,[17] specialising in the field of nationalism, for lacking depth and historical understanding. Anthony Smith maintains that post-national approaches present *'a lack of historical depth to so many of the analyses under this broad heading, in a field that demands such depth'*.[18] The overall salience and domination of identity politics and strategic essentialism in current national and international politics is potent evidence that we are far from the demise of the nation-state and its ability to set the conceptual and institutional agenda of the modern world.

Despite the sometimes romantic celebration of a modern, fluid, mobile, cosmopolitan, and plural world, where apparently people are free to move and reinvent themselves, the reality is that the ability to move freely is still strongly restricted and structured reflecting the global relations of power and dominance — the ongoing migration crisis on the Mediterranean being one of the many tragic outcomes of that inequality. States continue to control global flows through immigration controls, access to welfare state, increasingly restrictive asylum policies, and capital relocation. These policies are not static, however, and often change due to political conditions and the accumulated actions of thousands of

---

[16]   R. Hansen. 2009. The poverty of postnationalism: citizenship, immigration, and the new Europe. *Theory and Society* 38:1–24.

[17]   L. Basch, N. Glick Schiller, C.S. Blanc. 1994. *Nations Unbound: Transnational Projects, Postcolonial Predicaments, and Deterritorialized Nation-States*. Langhorne: Gordon and Breach.

[18]   A. Smith. 1998. *Nationalism and Modernism. A Critical Survey of Recent Theories of Nations and Nationalism*. London: Routledge, p. 218.

migrants. This is where the limits of the state and the structures of dominance become most evident and the power of thousands of individual households' and migrants' decisions may shape these very structures.

Although quite a few theoretical attempts to reinsert the power of the individual have been made, there is still a significant gap in actual detailed ethnographic accounts of how this happens. As an example, developed further in next chapter, I invite the reader to look at the decades before the EU enlargement in 2004 when Poles had a highly restricted access to British labour market. The structural conditions, it seems, were highly unfavourable for migrations, both in terms of access and patterns of settlement, as well as structures of opportunities. However, individuals, groups, and networks were far from accepting this status quo, subordinating to institutional regimes of entry control — on the contrary, they took action in order to better themselves and fulfil their culturally specific aspirations despite structural exclusions put in place by British immigration and labour restrictions. As we shall see in this book, a vast number of migrants from Poland prior to the EU enlargement came as 'visitors', 'tourists', and 'visiting relatives' violating immigration restrictions *en masse* — with previous cohorts, extending up to the Second World War refugees, travel agents, ethnic press, and British employers, complicit in these activities. As I will show, this movement has directly led to opening up the UK labour market, hence giving individual migrants a rare victory over state control. So global flows were shaped by power structures and social inequalities specific to particular nations, even though these structures and inequalities were, in turn, influenced by these flows — whether clandestine or not. What is vital, however, as we will continuously witness in the accounts presented in this book, is that individuals' ability to resist and by-pass these regulations have strongly contributed to the development of migration networks, which facilitated chain migration processes and better employment opportunities, which in turn led to the massive post-2004 inflows. In other words, opening of the labour market in the UK was not just a top-down process instigated by political process, labour shortages, or decisions of political actors in offices in Brussels, London, or Warsaw. The door was pushed open as well, by hundreds of thousands of clandestine or semi-clandestine migrants continuously testing the strength of structural boundaries since the early 1990s.

The interaction between global flows, national legal structures, and the sum of individual actions, which often resist, contest, and by-pass legal barriers can be most usefully understood as a transnational process underpinning all migration movements across the world. People's ability to move where they like is still influenced by national border controls and internal institutions, but their movement, whether officially sanctioned or not, creates (real or imagined) spaces across and between national borders, further stimulating flows of peoples, ideas, and goods. These spaces can be analysed by employing the social field perspective and the distinction made by Glick Schiller and Levitt between national and transnational social fields demonstrating how we can conceptualise and render empirically useful the role of state borders without falling into methodological nationalism—an illusionary perspective that society and social process are somewhat contained within the administrative borders of the nation-state. According to them, we should see a social field

> ...as a set of multiple interlocking networks of social relationships through which ideas, practices, and resources are unequally exchanged, organized, and transformed. Social fields are multidimensional, encompassing structured interactions of differing forms, depth, and breadth that are differentiated in social theory by the terms organization, institution, and social movement. National boundaries are not necessarily contiguous with the boundaries of social fields. National social fields are those that stay within national boundaries while transnational social fields connect actors through direct and indirect relations across borders. Neither domain is privileged in our analysis. Ascertaining the relative importance of nationally restricted and transnational social fields should be a question of empirical analysis.[19]

---

[19]   P. Levitt, N. Glick Schiller. 2004. Conceptualizing simultaneity: a transnational social field perspective on society. *International Migration Review* 38(3):1009.

The problem about how to empirically delineate both fields is a methodological one. From the perspective of interpretative anthropological enquiry, it is through peoples' actions and meaning-making practices that borders and boundaries are being recreated and remade. When we look more closely at how national discourses, ascribed identities, are constructed and human actions navigate through these, we can see that transnational social fields are a fundamental characteristic of how nation-states are produced, sustained, and remade to adapt to a new environment. In other words, transnational movements and nationalism or nation-state discourses are mutually dependent and connected – at the same time offering people comfortable space for individual manoeuvre and contestation. As Michael Peter Smith notes, the dynamic functional relationship between transnational processes and nationalism is still one that needs to be better explained[20] as transnationalism is inherently embedded into the conceptual framework of the nation-states – with its ideologies, symbols, legal structures, and the fundamental role played by borders – real, hard, or those produced through symbols, myths, rituals, and meaning-making practices.

This book, through looking at the case of Polish migration in the last decade, analyses how nation-states are made and remade transnationally through evolving, contradictory development of particular migration culture. Individual social actors may contest and negotiate these fields through their daily practices, and this has some very specific consequences for nation-building in Poland and the UK and, in a way, makes this process of nation-building happen, at the same time shaping British debates and problems around diversity, multiculturalism, and new forms of racism, and recently about the UK presence in the European project. However, at the very same time, individual actors are able to skilfully manoeuvre through diverse cultural and social environments in order to occupy privileged positions in each society, resisting social and economic constraints in both. This is done

---

[20]   M.P. Smith. 2001. *Transnational Urbanism*. Oxford: Blackwell, p. 3.

through a renegotiation of individuals' perceptions of class and ethnicity, and one of the arguments of this book is that we cannot fully grasp one without the other. Social class and ethnicity are interwoven into the fabric of modern global cities, and both represent dimensions of social relations that characterise modern polyethnic diverse societies.

Scholars note that transnational social fields can be understood not only spatially but also over time. Moreover, if we link the definition proposed by Glick Schiller and Levitt to Bourdieu's understandings of social field as a space of power struggle and competition for resources, we can understand how different hegemonic social constructs are reformulated and used within these fields. People operate across transnational fields, but they influence and are influenced by specific national histories, cultures, and social groups. Gupta and Ferguson see the ways in which people make sense of movement and belonging as a political process *par excellence*:

> The idea that space is made meaningful is, of course, a familiar one to anthropologists .... The more urgent task would seem to be to politicize this uncontestable observation. With meaning-making understood as practice, how are spatial meanings established? Who has the power to make places of spaces? Who contests this? What is at stake?[21]

It is not a coincidence that social anthropologists were able to make transnationalism one of the most frequently used concepts in contemporary migration studies.[22] Their ethnographic fieldwork focuses on people's self-definitions, perceptions, and meaning-creations in making sense of the world and they have a keen eye for the dynamics and relations between what people say and what they do in everyday life. A particular target for those working on transnationalism has been what they call 'methodological nationalism' — an analytical perspective which takes the nation-

---

[21]   A. Gupta, J. Ferguson. 1997. Culture, power, place. Ethnography at the end of an era. [in]: A. Gupta, J. Ferguson (eds.) *Culture, Power, Place, Explorations in Critical Anthropology.* Durham: Duke Press, p. 40.
[22]   S. Vertovec. *Transnationalism.* 2009. London: Taylor & Francis.

state as the natural and undisputable framework for conceptualising migration in social sciences.[23] This perspective reproduces a fictional perception of a neat world divided into 'states', 'cultures', and 'societies', omitting the crucial aspect of relationships between these entities, the whole sphere of border-crossing, hybridity, multiple identities, and less-than clear categories that social actors use in their everyday life.

Methodological nationalism is indisputably an outcome of how societies, cultures, and territories were conceptually contained in a post-Wesphalian political order. It belongs to the domain of a philosophical normative discourse that Western philosophy has taken for granted and, as Isaiah Berlin notes, did not give much intellectual attention until very late.[24] Transnationalism highlights not only the limitations of focusing only on what is happening within nation-state boundaries, artificially 'cutting off' analytically every aspect of the social life crossing the administrative boundary. Moreover, those contributing to the study of transnationalism have revealed the limitations of concentrating just on economic flows across national borders. In an increasingly interconnected world, the global links and flows of capital, ideas, and images are coupled and replicated by the very real and intimate physical movements of people, groups, and families. This shift of scope to the social actor and away from economic and social structures not only reminded scholars that the world has always been transnationally connected but also posed a question about social sciences' previous blindness — why have we only recently appreciated this history? Why have we only in recent decades recognised that the world has always been transnationally connected and constructed?

Here again, we find validation for specific anthropological enquiry as a close empirical examination of how individual actors

---

[23] N. Glick Schiller, A. Wimmer. 2003. Methodological nationalism, the social science and the study of migration: an essay in historical epistemology. *International Migration Review* 37:576–610.

[24] I. Berlin. 1997. *Against the Current. Essays in the History of Ideas.* Pimlico: Random House, p. 337.

construct class and ethnic identity using their own culturally spe-cific understanding of the changes they go through and social and economic forces they are faced with. It helps us to see the dynamic interaction between the dominant discourses and ideologies pro-duced, orchestrated, and ritualised by the nation-state and how people respond to these in pursuit of their goals. In other words, meaning-making takes place in specific contexts and uses different tools available to different individuals. Anthropologically, these tools are empirically available for analysis — they are words, texts, deeds, interviews, actions, symbols, rituals, norms, and values of a given group of people, and as a 'web of meaning', they inform, legitimise, validate, and make sense of people's actions. As Geertz argues, in order to act, people need to interpret the world around them and grasping these interpretations brings us closer to under-standing why people do things they do.

Transnationalism from below, ways of being, and belonging

Remaining faithful to Malinowski's understanding of social an-thropology as 'seeing the world through the eyes of the native', the transnational perspective foregrounds individual human agency and its ability to contest the structural constraints imposed by the modern nation-state, mobility-restricting regimes, capitalist order, and global power relations. In a situation where, due to human mobility, the volume of new interactions is rapidly in-creasing, we need to look at the ways in which people develop new meanings and innovative strategies for 'playing out' social class and ethnicity. As Smith points out in his study of 'transna-tionalism from below', research has to explore people's experience of crossing *political and cultural borders* and capture *the emergent character of transnational social practices* through people's narratives as they directly engage with the dominant structures of power, discourses, and collective constraints.[25]

It is theoretically beneficial to link Smith's exploration of transnational experience with Glick Schiller's distinction between 'ways of being' and 'ways of belonging'. 'Ways of being' refer to social relations and practices, whereas 'ways of belonging' involve identity categories generated by the 'institutions, organisations, and experiences', which operate within social fields and people's conscious connections with a particular group. Individuals *'can be embedded in a social field but not identify with any label or cultural politics associated with that field. They have the potential to act or identify at a particular time because they live within the social field but not all choose to do so'*.[26] Social actors can be engaged in transnational ways of *being* but not *belonging* or the other way round. Additionally, people who engage in transnational social relations and explicitly recognise this, exhibit both transnational ways of being and belonging. As we shall see later in this book, for Polish migrants in London, the concept of social class and ethnicity and their perception of both stratification and ethnicity is closely associated with the extent to which they see their migration as a *way of being* or *belonging*. At the same time, from a different anthropological perspective, differences between two ways of conceptualising these processes refer to inescapable tensions in social life born out of discrepancies between the normative ordering and actual life praxis. People prescribe some things but follow others and the tension between the 'ought' and the 'is' remains one of the cornerstones of myth constructions, representations, and cultural production.[27] Ethnographic method offers here a way forward — decoding the various discourses utilised by Polish migrants whilst directly observing them during their social interactions generates

---

[25] M.P. Smith. 2001. *Transnational Urbanism*. Oxford: Blackwell, p. 138.

[26] N. Glick Schiller, A. Wimmer. 2003. Methodological nationalism, the social science and the study of migration: an essay in historical epistemology. *International Migration Review* 37:606.

[27] C. Lévi-Strauss. 1963. The structural study of myth. [in]: C. Jacobson, B.G. Schoepf (trans.) *Structural Anthropology*. London: Basic Books Inc., p. 229.

directly verifiable data on what it means in practice to *belong* or *be* in a transnational social field.

There is one crucial point to be made here. The non-economic aspects of migration are sometimes seen in public discourse as a process involving people moving from one *culture* to another *culture*, and any problems that migration generates are regarded as cultural/ethnic ones. In her important article, Stolcke criticises this 'culturalisation of migration', which presents people as containers for specific cultural traits, naturalising and biologising culture, thus creating a new form of racism, shaped and entrenched by the anti-immigration backlash across contemporary Europe.[28] This culturalist version of methodological nationalism obscures the fact that modern transmigrants come from various social class, educational, and economic backgrounds. Putting them into one 'ethnic' or 'cultural' box not only ignores the ways in which individuals use various strategies and cultural resources to resist them, but it also creates distinct units and boundaries, which reify groups and their cultural content.

There are numerous critiques of that theoretical fallacy, but it is through detailed ethnography of peoples' actions and meanings they construct that reveals how individual strategies contest or use to their own advantage for this reification of ethnicity, culture, class, or gender. The logical conclusion is that there is a clear need to place the discourse of social class at the centre of ethnic and nationalism studies. Indeed, there is ample evidence that the overemphasis on ethnicity and culture has obscured the relationship with how hierarchies and stratification is produced in the domain of the symbolic. As Bottomley notes:

> One of the complexities of this area of study [immigration] is its inevitable association with political programs and debates, a field of struggle within which the role of the 'disinterested observer' is not readily available and hegemonic forms of knowledge not easily contested. In the US, for example, an emphasis

---

[28]   V. Stolcke. 1995. Talking culture. New boundaries. New rhetorics of exclusion in Europe. *Current Anthropology* 36(1):1–24.

on ethnicity, race and, more recently, gender, has tended to subsume class as an analytical category.[29]

In similar tone, Stolcke argues, the *culturalisation of migration* has been a complex process linked with multicultural policies and a popular understanding of migrants as 'bearers' of specific traits separating them from the majority. It is, nevertheless, crucial to ask why the notion of social class has not been treated as part the process of 'cultural ordering' in popular multicultural discourse. It is almost as though the notion of ethnicity, with its egalitarian overtones (rich or poor, everyone is English, Polish, or something else), has removed questions about social class, inequality, poverty, and social justice. It has certainly done so on the level of hegemonic public, state-centric discourse, but what about the one used on the everyday basis, one that assists social actors in orienting in the social world around them?

Ethnicity: dominant and demotic discourses

An anthropological approach towards Polish migration to Britain involves, therefore, understanding of the interplay between the two sets of discourses and practices. On the one hand, social actors are confronted with a dominant set of values, norms, and behaviours which are frequently assumed — through the production of nationalist ideologies, history textbooks, state-orchestrated rituals, symbols, everyday actions, etc. — to define the essence of a particular group, its representation, and the 'outside' face. On the other hand, they are continually required to adapt these norms and values to the new circumstances in which they find themselves — a demotic process, involving thousands of individual choices, modes of behaviour, strategies of interaction, and meaning-creation. Gerd Baumann in his study of a multicultural Lon-

---

[29]   G. Bottomley. 1998. Anthropologists and the rhizomatic study of migration. *The Australian Journal of Anthropology* 9(1): 31–44. For a similar argument, see also: C. Brettell. 2002. *Anthropology and Migration; Essays on Transnationalism, Ethnicity, and Identity.* London: Routledge.

don suburb—Southall[30]—introduces this duality and the notions of dominant and demotic discourse to analyse how individuals and groups engage with the British model of multiculturalism, which on the policy level equates it with a mosaic of distinct, reified groups, and essentialistically treats cultures and ethnic groups as interchangeable concepts. He traces the various ways and strategies that groups and individuals employ to maintain boundaries or transcend them in order to communicate with other groups, negotiate their position, diffuse conflicts, or form partnerships.

Baumann's approach is rooted in the anthropological tradition of analysing human understanding of norms, values, perceptions, and how this understanding is implemented, applied, and made meaningful in real life. There is an inescapable tension between the two orders, mirroring the naturalistic fallacy—the tension between the world as 'it should be', prescribed in norms and values, and the practice of the 'world as it is'; between the normative order—which in turn is explained in cultural terms—and real-life dynamics. This tension demonstrates the core problem involved in the popular notion of culture as a uniform set of variables rather than as a set of competing discourses, contested narratives, and complex meanings. Polish migrants in London come to Britain with their own dispositions, perceptions, sets of norms, and discursive practices, and to understand what they say and do, we need to examine the symbols, traits, notions, and implicit images that are evoked in Polish culture, whenever migration, boundary, foreignness, strangeness, home country, mobility, and settlement, notions of home and abroad are evoked. It is to this domain of symbolic actions that social actors refer when speaking about class or ethnicity, community or solidarity, animosity, and cooperation, and in a context of migration, it acquires new meanings through legitimising new practices of cultural production. On the other hand, these meanings are not random—they stem from a

---

[30] G. Baumann. 1996. *Contesting Culture*. Cambridge: Cambridge University Press.

long history of socially constructed transnational social fields, which is fundamental for grasping the process of nation-state and national identity formation in Polish society.

Inevitably, this perspective puts ethnicity at the centre of attention. Since Barth's seminal work,[31] anthropological literature has been strongly influenced by an instrumentalistic and rational-goal-oriented perspective, which treats ethnicity as a form of social organisation and a political resource and a dynamically constructed mode of being and belonging.[32] However, if ethnicity is something that people *do* rather than *have*, clearly it can be 'done' in many different ways and with various different strengths depending on the context and type of social interaction. For example, as many studies have demonstrated, ethnicity can be deliberately 'shown off' or, in poly-ethnic situations, individuals may seek to play it down.[33] Yet, as we shall see, the relational construction of ethnicity by Polish migrants is not shaped by solely participating in the British multiethnic environment; it also involves their own understandings and awareness of Polish dominant collective discourses concerning ethnicity, the nation, and the moral obligations which co-ethnics have to one another, and what it means to be Polish abroad.

In other words, when adopting Barth's view of ethnicity as a strategically chosen way of boundary construction and differentiating one group from another, we must be aware that, in plural urban societies, ethnicity may also be a differentiating factor 'within' groups and that looking at what anthropologists may regard as performances of ethnicities, we see social class positioning and power relations within a particular social field of which ethnicity is just one part. As Jenkins emphasises:

---

31   F. Barth. 1969. Introduction. [in]: F. Barth (ed.) *Ethnic Groups and Boundaries. The Social Organization of Culture Difference*. Oslo: Universitetsforlaget.

32   T.H. Eriksen. 1993. *Ethnicity and Nationalism*. London: Pluto Press, p. 34; Comaroff and Comaroff. 1992, p. 54.

33   T.H. Eriksen. 1993. *Ethnicity and Nationalism*. London: Pluto Press, p. 21.

In the practical accomplishment of identity, two mutually interdependent but theoretically distinct social processes are at work: internal definition and external definition. These operate differently in the individual, interactional and institutional orders. .... Identity is always the practical product of the interaction of ongoing processes of internal and external definition. One cannot be understood in isolation from the other.[34]

Following Jenkins' argument, one must also recognise that there may be many levels of 'externality' and from the perspective of an individual actor the boundary may be far from clear. For instance, Poles may define themselves in many different ways towards other Poles and this process of 'othering' towards what an external viewer may see as one ethnic group is crucially important for understanding how ethnicity obscures and hides certain power relations, hierarchies of what is ultimately cultural embodiment of social stratification. Throughout this book, many examples of these strategies are analysed, which people employ in order to reformulate their identities as they both engage with new significant others—other Poles, English, ethnic minorities, British Poles, etc.—and continually relate to Polish dominant discourses about migration, nation-state, the community, how ethnicity translates itself into particular norms and values in the everyday life, and consequently about the moral fundamentals of human relationships. What is crucial here is that these are constructed and used in a transnational context and the notion of the border—the boundary dividing 'Poland' and the 'rest'—is fundamental for understanding the complex development of Polish national identity, history, tensions between localised traditions, and how individuals understand it and, consequently, act upon it. How that boundary is reproduced, and in what contexts, is vital for our understanding of the transnational social field, which links various locations in Poland and the global city of London, and will be the main theme in Chapter 2.

---

[34]   R. Jenkins 1997. *Rethinking Ethnicity. Arguments and Explorations*. London: Sage publications, p. 64.

Class: objective and subjective dimensions across national borders

When we come to social class, the issue is also rather complicated. Class refers both to the objective features of social inequality and to subjective understandings of that inequality. As Diane Reay points out:

> class is more than income ... [it] is a rather complicated mixture of the material, the discursive, psychological predispositions and sociological dispositions being played out in interactions with each others in the social field.[35]

Like the anthropologist Michał Buchowski,[36] who has extensively written about social class in Poland, I contend that the process of class differentiating and structuring is deeply embedded in culture, and it is through this culturally contingent meaning-making that class manifests itself in the social world. The issue of class is further complicated by placing it in a transnational migration context, where again it is obscured by methodological nationalism where societies and economies are seen as separate, distinct, and nonoverlapping (as, for instance, in such widespread distinctions between internal and external markets, internal and international migration). People are moving between different classed discourses and hierarchies, shaped by two different national histories with different relations to modernity, capitalism, and state intervention — but how do they make sense of them and how do they redefine or contest them? And what are the consequences of their transnational position in the process of making sense of the world? Clearly, we need to appreciate both national and transna-

---

[35]   D. Reay. 1998. Rethinking social class: qualitative perspectives on gender and social class. *Sociology* 32:259–275.

[36]   See, for instance: M. Buchowski. 2004. Redefining work in a local community in Poland. Transformation and class, culture and work. [in]: A. Procoli (ed.) *Workers and Narratives of Survival in Europe. The Management of Precariousness at the End of the Twentieth Century.* New York: State University of New York Press; or M. Buchowski, E. Conte, C. Nagengast (eds.). 2001. *Poland Beyond Communism: 'Transition' in Critical Perspective.* Fribourg: Fribourg University Press, pp. 259–279.

tional contexts if we are to understand, for example, the situation of a Polish migrant, who lives in London for one year mainly to build a house in Poland or a Polish family that tries to make sense of the British class stratification as it plays out itself in London neighbourhoods, schools, and workplaces.

In a transnational context, then, the subjective perception of class informed by cultural meanings attached to social hierarchy, the symbols and values attached to work, labour market, capitalism, role of elites, power, and the markers of class becomes even more important for individual social actors trying to make sense of the world around them. In this book, I trace the cultural dimension of social class construction and show how it intersects with ethnicity, with dominant and demotic understandings of what it means to be a Pole abroad and the resulting construction of a Polish community in a specific time and place — 21st-century London with its own problems and debates around multiculturalism, inequality, social justice, race, and diversity. My main argument in this book is that neither class nor ethnicity can be treated as separate, distinct characteristics of social actors operating in a transnational social field. Human reception of specific ideologies — be they related to neo-liberalism, modern capitalist market, the nation-state, nationalism, or multiculturalism — are all closely interconnected in a way that to analytically separate them would remove the role of individual choices and freedom of manoeuvre in a complex modern world. This holistic approach is a logical extension of the central role we assign to individual actors' agency in the transnational social fields.

People migrate from villages, towns of various sizes, and great cities. In this book, the focus will be on migration between Poland and London, one of the world's global cities, and people's reflections on their movement between these different worlds constitutes a kind of social commentary about the differences between the Polish villages, smaller and larger towns from which they came, and London's social, cultural, and economic complexity. Although many had little attachment to London and its localities, they still had to take these places into consideration for jobs, accommodation, welfare services, and leisure. Engagement with place informed their ways of both behaving and belonging and shaped the development and significance of national and transnational fields outlined earlier. Through this commentary social reality is produced and I argue that—true to the anthropological tradition of seeing culture as a web of meanings—Polish migrants shape actively the world around them using the best available resources: freedom of movement, EU citizenship, independence from the state and its political and economic constraints, and powerful possibilities made due to the existence of the transnational social field.

This book is thus about individuals and their networks living in a transnational world where, on the one hand, states (both at the level of institutions and the ideologies that underpin them) constantly seek to control their lives and, on the other hand, individuals manage to use their own perception of transnational social field and their position to their own advantage contesting and questioning the encroachment of the state.

Data for this book and the problem of 'waves' of Poles

This monograph arose from numerous research projects which I carried out in the decade between the years 2003 and 2013 and combined they offer a body of data that are multidimensional and both qualitative and quantitative. The body of qualitative data draws on my doctoral dissertation that dwelled on cultural and social determinants of constructions of Polish ethnic associations in London in the 1990s and the first decade of 21st century.[37] The thesis draws from data collected during a fieldwork phase, when I was a part-time reporter for the media outlet catering to the old

---

[37]   M. Garapich. 2008. *Migracje, społeczeństwo obywatelskie i władza. Uwarunkowania stowarzyszeniowości etnicznej wśród polskich emigrantów w Wielkiej Brytanii.* Doctoral thesis. Kraków, Poland: Instytut Socjologii, Uniwersytet Jagielloński.

Polish diasporic associations, the *Polish Daily*, along with other research projects in the years 2005–2007. Working in the ethnic media during the build up to the large influx of Polish migrants, and observing the debates by older generations of Poles along with their British offspring, offered me valuable data about the dilemmas and conflicts between specific ethnic ideologies, class interests, and values. A number of publications borne out of that study dwell on the tensions and power relations between these groups.[38] Another body of qualitative data came from an Economic and Social Research Council-funded study[39] on Polish migrants in London, carried out between 2005 and 2006 during which I conducted 70 in-depth interviews with Poles both in London and in three locations in Poland along with extensive periods of participant observation. This study specifically looked at constructions of social class and ethnicity among Polish migrants in London. Data for this book come also from several small-scale studies commissioned by local authorities in London who were increasingly intrigued by their booming populations from Poland and other Accession States.[40] These, usually two to three months long ethnographic enquiries were commissioned by the following London Boroughs: Greenwich, Hammersmith and Fulham, Redbridge, and Lewisham. Although focusing on A8 migrants in general, in each of them, at least 50% of respondents were Polish. They involved usually a small survey of 100 Polish nationals,

---

[38] M. Garapich. 2008b. Odyssean refugees, migrants and power: construction of the "Other" within the Polish community in the United Kingdom. [in]: D. Reed-Danahay, C. Brettell (red.) *Citizenship, Political Engagement and Belonging. Immigrants in Europe and the United States.* New Brunswick/New Jersey/London: Rutgers University Press, pp. 124–144; M. Garapich. 2010. Wyjechalem, ot tak i nie jestem emigrantem. Polski dominujacy dyskurs migracyjny i jego kontestacje na przykladzie Wielkiej Brytanii. *Przeglad Polonijny* 1:2010. Je suis parti juste comme ça… Je ne suis pas un émigré… Le discours migratoire dominant dans la culture polonaise et ses contestations. *Ethnologie Française* 40:235–243.

[39] J. Eade, M. Garapich, S. Drinkwater. 2007. *Class and Ethnicity. Polish migrants in London.* ESRC RES-000-22-1294.

[40] Some reports from these studies can be found on University of Roehampton website.

complemented by one or more focus group discussions, in-depth interviews, or interviews with local community leaders. These studies mainly looked at migration strategies, patterns of mobility, and intentions of stay along with labour market outcomes and social networks. They also generated data on Poles' perceptions of race, multiculturalism, and their own attitudes towards Polishness. The picture is also completed by data from a few large-scale surveys that I conducted among Polish migrants, not specifically in London. In 2006, I conducted a survey among a sample of 505 Polish migrants in the UK (commissioned by BBC Newsnight). In September 2007, ahead of elections in Poland, a large sample survey (1100 Poles across England, Scotland, and Ireland) was also carried out. Between 2009 and 2010, I also lead an ethnographic study on homeless Eastern European migrants living in London funded by the Methodist Southlands Trust.[41] Thirty in-depth interviews were carried out, mainly with Polish homeless migrants along with extensive participant observation undertaken over six months. Another strand of my research interests looked at Polish migrants' political participation and various forms of political activism. Ahead of the Mayoral elections in London, three focus groups with Polish residents were carried out in April 2012, exploring their political views and attitudes towards the democratic process in Britain.[42] In 2013, I took part in a study led by Warsaw-based think-tank, Instytut Spraw Publicznych, looking at various forms of social and political activism of the Polish immigrants, in particular looking at political participation and the internal diversity of Polish diaspora in the UK.[43]

---

[41] M. Garapich. 2011. "It's a jungle out there. You need to stick together": anti-institutionalism, alcohol and performed masculinities among Polish homeless men in London. *Liminalities: A Journal of Performance Studies* 7(3): Autumn.

[42] S. Driver, M. Garapich. 2012. 'Everyone for themselves'? Non-national EU citizens from eastern and central Europe and the 2012 London elections. http://www.sociology.ox.ac.uk/documents/epop/papers/EPOP_article_gara pichdriver_SEPTEMBER_07_mg.pdf

[43] M Garapich. 2013. Między apatią a aktywnością — partycypacja polityczna migrantów z Polski w Wielkiej Brytanii. [in]: J. Kucharczyk (ed.) *Nic o nas bez*

All this, however, in itself would not be enough without a more subtle anthropological approach and immersion into the subject of this book. As an immigrant from Poland living in London since 2001, I was constantly a keen observer of issues concerning Polish migrants in both Poland and Britain — in public debates, discussions on websites, the ethnic press, through participation in events, rituals, public meetings, masses, private gatherings, informal discussions, and so on. While quantitative data offer us important information about various aspects of Polish migration to the UK, in order to gain a more rounded view, a more subtle and multidimensional analysis is fundamental. From an ethnographic perspective, when explaining the social and cultural factors behind peoples' attitudes, perception, cultural norms, or behaviour, I consider that data from casual talk and gossip are just as valid as a large survey. I strongly believe that data which are sometimes thrown into the non-scientific bin of just being 'anecdotal' are equally valid. If we look beyond mere descriptions of Polish migrants' life worlds and try to offer an explanation as to why a particular type of behaviour, norm, or discourse is prevalent over another, we must go deeper into the very meanings of individuals' perceptions, attitudes, and actions. In essence, then, the textual data from the interviews will be frequently coupled with the notes from the field or my own descriptions of certain activities of Polish migrants.

There are clear limitations of this approach, mainly in terms of statistical representativeness and interpretative power; however, the richness and variety of sources of data used for this monograph will off-set these. Anthropology seeking to understand the contemporary processes in the transnational social field between London and Poland through careful listening to social actors has — I believe — few important things to say, not just about Polish migrants, whose presence in Britain seems to be a permanent fixture, but also about social conditions in contemporary Britain in

nas. *Partycypacja obywatelska Polaków w Wielkiej Brytanii*. Warszawa: Instytut Spraw Publicznych, pp. 133–162.

particular, London, the global city. This uniqueness of London as the main node of a multitude of transnational social fields reveals a new, vital face of modern urbanism closely linked with nationalism and political debates—something I will dwell upon in Chapter 7. From the perspective of the political meanings produced by some Polish diasporic institutions, this will offer an insight into the role played by London in current debates concerning British multiculturalism, its compatibility with the welfare state, and role of constructions of whiteness in that process.

A typical, commonly found in literature account on the Polish presence in Britain usually refers to 'waves' of Poles arriving at British shores, mainly as the result of the turbulent history of their homeland.[44] This is usually composed of historical accounts of a small band of revolutionaries after the 1830 November Uprising, followed by a small group of workers at the beginning of the 20th century. The establishment of the Polish community is associated with the veterans of the Polish Army who refused for various reasons to return to a communist Poland after the Second World War. It was then that London became the political centre for the Polish diaspora as it was the base of the government-in-exile until 1991 when the pre-war Poland presidential insignia were brought back to Poland and given to the first elected president of post-communist Poland, Lech Wałęsa. The next group described in these accounts consists of Poles, who escaped the communist regime after the imposition of martial law by General Jaruzelski in the winter of 1981. The latest 'wave' consists of Poles who came before and after May 2004.

Although to some extent representing a statistical reality, these classifications are also quite politically constructed and borne out of a very specific state-centred and deterministic version of Polish history, something dwelled upon in the next chapter. In this vision, Poles 'naturally' belong to their territory and only foreign-initiated oppression or internal calamity can remove them

---

[44]   See, for example, P. Stachura. 2000. *The Poles in Britain 1940-2000*. London: Franck Cass; or K. Sword. 1994 . *Community in Flux*. London: SSEES UCL.

from there. Poles in this narrative are presented thus as passive victims of history and the source of evil, and its turbulent history is always 'outside' — the occupiers, foreigners, outsiders, communist. As we shall see in detail in next chapter, these classifications — widely used in speeches, the media, and academic literature — carry an implicit distinct hierarchy and ethnic classification that is present in the Polish nationalist ideology of emigration. For instance, in standard Polish accounts, there is usually no mention of the massive influx of Jews from Polish territories under Russian rule at the end of the 19th century and the beginning of the 20th century or after the anti-semitic actions of the Polish state in 1968. The standard accounts also interestingly omit the massive outflow of Polish Roma, who after an increased wave of racist attacks in the early years of post-socialist Poland, began their journey to Britain at the beginning of the 1990s in search of asylum. In a subtle way, through dominant representations, Polish migration is being 'ethnicised' — that is, not everyone migrating from Poland falls within a category of a Polish migrant. In a mysterious way, the standard narrative then becomes a tool in discursive ethnic cleansing of what was once a richly diverse and multicultural society.

These omissions are vital if we are to better understand the process of construction of an ethnic community in 21st-century London and how multiculturalism operates in that city from within a particular group of white migrants. Despite distinct histories, identities, and often very different outlooks and cultures, the links between various 'waves' are being forged, and Poles from various groups do interact, create alliances, or sometimes act together. In other instances, however, their relationship is marked by deep suspicion, distance, and hostility. The classification that people use in describing different histories of Polish immigration to Britain represent, then, different positions of power and places in local hierarchies, diverse abilities to be able to turn 'spaces into places'. As I move on to describe various groups of Poles in London, it is vital to understand that, although the focus of recent scholarship has been predominantly on the post-accession migrants, in order to understand how ethnicity and social class is constructed and used, we need to look back at the links, connections, and interactions with co-ethnics from previous 'waves' and look at how these connections are represented through dominant narratives of Polish culture and imagined community. The last substantive chapter will look at this process more closely, summarising not only the entire argument of the book but also contextualising these constructions and showing how London's multiculturalism on the ground is understood and used by white migrants and their political supporters, who are often British citizens using the recent wave of migrants to their own advantage.

This monograph starts with an anthropological and historical account of meanings and symbols associated with migrations and the role they played in Polish culture throughout the last century and how these structures of meanings still remain important today. Chapter 3 traces the development of the migration system between Poland and London from early 1990s to EU enlargement, linking various resistance strategies of Polish migrants with the rise of neoliberal ideology of post-communist Poland and also the emergence of the 'migration industry' that played, as it still does, a crucial role in formation and development of the ethnic community in London. Chapter 4 offers analysis of transnational social fields within which people operate and the interconnection of various migration strategies people employ. The following two chapters analyse the transnational social fields in the context of this book's two central concepts—ethnicity and social class—and introduce the core arguments of the monograph, that both dimensions of identity, from the social actors' perspective, have to be treated in tandem, as they offer crucial reference points for conceptualising the modern world and its socio-economic constraints. Offering both a way to deal with inequality and hierarchy, and still hold an essentially egalitarian and anti-institutional outlook, this cultural resource employed by Polish migrants is explained in detail in these two chapters. The last chapter looks, however, at what this all means for Polish migrants in their socio-political context as an ethnic group in multicultural London and how Poles position themselves towards various, new 'others'.

In academic literature, there is always a tension between the theoretical weight of the analysis and its usefulness in explaining specific social phenomena. An exploration into Polish migrants' social and economic experience in terms of two social identities — ethnicity and class — needs to look at the different contexts in which this process takes place; it needs not only to consider the cultural and historical background within which Polish migrants operate, but also London's contemporary social and cultural environment. So, the focus will not only be on migrants' life in London but also on their continuing ties with Poland. In so doing, concepts introduced earlier will be used to explain diverse forms of action, but my primary aim is to bring the migratory experience alive through the interviews and other ethnographic material. This is not an exercise in justifying a particular theoretical framework — rather, I will use the concepts and theoretical debates to help understand what people told me and what I observed. In other words, the guiding light of this monograph is why certain people do and say things they say and what it tells us about the social life of one of the most diverse cities of the world. The factors behind the rapid rise of Poles into one of the largest British ethnic minorities are multifold, complex, and approachable from various perspectives. This one aims at bringing forward not theoretical complex contractions but three-dimensional social actors operating, living, coping across state boundaries, and making some human sense of it.

Chapter 2

The power of leaving — nation and class in Polish migration culture

There is an epistemological interdependence between conceptual tools with which migrations are studied and theorised and the context of the birth, development, and establishment of nation-states.[45] The whole migration discourse is strongly intertwined with hegemonic notions of the nation-state and its power. The very act of leaving the borders of the administrative unit generates a specific set of cultural meanings and symbols, which can easily be intertwined with narratives about imagined community and its boundaries and hegemonic, naturalised, and biological concepts of the nation, belonging, and territory. This book traces numerous versions of these hegemonic constructions created by elites, which frame and explain population movements in a collectivist and nationalist framework, explaining individual cases through a historical narrative of the fate of the nation. At the same time, it traces ways in which migrants themselves resist and contest these dominant discourses. Methodological nationalism is not, of course, simply a problem of academic discourse — it also finds its way into wider societal meanings and discourses resulting in the prevalence of what is called by Stephen Castles 'sedentary bias'[46] or specific 'sedentary metaphysics', as Lisa Malkki names it.[47] This

---

[45] N. Glick Schiller, A. Wimmer. 2003. Methodological nationalism, the social science and the study of migration: an essay in historical epistemology. *International Migration Review* 37:576–610.

[46] S. Castles 2010. Understanding global migration: a social transformation perspective. *Journal of Ethnic and Migration Studies*. 36(10):1565–1586.

[47] L. Malkki. 1997. National geographic: the rooting of peoples and the territorialization of national identity among scholars and refugees. [in]: A. Gupta, J. Ferguson (eds.) *Culture, Power, Place. Explorations in Critical Anthropology.* Durham/London: Duke University Press.

sees migratory behaviour as an abnormality and a social 'problem' to be dealt with, rather than, universal fact of life or modernity-driven aspect of social change. Yet, as part of how societies view themselves, different discourses of mobility are not static or given. They are being constantly shaped and reshaped by everyday meaning-making and social practices by people directly engaged in transnational processes. How individuals relate to these discourses and how new conceptualisations of ethnicity, class, and identity are being formed as a result of manipulation, use, or contestation of these hegemonic discourses, forms the ethnographic core of this monograph.

Transnationalism is an established theoretical framework in migration studies these days, and it is not my aim here to add to its complexity. Rather, I pragmatically use it to interpret individual actions. Transnational processes are understood here as *processes by which immigrants forge and sustain multi-stranded social relations that link together their societies of origin and settlement.*[48] These relations and their social significance may enter into direct competition and confrontations with the way states and hegemonic discourses see them and construct migrations and migrants. Hence, first, it is vital to understand what these dominant discourses constitute in the case of Polish culture and what historical, political, and social factors shaped them. For this reason, an anthropological gaze at Poles in London is, in fact, an exploration of cultural meanings, their actual application in real life, contestations, and tensions, which characterise Polish society in general. The case of Poland is important theoretically because its modern nation-state building process was a transnational and de-territorialised affair from the very beginning. In fact, as Ulrich Beck would argue, this is a feature of all nationalisms — they are by definition transnationally formed in relation to other groups, nations, ethnicities, internal minorities, etc. The complex set of meanings, traits, and

---

[48]   L. Basch, N. Glick Schiller, C.S. Blanc. 1994. *Nations Unbound: Transnational Projects, Postcolonial Predicaments, and Deterritorialized Nation-States.* Langhorne: Gordon and Breach, p. 7.

symbols referring to emigration were not invented and constructed overnight—they follow a long tradition of not only emigration
from one of the largest sources of labour for the Western market,
both in Europe and USA, but a tradition of political transnational
activity that throughout the last 200 years has produced an array
of political refugees, émigrés, activists, soldiers fighting from
abroad, governments-in-exile, political dissidents, poets, romantic
prophets, ideological mercenaries, upper-class nomads, and so on.
This transnational social field, constructed and continually redefined and reproduced throughout the last two centuries, is im-
pressively stable at the symbolic level, showing us how old structures of domination, power, and national narratives are adapting
themselves to the new socio-economic environment of 21st-
century Europe. In order to decipher the contemporary place of
migration from Poland, especially to Britain, both at the level of
individual agency and structural constraints, we need to explore
the cultural milieu, in which migrants are socialised, and the hegemonic ideologies of the nation that Poles are immersed in
through textbooks, rituals, symbols, imagery, arts, and state-
orchestrated historical narratives. As we shall see, these specific
ideologies and discourses are strongly intertwined with the concepts of ethnicity, class, role of the state, national identity, and
resistance that I will trace through this book, in individuals' lives,
their agency, and the dominant discourses of collective and national symbols.

De-territorialised nation-state

Poland has long been a typical emigration country.[49] Its economy
was primarily based on agriculture, which, in turn, was dominated by vast feudal estates untouched by land reform and the industrial revolution until the late 19th century or even, in some areas,
after the Second World War, when the new socialist state acceler-

---

[49]   P. Kaczmarczyk, M. Okólski. 2008. Demographic and labour market impacts of
       migration on Poland. *Oxford Review of Economic Policy* 24(3):601.

ated a massive industrialisation programme—the number of people employed in agriculture or living in rural areas decreased from 70% in the late 1940s to 20% by the late 1990s. This important feature of social structure had a crucial impact on social mobility and social stratification. During the last two centuries for millions of Polish Catholics and Jews, as well as their neighbours such as Lithuanians, Ruthenians, and Ukrainians, emigration has been the main or even the only option avenue for moving up the social ladder, escaping exploitation, starvation, and political oppression. This did not necessarily mean escaping from foreign occupiers as the nationalist narrative pictures it, but crucially also from the mainly Polish land-owning elites and local hierarchies of power. Estimates vary, but historians generally agree that, between the second half of the 19th century and the Second World War, around 10–15 million Poles emigrated, mainly to the USA, France, and Germany.[50] These emigrants worked in mines, farms, factories, and industries from Westphalia to Chicago,[51] joined industrial disputes with employers from Berlin to Cleveland,[52] and established their ethnic neighbourhoods from Lille to Toronto. They were, therefore, an integral part of 19th- and 20th-century population movements, trade unionism, the spread of capitalism, and the multiethnic face of emerging modern cities.

The creation of the Iron Curtain after 1945 cut the West off from this labour force reservoir and forced West European economies to open up to Southern Europe[53] and consequently to other

---

[50]   A. Walaszek. 2001. Polska diaspora. [in]: *Diaspory. Migracje i społeczeństwo*, t. 6, red. J.E. Zamojski, A. Pilch (eds.) *Emigracja z ziem polskich w czasach nowożytnych i najnowszych (XVIII–XX w.)*. Warszawa: Państwowe Wydawnictwo Naukowe, 1984; D. Praszałowicz. 1999. Wokół mechanizmów migracji łańcuchowych. *Przegląd Polonijny* 28(4):9–40.

[51]   Z. Mach. 2005. Polish diaspora. [in]: M.J. Gibney, R. Hansen (eds.) *Immigration and Asylum. From 1900 to the Present*. Santa Barbara/Denver/Oxford: ABC Clio.

[52]   J. Bukowczyk. 1996. *Polish Americans and their History Community, Culture and Politics*. Pittsburgh: University of Pittsburgh Press.

[53]   A. Favell, H. Randall. 2002. Markets against politics: migration, EU enlargement and the idea of Europe. *Journal of Ethnic and Migration Studies* 28(4):581–601.

sources of labour in Africa and Asia. From this perspective, the entry of Poland and the other European states into the EU in 2004 can be seen as a return to the pre-Second World War pan-European labour market. One can easily argue that this traditional pool of labour migrants has opened up again, enabling people to escape the social and economic constraints of their own under-developed and under-urbanised economies. This also meant that, in the new structural environment, vast parts of Polish society found themselves in a familiar position and once again engaged in large-scale mobility akin to that of the end of the 19th century.

This tradition of mobility has deeply influenced the devel-opment of Polish national identity and is clearly evident in con-temporary debates about migration, both publicly and among the migrants themselves. The era of the great migrations occurred during the period of partitions (1789–1918), when Poland did not exist as a state, divided between Prussia, the Austro-Hungarian Empire, and Russia. In the era of growing nationalism and the establishment of the centrally controlled nation-state, the absence of a Polish state administration[54] had profound consequences for the development of Polish national identity and its relationship with the central administration and legal culture of the state. Lack of state borders and associated regulations, which could control outsiders and identify the population through structural exclusion and inclusion, led the emerging class of intellectuals, mainly from the Russian part of Poland[55] — the active participants in 'print capi-

---

[54]   However, one needs to remember the considerable differences between the situation of the three provinces and in different periods of time. In some — like the Galicia region during the second half of the 19th century or Warsaw in late 19th century, despite the lack of state administration, Polish culture flourished, and a large number of Poles were actually part of the Russian or Austrian ad-ministration. This fact is frequently missed by nationalistic discourse as it puts a grain of doubt that Poland was somewhat 'unfree'. The fact that Poles were enjoying considerable freedoms and were elected to the Austrian and Russian parliaments proves that things were much more subtle.

[55]   B. Jałowiecki, M. Szczepański. 2008. Dziedzictwo polskich regionów. [in]: *Jedna Polska? Dawne i nowe zróżnicowania społeczne.* PAN 2007.

talism'[56] — to focus on defining the cultural and social boundaries, which would maintain the 'essence' of Polishness — its language, historical legacy, and later its (Roman Catholic) religion. These boundaries were not administrative structures and state regulations; they were reproduced in 'softer' spheres of social life through literature, popular culture, myths, symbols, and rituals.

The function of these cultural boundaries helps to explain the powerful place which the theme of emigration plays in Poland. As Koslowsky argues, states with large volumes of emigration, such as Germany, developed specific laws of nationality based on imagined kinship (*jus sanguinis*), because this encouraged migrants to retain or pass on their nationality to descendants, and thereby sustained their loyalty and sentiments to the homeland.[57] This policy of de-territorialising the nation-state through ideological tools aimed at retaining the loyalty of emigrants played a crucial role in the past[58] and also in contemporary global modernity,[59] but what happens if a country has no state apparatus and cannot identify its population through passports, citizenship, and nationality laws?

If structural boundaries are weak or absent they are typically reinforced through symbols, cultural meanings, and rituals.[60] Polish migration provides a classic illustration of this process. The main way to remind emigrants and their descendants about the places which they had left and to construct a commonality of de-

[56]   B. Anderson. 1991. *Imagined Communities: Reflections on the Origin and Spread of Nationalism*. London: Verso.

[57]   See R. Koslowski. 1997. Migration and the democratic context. [in]: E. Ucarer, D. Puchala (eds.) *Immigration into Western Societies*. London: Pinter, p. 80; see also R. Brubaker. 1990. Citizenship and Nationhood in France and Germany. Cambridge: Harvard University Press, pp. 169–172.

[58]   N.L. Green, F. Weil (eds.). 2007. *Citizenship and Those Who Leave: The Politics of Emigration and Expatriation*. Chicago: University of Illinois Press.

[59]   L. Basch, N. Glick Schiller, C.S. Blanc. 1994. *Nations Unbound: Transnational Projects, Postcolonial Predicaments, and Deterritorialized Nation-States*. Langhorne: Gordon and Breach.

[60]   A.P. Cohen. 1985. *Symbolic Construction of Community*. London: Routledge, pp. 70–96.

scent and an imaginary kinship was to develop a specific set of discursive and symbolic practices, meanings, and traits—a set of features commonly described as migration culture. This cultural set defined the imagined national community and placed specific moral obligations on emigrants by presenting them as part of a wider whole, the newly invented community, the nation. Norms were established about not only how to 'be' or 'become' a Pole while abroad but also how and for what purpose the imagined community should be reconstructed while abroad by forming specific ethnic communities with a primary task of maintaining a set of cultural norms, which were bound with nation-state building processes. It was then at the peak of migration from Poland in late 19th and early 20th centuries during the coming of age of Polish nationalism that the term *Polonia* describing Polish communities abroad evolved describing a sort of parallel Polish society.[61] The idea was that, although removed from sacred contact with the national soil, the *Polonia*, nevertheless, maintained its Polishness and connection with Polish traditions and cultural traits. In the process of new boundaries demarcation in urban settings of USA and Europe, Catholicism, language and a binding perception of hostility towards non-Polish neighbours (Jews, Germans, and others) became increasingly important.[62]

A continual debate about the tasks and meanings of emigration and Polish communities abroad, both in political and academic literature, proves how vital the existence of that 'Poland abroad' was for the nationalist struggle. For nationalists, observing mass migrations of the late 19th century, migrations from Poland were a

---

[61] On the development of the notion of *Polonia*: M. Drozdowski. 1974. Ewolucja pojęcia "Polonia" w XIX-XX wieku. [in]: M.M. Drozdowski (ed.) *Dzieje Polonii w XIX i XX wieku*. Toruń, p. 5; or A. Paluch. 1976. Inkluzywne i ekskluzywne rozumienie terminu "Polonia." *Przegląd Polonijny* 2:37–48.

[62] D. Praszałowicz. 1999. Wokół mechanizmów migracji łańcuchowych. *Przegląd Polonijny* 28(4):9–40.

worrying sign of weakening the 'national substance'.[63] Yet, they also saw a potential political capital in 'awakening' their national sentiments abroad and mobilising politically. Crucially, nationalists did not oppose or regarded as a threat mass migrations from the same regions by Jews, local Russians, or Ruthenians since their migrations were perceived as facilitating the 'polonisation' of the land.[64] This form of migration encouraged the assertion of control over territory by one particular group and strengthened the claim that 'Polish land' should be occupied by 'Poles' only—a claim which was difficult to apply in a region marked at this time by huge ethnic, religious, and cultural diversity.

That moral hierarchy of migrations had profound consequences. By judging differently the migrations of different people leaving the land, the nationalists were able to ethnically purify it and select the mobile population on the basis of its newly constructed and invented 'Polishness'—something which was often very alien for rural Poles and did not reflect their real-life experiences, more concerned with local identity and status acquisition.[65] The discourse about the status of non-ethnic Polish citizens within the Polish state and the political significance of minorities is far from being just a historical discussion about past. Its function emerges full scale during structural shifts of the political landscape—such as the collapse of Communism or accessing the EU. Thomas Faist, for instance, notes that the problem of non-Polish minorities' and their descendants' place in the Polish social landscape resurfaced in the debates over dual citizenship after the

---

[63]   As one 19th-century politician noted, emigration is "Galicia gravest social sickness"—quoted in D.R. Gabaccia, D. Hoerder, A. Walaszek 2007. Immigration and nation building during the mass migration from Europe. [in]: N.L. Green, F. Weil (eds.) *Citizenship and Those who Leave: The Politics of Emigration and Expatriation*. Chicago: University of Illinois Press, p. 75.

[64]   D.R. Gabaccia, D. Hoerder, A. Walaszek 2007. Immigration and nation building during the mass migration from Europe. [in]: Nancy L. Green, François Weil (eds.) *Citizenship and Those Who Leave: The Politics of Emigration and Expatriation*. Chicago: University of Illinois Press, pp. 75–78.

[65]   L. Stomma. 1986. *Antropologia wsi polskiej XIX wieku*. Warszawa: Instytut Wydawniczy Pax.

collapse of Communism.[66] In a study on Polish–Ukrainian relations in the town of Przemysl, Chris Hann also documents that ethnic boundaries, which were subdued during the communist period, resurfaced once a new political arrangement was in place.[67]

The cultural and symbolic environment surrounding the notion of emigration in Polish culture is, therefore, laden with meanings that accumulated during a long history of migratory movements and nation-building projects. The very term *emigracja* [emigration] evokes specific connotations, like the notion of *wychodźstwo* [noun from *wychodzić*, to go out]. They both evoke the boundary, the crossing, and change of status – being out there, not at home. This dominant discourse of emigration resonates through Polish culture and politics. Not only were the major Polish literature works of the 19th century written in exile, the symbols of the nation also refer to the act of being 'out' and coming back – the national anthem is a poem written during the Napoleonic wars about soldiers-emigrants returning from exile to 'free' their oppressed homeland. Throughout the pre-war period of independence, the Polish state saw Polish communities abroad as an extension of its foreign policy, funding diasporic activities and even seeing some Polish settlements – mainly in South America – as potential colonisers in their rather overgrown ambitions placing Poland in the powerful family of imperial states with their own overseas territories.[68] After the Second World War, the communist state not only fought to gain legitimacy from but also control over the Polish diaspora,[69] and today, there is a pervasive, taken-for-granted belief among Polish politicians, intellectuals, and wider society that Poles abroad *should* represent the nation-state and *should* behave

[66] T. Fais. 2007. *Dual citizenship in Europe: from nationhood to societal integration.* Surrey: Ashgate Publishing, p. 160.

[67] C. Hann. 1998. Post-socialist nationalism: rediscovering the past in southeast Poland. *Slavic Review* 57(4):840–863.

[68] M. Kicinger. 2005. *Polityka emigracyjna II Rzeczypospolitej;* CEFMR Working Paper, 4/2005. http://www.cefmr.pan.pl/docs/cefmr_wp_2005-04.pdf

[69] S. Cenckiewicz. 2002. Geneza Towarzystwa Łączności z Polonią Zagraniczną "Polonia." *Pamięć i Sprawiedłowość* 1(1):161–168.

and act in certain ways to maintain a set of cultural meanings, values, and norms of behaviour. State funding of Polish institutions and organisations abroad,[70] symbolic capital distribution and participation in the transnational political field — are all familiar strategies of the de-territorialised nation-state described by scholars.[71] They are underpinned however, in the Polish case, by long-established, institutionalised, and culturally embedded dominant meanings around the notion of *emigracja*. Explaining the origins and power of these meanings employed by the state and its elites is crucial for exploration of the migration culture in which Poles are socialised and which forms part of their cultural resource used in real-life situations. It is also vital for understanding ways with which they are also resisting and sometimes contesting these meanings.

Emigration as a moral issue

If the meanings ascribed to space and place are universal characteristics of human cultural production,[72] logically the same applies to the very act of leaving that space, of separation from it. As Mary Erdmans notes '*both home country and host country nationals have varying attitudes towards individuals seeking to change their place of residency*'.[73] The major theme in Polish literature, popular culture, and official political symbolism is that physical movement beyond boundaries constitutes an important morally charged act with political consequences, as it essentially defines an individual's relationship with the larger imagined community — the nation. In fact, the very act of leaving the sacred territory — which, in the

[70]   The expenditure of the Polish Senate for support to Poles abroad is substantial — in 2008, 75m PLN (est. 17m GBP); in 2012, it was 80PLN: for full details, see: http://www.money.pl/archiwum/wydarzenia/wydatki;na;polonie.html

[71]   L. Basch, N. Glick Schiller, C.S. Blanc. 1994. *Nations Unbound: Transnational Projects, Postcolonial Predicaments, and Deterritorialized Nation-States*. Langhorne: Gordon and Breach.

[72]   V. Turner, E. Turner. 1978. *Image and Pilgrimage in Christian Culture*. New York: Columbia University Press, p. 241.

[73]   M.P. Erdmans. 1992. The social construction of emigration as a moral issue. *Polish American Studies* 99(1):7.

domain of the profane, was occupied by foreign powers before 1918 — constitutes its boundaries and reifies the nation, the collective. Since the absence of formal state borders entailed moving the Polish border into the domain of symbol and ritual, the very boundary of Poland could only been imagined, revitalised, reproduced, and communicated by crossing it, by being outside of imaginary homeland. Put differently, leaving Poland recreated its ontological status as a real, true, reified entity. By crossing the border, a person proves the existence of the imagined community of Poles, being outside immediately assumes a state of being inside, of the existence of the inside — reified and seen as a bounded whole. Metaphorically speaking then, leaving Poland means *making it* and the very existence of boundary is defined by crossing it. This is why 19th-century elites did not use the term *emigracja* to describe the movements of Poles between Austrian, Prussian, and Russian parts of former Polish territory.[74] The symbolic boundary did need not to be asserted there; even though in the strict technical sense, this was an international migratory movement. And *vice versa*, someone, who moved within the Russian empire from Warsaw to Moscow, was an emigrant for the nationalist, although administratively, remaining an internal migrant. Additionally, these kinds of people were also morally dubious since they were emigrating to work for the occupier,[75] even if from state's view they were simply moving from one city to another within the same country.

As a result, in Polish culture, emigration was, and still is, not only a key element that helps to define an individual's relationship to the collective imagined community but also one of the main ways in which *the collective is produced*, made to happen, imagined.

---

[74]   D.R. Gabaccia, D. Hoerder, A. Walaszek. 2007. Immigration and nation building during the mass migration from Europe. [in]: N.L. Green, F. Weil (eds.) *Citizenship and Those Who Leave: The Politics of Emigration and Expatriation*. Chicago: University of Illinois Press, pp. 70–71.

[75]   M. Micińska. 2004. Zdrada, dezercja czy jedyna szansa? Dyskusje wokół tzw. emigracji talentów z ziem polskich w drugiej połowie XIX wieku i na początku XX w. [in]: J.E. Zamojski (red.) *Migracje i Społeczeństwo t. 9*. Warszawa: IH PAN, MWSH-P, Wydawnictwo Neriton, pp. 91–109.

Through the act of leaving one's home, village, town, country the individual act merges into the collective experience of the whole imagined community. This was the message of one of most revered romantic poets, Adam Mickiewicz, who combined theology, millenarianism,[76] and nationalism with emigration (or what he called pilgrimage). In his strongly religious vision, the Poles, who were scattered across Europe and were fighting their oppressors, were redeeming Europe from its sins and were defending endangered freedom and equality of humankind. Genevieve Zubrzycki uses the notion Victor Turner developed, that of a root paradigm[77] in Polish culture — one which aims to off-set the peripheral status of Poland within Europe, regain its former glory at the same time placing its values in a religious-republican ideological framework:

> Romantic poets played a critical role in the creation and diffusion of this novel notion of the Polish nation, they were proclaimed the nation's 'apostles' the 'missionaries of the Polish soul', moral authorities describing in their work the suffering of the enslaved nation and supporting personal sacrifice in the name of the fatherland, supreme ideal and sacred value. For Romantics, the nation was a community of history and tradition guided by a unique mission: to free nations from oppression, thereby placing them on the road to universal salvation. Poland was represented as the Christ of nations: crucified for the sins of the world, it would be brought back to life to save humanity from dangerous political idols and satanic rulers....[78]

Nation, according to this tradition, is then linked with the soil, and the connection with the territory is understood as a moral one; hence, physical distance requires the reinforcing of moral obligations to it. If the source of morality and social order lies in physical connection with the land, then migration potentially threatens to disrupt this order and leads to moral confusion and chaos. The

---

[76] D.R. Gabaccia, D. Hoerder, A. Walaszek 2007. Immigration and nation building during the mass migration from Europe. [in]: N.L. Green, F. Weil (eds.) *Citizenship and Those Who Leave: The Politics of Emigration and Expatriation*. Chicago: University of Illinois Press, p. 75.

[77] V. Turner. 1974. *Dramas, Fields and Metaphors: Symbolic Action in Human Society*. Ithaca: Cornell University Press, p. 64.

[78] G. Zubrzycki. 2006. *The Crosses of Auschwitz. Nationalism and Religion in Post-Communist Poland*. Chicago/London: The University of Chicago Press, pp. 44–45.

moral message of obligation had to be reinforced, since migration as a liminal state is laden with the potential to reinforce the dominant symbol but also with the threat of individuals going astray, 'losing' their moral compass, weakening the magical connection that makes Poles of them, 'de-polonising' themselves, abandoning the ethnic and thus the moral community altogether. This discourse was vigorously communicated by equating emigration with rupture, the traumatic destruction of the natural order, loss, and drama. The border-crossing of an imaginative, non-existent state territory did not just entail physical movement—it was a tragic crossing of the Styx, the movement from 'our' to 'their' land, a change from 'here' to 'there', from the 'known and secure' to the 'unknown and threatening'. Conceptually, thus, through emigration, a binary opposition of 'here' and 'there' is constructed, but also specific power hierarchies are legitimised. So in order to maintain its power and grasp over peoples' minds, the hegemonic construction of the nation border-crossing was presented as a dramatic rupture, which led to a radical juxtaposition of 'us' versus 'them' and 'our' territory' with an 'alien' one. Emigration, from this romantic, nationalist perspective, is then essentially valued negatively, as something that unfortunately happens but should be treated as a threat and the negation of how things should be, how nature has designed things to be—nations rooted in land and culture and people populating the land of their ancestors. It sees the nation as a biological entity, which encloses individuals, and the territory as the source of its biological vitality and a guarantee of maintaining Polishness and, hence, moral and social order. When the Polish PM, Jarosław Kaczyński, described modern post-2004 Polish migration as a 'bloodletting'[79] and a national tragedy, or later his opponent, Donald Tusk, also as PM described the same migratory movement as 'national trauma',[80] he

---

[79] Exactly the same term was used by 19th-century intelectualls expressing worries about migrating Poles. See D.R. Gabaccia, D. Hoerder, A. Walaszek 2007. Immigration and nation building during the mass migration from Europe. [in]: N.L. Green, F. Weil (eds.) *Citizenship and Those Who Leave: The Politics of Emigration and Expatriation*. Chicago: University of Illinois Press, p. 75.

[80] D. Tusk. 2009. Speech at the Polish Embassy in London. Fieldwork notes.

implicitly refers to the collective as a functional, bounded, and clearly defined biological entity. The fear that Poles will *wynarodowią* ['de-nationalise'] themselves abroad implies that this does not happen at home. Contact with the territory (and the state) is physical; it is the soil and its magical powers that naturally makes 'a Pole' and once removed from it, the threat of no longer being one becomes real. When Pope John Paul II referred to emigrating as a sometimes necessary but essentially a bad thing to do[81] and that all emigrants owned a particular debt to their homeland, he employed a 'sedentary metaphysics', which assumes that the natural way of being is to live in one's national territory and leaving it keeps the bond of debt, service, and submission to the collective very much alive. In that sense, the link between the moral spine of the collective and the territory — imagined, as the physical territory kept changing in the Polish case — is established and maintained.

Migration, then, becomes the conceptual axis and root paradigm that structures relations between individuals, between tradition and modernity, and between the individual and the collective. In this way, it becomes the ultimate test of how effectively the collective organises individuals, how dominant norms and values are being enforced and practised by society. As Erdmans notes in her analysis of the attitudes of the Polish Church and anti-communist opposition towards emigration: *The moral authorities in Poland defined emigration as a collective act. The decision to emigrate, though acknowledged to be one of individual choice, was embedded in national issues and framed in the context of a moral decision. Religious and oppositional leaders especially have instructed Poles to place collective good — i.e. the good of the nation — over the individual gains one may receive from emigrating.*[82]

This structure of meanings shows an impressive stability over time. Today, in sermons, debates, literature, and arts, emigration from Poland is also treated as a dangerous rupture of sacred space, as a traumatic breach of the continuity of human life (which

---

81   See, for instance: J. Paul II. *Laborem Exercens: O Ludzkiej Pracy*, par. 23, p. 198.
82   M.P. Erdmans. 1992. The social construction of emigration as a moral issue. *Polish American Studies* 99(1):13.

assumingly is only righteous, natural, and morally correct when sedentary, or at least confined to the administrative borders) and in radical interpretations as a deeply suspicious, morally ambiguous socially pathological unnatural act. It may be beneficial to the individual but the nation suffers. Leaving Poland breaks the sacred link between people and territory.[83]

This is not just a historical debate but one that permanently shapes the modern understanding of the community, group, and moral obligations individuals should have towards the collective. A recent example illustrates the extraordinary stubbornness and stability of the entanglement between the notion of leaving and the collective prescription laden with sedentary metaphysics. A poster campaign, sponsored by the Polish Ministry of Culture and National Heritage and called 'Patriotism of tomorrow', tried to provide young Poles with a modern interpretation of patriotism by drawing on the past. The picture below is a classic example of how migration through dominant discourse is constructed as a moral issue that defines individual relations and moral worth for the nation:

łączy nas
patriotyzm
jutra

Mjr Janusz Brochwicz-Lewiński „Gryf"
86 lat, dowódca obrony
pałacyku Michla
podczas Powstania Warszawskiego,
walczył o Polskę.

Filip Wolski
19 lat, mistrz świata
olimpiady informatycznej
w Meksyku 2006,
zostaje w Polsce.

Source: Ministry of Culture and Nationl Heritage, Poland 2006.

The person on the left is an 86-year-old commander of the Warsaw Uprising. The text referring to him reads: *Major Janusz Brochwicz-*

83   D. Mostwin. 1986. Emigrant polski w Stanach Zjednoczonych 1974-1984. [in]: M. Paszkiewicz (red.) *Polskie więzi kulturowe na obczyźnie*. Londyn: Prace Kongresu Kultury Polskiej na Obczyźnie, t 8, pp. 210–212.

Lewiński 'Gryf'. Commander of the Pałacyk Michla, during the Warsaw Uprising. He fought for Poland. The description of the person on the right reads: *Filip Wolski, winner of IT championship in Mexico. He stays in Poland* [emphasis added].

In this intergenerational juxtaposition, several important messages are communicated. First, individual talents, abilities, resources may manifest themselves in the individual, but they do not belong to him in their totality; they constitute a collective resource, and the collective has a right to determine its use, or more precisely its geographical application. Hence, it is the individual's duty to employ them within the boundaries of the nation-state. 'Staying' is the contemporary version of resistance to foreign influence, power, and wealth. The moral prescription is clear: in the same way that Mjr Brochwicz-Lewiński 'Gryf' resisted the German army's attack on the Polish capital in August 1944, so Filip ought to resist foreign headhunters, multinationals, and foreign capital. It is a patriotic duty, which corresponds with the same principles guiding Polish freedom fighters 60 years ago. Migration, then, in this hegemonic discourse, is intertwined with the root paradigms of Polish national culture — the notion of Poland the defender, the last outpost of European civilisation, the militaristic, male-centred perspective of a member of national body which is constantly reminded of the ultimate sacrifice he has to make in guarding the territory — by dividing for it, or in conyemporary version, not leaving it.

Established political transnationalism and the production of Poles

Evolution of this nationalist discourse and set of moral guidelines related to emigrating and living abroad was historically driven mainly by a small[84] but highly visible presence of Polish political

---

[84]   The so-called Great Emigration in Paris triggered by the fall of the November Uprising in 1831 numbered around 5,000 to 8,000 people but among which one could count most influential Polish romantic writers.

refugees and revolutionaries throughout the 19th century. They primarily came from the land-owning class which found itself competing with new rulers or destitute due to the confiscation of their property or simply modernisation. From the Polish Legions in the Napoleonic Wars to the First World War Polish regiments recruited from emigrants, up to the Second World War government-in-exile in London, soldiers, mercenaries, and legions from Poland have been omnipresent and have imprinted a set of specific emigration ideologies, political ideas, norms, and values. Like the educational travels of the Polish elite during the Renaissance, political emigration became the norm in practice and performed often in literature and high culture. In 19th-century Paris, Brussels, London, Istanbul, and Berlin, Polish political parties fought fierce debates and the Polish nomad-revolutionary became a familiar, sometimes stereotypical figure.[85]

It is not surprising, then, that some historians began to conceptualise the great migrations during the 19th and 20th centuries from Eastern Europe using theories of transnationalism highlighting circular migration, transnational networking,[86] and economic and political connections linking sending and receiving countries. If one looked at the functional relationship between nationalism and transnational connections, then the Polish case would offer a paradigm example. In constructing its myths, symbols, and dominant narratives, Poland was very much invented abroad, in Warsaw as well as in Paris. What is crucial is that this ideology was based on the distinction between migration for political reasons — for the collective good — as opposed to far more numerous economic reasons — which were presented as for individual gain only. This distinction gave moral force to the boundaries between the collective and the individual, duty and freedom, the self and the

---

[85] It was also a figure much mocked and ridiculed as in Fiodor Dostoyevsky's books, like *The Idiot*.

[86] E. Morawska. 2001. The new-old transmigrants, their transnational lives and ethnicisation: a comparison of 19th/20th situations. [in]: W.J. Mollenkopf, G. Gerstle (red.) *Immigrants, Civic Culture and Modes of Political Incorporation*. New York: Sage and Social Science Council, pp. 175–211.

imagined community, the material and the ideal. It was also a tool for reproducing feudal Polish class relations abroad since it separated the gentry, who were 'fighting for independence', from 'simple folk', peasants and working-class people who, in their millions, were seeking a better life abroad escaping economic hardship often induced by these very same elites.[87]

During the 19th and 20th centuries, this hegemonic emigration culture served as a nationalist tool for delineating membership into the nation, a tool which in the context of lack of administrative structures of inclusion and exclusion of the state served to decide who was a rightful Pole and who was not, who was an alien, a foreigner. In that practice, there was little place in it for minorities who were also migrating from Poland: Jews, Roma, Germans, Ukrainians, and many others. Even if Jews migrating from 19th-century Poland did so for political reasons, these migrations do not form part of the national narrative of Polish migrations reproduced in the text books and dominant perceptions — in standard accounts of history of emigration from Poland, one would not find members of Zionist movement or Jewish anarchists. 'Political' emigration in that case was strictly Polish state-oriented. The mass escapes of Polish peasants from feudal systems prior to the great partitions also find no place in these accounts. For the very same reasons, the emigration of Polish Roma since the 1980s in order to escape persecution and discrimination is rarely described as 'political' in public discourse, which contrasts with their political status as asylum seekers in their countries of destination. In this way, Polish romantic nationalism ensured that political migration was seen as morally superior to migration for economic gains. Political exile was a sacred act, almost a rite of passage for political transnational entrepreneurs in the fight for freedom while economic migration was a necessary evil, cowardice, egoism, or an ambiguous act of turning away from the nation's destiny. This ideology plays on a Christian/Platonic dichot-

---

[87] L. Stomma. 1986. *Antropologia wsi polskiej XIX wieku*. Warszawa: Instytut Wydawniczy Pax.

omy between the ideal and the material, the soul and the body, patriotism and narrow particularism or egoism. By reducing the individual's set of motivations to the dichotomy of 'ideas' versus 'bread',[88] a hierarchy of migrants is created and the main criterion is the political fight for the Polish state. Consequently, the political engagement by Polish Jews in the construction of the Israeli state, the participation of Polish workers in trade union struggles in the USA,[89] the involvement by Polish migrants in foreign armies in the colonies is never described as 'political' and is omitted from the dominant discourse. The distinction between political and economic migration was also fixed, since it referred to the initial motivation for migrating. People who migrated for political reasons to the West half a century ago are seen as morally superior, even if their original reasons were overtaken by the evolution of political events. By fixing peoples' motives once and for all, that ideology attempts to establish the politicisation of individual motives as the main source of authority, power, and symbolic capital.

However, as the later chapters of this book will demonstrate, a specific emigration ideology is not only concerned with the reproduction of the nation-state—it also involves a prescription for particular power relations within an immigrant community and keeping contestants at bay. Furthermore, these power relations reflect the attitudes of those within the country of destination towards their increasingly diverse populations. Since romantic nationalism located social morality in the sacrificial fight for freedom of the nation and the creation of the state, anything with an aura of individualism or self-fulfilment was treated suspiciously. It is the poet Adam Mickiewicz, dying of cholera in Istanbul trying to organise a legion to fight for free Poland, who is the paradigmatic émigré of Polish nationalism, the embodiment of what a

---

[88]   In Polish vernacular statement, to 'migrate for bread' (emigracja za chlebem) denotes economic migration.

[89]   A. Walaszek. 1988. *Robotnicy polscy, praca i związki zawodowe w Stanach Zjednoczonych Ameryki 1880-1922*. Wrocław/Bukowczyk: Ossolineum; J. John. 1996. *Polish Americans and their History Community, Culture and Politics*. Pittsburgh: University of Pittsburgh Press.

Pole abroad *should do*, rather than Bronisław Malinowski, who was developing modern anthropology through fieldwork in Tro-briand Islands. Polish emigration ideology bears the deep impression of political refugees, who were and still are the high priests of Poland's nationalistic ideology of emigration. They still enjoy the power to decide who left Poland 'just for bread' and who did so for spiritual purposes. In this way, they also control the local topography of power. The only chance for the working/peasant class to enter the domain of higher status of 'political' émigrés was to actively engage in the fight for the Polish nation, which frequently happened thanks to the activities of leaders, priests, national activists, or ethnic entrepreneurs. This 'politicisation' and collectivisation of the migration experience not only involved political elites, but it can also been seen in the work of Polish migration scholars. Jerzy Zubrzycki, a distinguished sociologist, a disciple of Florian Znaniecki, and the author of the first monograph on Polish migrants in Britain, and later one of most prolific theorists of Australian multiculturalism, writing about Poles in the USA in the aftermath of the Second World War, observes that: *And so again those men, who represented no more than a little tradition of their community transplanted to a foreign soil, became bearers of the great tradition which illuminates and articulates so much of Polish migration experience. Peasants and soldiers, peasants or soldiers are indistinguishable in the sociology of Polish migration, in its social structure and social organization.*[90]

The 'great tradition' — the collective fate of the nation — in his words, thus overrides the 'small' traditions of rural folk, who seem to be child-like, barbarians almost from this perspective — they need special care in order to 'become' full Poles. Zubrzycki's observation also implicitly alludes to class hierarchy. Peasant and working-class migrants only achieve the high status of participating in the national narrative and dominant historical discourse when they become 'soldier' migrants, when they aspire to a par-

---

[90]   J. Zubrzycki. 1988. *Soldiers and Peasants. The Sociology of Polish Migration.* The Second M.B. Grabowski Memorial Lecture. London: Orbis Books, p. 24.

ticular hegemonic nation-state ideology. In the same way that rural 'folk' were made into 'Polish' abroad, 'peasants' were turned into 'soldiers'. Polishness, in this emigration discourse, brings the aura of military training and initiation to a male-only, politically defined and hierarchical collective.[91] Emigration in that ideological construction is, thus, the rite of passage through which young, unaware, undeveloped individuals through separation from the land become complete members of the national community. Reproduction through separation achieves another dimension here, since migrants are required to rebuild what they have left, but in strongly militaristic and state-centric overtones. Migrants are not only turned into freedom fighters and bearers of a particular nationalist tradition but they are men turned into cannon-fodder. Women are explicitly excluded from the discourse, and apart from a strong emphasis on the suffering of the family, this is a purely male-dominated view.

In this cultural code, while working-class and male peasant migrants have the potential to be authentically Polish, they still need to prove it, and it is the elites that have the power to decide on the validity of such proof. However, the liminal status of the working class and peasantry means that, as well as turning into soldiers/Poles, they could also disassociate themselves from this collective and national ideology. Liminal space is not only potentially reproductive but also subversive for constructions of symbols and meanings.[92] Hence, the need to confine the working-class related 'small traditions' to subordinate positions and restrict the control of symbols to 'political' emigration. Hence, becoming Polish means rejoining the community, and this automatically assumes that the community has been broken by the very act of leaving one's home. Joining the community at the same time hap-

---

[91]   A striking similarity with the process of turning peasants into Frenchmen through military service as described by E.J. Weber. 1976. *Peasants into Frenchmen: The Modernization of Rural France, 1880–1914.* Stanford: Stanford University Press.

[92]   V. Turner. 1995. *The Ritual Process: Structure and Anti-structure.* New York: Hawthorne.

pens under the terms of the power holders. In result, becoming Polish through emigration means accepting a given hierarchy of power, class stratification, and legitimacy of domination.

The political making of the Polish diaspora

Benedict Anderson coined the term 'long-distance nationalism'[93] to describe the diaspora's political activities in creating and maintaining the nation-state or stimulating an ethnic revival. The contemporary Polish state, with 200 years of tradition of engaging in political transnationalism on a large scale, not surprisingly sees the diaspora as making a significant contribution to Polish nationalism.[94] After all, in order to gain symbolic legitimacy, the first elected president of post-1989 Poland, Lech Wałęsa, received the presidential insignia — a sort of sacred totem of power — from the last president-in-exile in London — Ryszard Kaczorowski. In official Polish discourse, Poles abroad are frequently seen as somehow preserving the 'true' meaning of Polishness. This 'authenticity' is a source of inspiration, strength, and worship by many on the right of the Polish political spectrum. They, we may call them shamans of Polish nationalism, who, through their separation from the national territory, have truly preserved its essence, are also the guardians of tradition and moral order; they are the only ones who *really* have preserved the essence of Polishness. This is why the Polish prime minister, who visited Britain in November 2005, said to a gathering of the Second World War Polish émigrés in their 1980s that he *'doesn't have to worry about these young Poles that come to England now, because I know that they have role models of true Polish patriotism and Polishness over here'*.[95] The young Poles — the post-Accession migrants — in his view needed special care, since they were in a liminal position where they could experience

93   B. Anderson. 1992. *Long-Distance Nationalism: World Capitalism and the Rise of Identity Politics*. Amsterdam: The Wertheim lecture, Centre for Asian Studies.
94   A. Walaszek. I*bidem*, pp. 8–12.
95   Own fieldwork notes.

moral collapse, question their national identity, and betray their heritage. Luckily, there were individuals, who—like Mjr Brochwicz-Lewiński 'Gryf' from the poster described earlier—are able to take guard and remind Poles what it means to be Polish. Again this perspective arises from a very specific, nationalistic account of Polish history, the one that according to Polish sociologists Jałowiecki and Szczepański[96] originated from very specific conditions of late 19th-century Warsaw and the part of Poland under Russian administration, the so-called *Kongresówka*. Its core referred to the idea that fighting for the independence of the state constitutes the essence of Polishness and that being a Pole was defined in terms of military struggle directed towards the resurrection of the state. However, as they and many others note, traditions and political conditions in other parts of Poland differed, and most people were rather indifferent or even hostile to this ideology.[97] Nevertheless, this discourse managed to become a dominant one, to the point that it is treated unquestionably even by reputable historians. For instance, Peter Stachura writes that: '...*regardless of the most inauspicious circumstances, the Poles always, without fail, find a way to continue the fight. National tradition dictates them that this should be so'.*[98] The anthropological problematisation of this statement is, of course, 'who' dictates and why and who has the power to define the direction of that 'fight'? What is the purpose of this 'soldier narrative' and in what contexts does it become salient to the point that historians are reproducing such blatant stereotypes without mentioning that this Polish 'love for freedom' was hardly a black and white issue, often more controversial that officially acknowledged? Not only historians of the past but also present omit or belittle the participation of the Polish

---

[96]   B. Jałowiecki, M. Szczepański. 2008. Dziedzictwo polskich regionów. [in]: *Jedna Polska? Dawne i nowe zróżnicowania społeczne.* PAN 2007.

[97]   L. Stomma. 1986. *Antropologia wsi polskiej XIX wieku.* Warszawa: Instytut Wydawniczy Pax; Z. Mach. 1993. *Symbols, Conflict and Identity.* Albany: SUNY Press.

[98]   P. Stachura. *The Poles in Britain. From Betrayal to Assimilation.* London: Franck Cass, p. 2.

gentry and elites in Austrian, Russian, and Prussian colonial administration in partitioned Poland and choose instead to overem-
phasise the actions of a minority as the makers of the 'national
tradition'. In consequence, they seem to like to portray the mass
migrations of 19th century as a result of political oppression from
occupying powers, rather than political and economic response to
structural condition in what was still feudal social relations with
Polish gentry holding considerable power on the local level.[99] The
standard perception of Polish society as universally engaged in
military struggle for freedom ignores the fact that vast sections of
Polish society and the ruling classes participated in Russian, Austrian, and Prussian politics and regarded themselves as subjects of
the Habsburgs, Romanovs, and the Reich. The current fashionable
nostalgia for the Austro-Hungarian past, evident in popular culture in towns like Krakow, is at odds with the claim made by Stachura and many others that Poles are essentially a freedom-loving
folk with hatred for occupying powers.

It is one of many paradoxes that Poles are constantly confronted with while constructing the dominant narrative of their
national story. On one hand, the 'soldier narrative' or the root-
paradigm described by Genevieve Zubrzycki brings certain benefits for a relatively economically poor society on the margins of
Europe. Yet, on the other hand, it creates a tension within this
society, since individual, regional, and local stories contrast sharp-
ly with these grand nationalist narratives. Evidence of this tension
usually becomes apparent during elections when opponents confront each other using historical arguments. For example, the 2005
presidential campaign turned against Donald Tusk after it was
disclosed by his right-wing opponent that Tusk's grandfather
served in the Wehrmacht during the Second World War. No one
dwelled on the local context of Pomerania (where Tusk's family
comes from) where, in 1939, locals were forced into the German

---

[99]   S. Kieniewicz. 1969. *The Emancipation of the Polish Peasantry*. Chicago: University of Chicago Press; L. Stomma. 1986. *Antropologia wsi polskiej XIX wieku*. Warszawa: Instytut Wydawniczy Pax.

army *en masse*. The very fact that Tusk could not claim the 'soldier narrative' as his own was enough for him to lose the vote.

Migration counter-discourse from below

Why does this matter for an ethnographic analysis of the lives of contemporary Poles in London? In making sense of the world, its constraints and freedom, social actors refer to the known symbolic and mythical vocabulary—whether in order to serve their own interest or reproduce particular positions in the field of power. On the other hand—as banal as it may sound—people say one thing and do another one and it is the resulting cognitive and ethical tension between the world as imagined in ideologies, moral guidelines, and normative systems of rules and values borne out of a process of tradition-making, on the one hand, and everyday reality, its complexity and context, on the other, which produces an array of social and cultural responses to a given situation—in this case, migrating and settling in London. These tensions, contradictions, and conflicting world perceptions are dealt with in numerous ways. Anthropologists in this situation focus on the role played by myth-making and the production of specific narratives that aim to overcome, control, or obscure the apparent contradictions between what people say and do, between the sets of norms and values and mundane, everyday practicalities of the everyday. Myths, as Anthony P. Cohen observes, among many features and functions are: '... *a means by which men make use of elements in their sociocultural experience to mediate the contradictions with which social life confronts them* ... and ... *used to reconcile society to inevitable truths, and to resolve or render tolerable the contradictions which appear in social life*'.[100] Also, according to Claude Levi-Strauss, the '*the purpose of myth is to provide a logical model capable of*

---

[100] A.P. Cohen. 1975. *The Management of Myths: The Politics of Legitimation in a Newfoundland Community*. St John's: Institute of Social and Economic Research, Memorial University, p. 13.

overcoming a contradiction'[101] — hence, they resolve an internal, logical conflict between the ideal and the practical. In many ways, the processes of meaning–making, conducted by part of the Polish elites preoccupied with legitimising their power position through the 'invention of traditions' and the role of emigration and political exile, involve myth-making. The dominant discourse, by emphasising the dominance of the collective nation over individuals, moral obligations on members, John Paul II's idea of indebtedness to the nation and the doctrine of sacrifice in order to liberate the state, *is* an ideal par excellence, it belongs to the domain of normative guidelines and describes what *ought to be*. In that way, it manages also to explain why ideals of nationalism are not yet realised, why a majority of members of Polish society were not actively engaged in the nationalist struggle of the 19th century, why the message of the elites falls on deaf ears so many, actually a vast majority of population. However, we must be careful not to overestimate the ability of the elites to project their myths and narratives over members of society, who do not share their positions of power. In fact, strong counter-narratives are also at play, and these off-set the control of cultural production on the part of the elites, creating a space for autonomy for groups in subordinate positions.

In the light of structuration theory, Baumann's or Cohen's position would be empirically inaccurate and theoretically incomplete, thus, to take the dominant discourse at face value and treat it as the sole force determining people's agency — as, for example, Stachura sees it when mentioning that *'national tradition dictates them to do so'*. The description and analysis of people's actions and narratives in this book looks how people deal in their daily lives with dominant structures of representations and cultural traits produced by the nationalist narratives, public discourses, and resulting power relations. People are not passive recipients of dominant categories and ascribed identities. Polish migrants

---

[101] C. Lévi-Strauss. 1963. The structural study of myth. [in]: C. Jacobson, B. Grundfest Schoepf (trans.) *Structural Anthropology*. London: Basic Books, Inc., p. 229.

maintain various ties along ethnic, class, and gender lines, for example, which are imbued with meanings. These vary from person to person, and they are dynamically and situationally reconstructed against the backdrop of new cultural and social encounters in a global city like London. Because, social identities are transactional, exist only in human interaction, and are formed through a dialectical interplay between *internal and external definition*.[102] Therefore, the situation migrants find themselves in and have to make sense of, offers a particularly good opportunity to understand how social identities change when 'external' environments change. The power of Polish dominant emigration discourse forces individuals to manoeuvre between the complex contradictions of duty and sacrifice, on the one hand, and self-development, aspirations, and individuality, on the other. These contradictions designate different levels of cultural response to the act of migrating — the level of the nation and the state and the level of individuals, families, households directly engaged in transnational movements.

Although nationalist ideology is buttressed by the state and powerful diasporic lobbies, it is still the product of numerous other social actors. Moreover, the power of collective ideas about Polish nationalism forces 'ordinary people' to assert their individuality in an equally powerful way through myths and narratives. These myths are multifaceted and have many meanings, and for the sake of further analysis, it is useful to use a particular example of the relational character of these constructions. As many other scholars' studies note,[103] Polish migrants frequently emphasise their assertiveness, self-reliance, individuality, can-do attitude, and the omnipresent pull-yourself-by-the-bootstraps mentality of the rational, individualistic economic actor — something that was

---

[102] R. Jenkins. 1997. *Rethinking Ethnicity. Arguments and Explorations.* London: Sage Publications, p. 53.

[103] A. Triandafyllidou (ed.). 2006. *Contemporary Polish Migration in Europe. Complex Patterns of Movement and Settlement.* Lewiston: Edwin Mellen Press; A. White. 2011. *Polish Families and Migration since EU Accession.* Bristol: Policy Press, University of Bristol.

observed both in pre-accession migrants[104] as well as early 20th-century emigrants in USA.[105] In the light of the aforementioned facts, this individualistic discourse should not be treated in separation as it is also a response to a cultural environment where the act of leaving is deeply entangled with the individuals' obligations to the collectivity and the dominant narrative, which is highly communitarian in its essence. In other words, the strength and persistence of the collectivistic dominant discourse produced by the elites in Polish culture is matched relationally by the importance and strength given to resisting it and contesting it at the individual level. The more the discourse of obligation and moral duty is imposed in national narratives — through the actions of politicians, media, narratives, church sermons, social policy, informal debates — the more it has to be contested, qualified, and questioned by individuals in order to allow them to pursue their particular goals and interests.

It is here that we encounter one of many paradoxes in the life of Poles, or more generally in Polish society. This is the quite distinct and important disparity between what is being said, what is thought of as right and the reality, the contrast between the ideal and the fact, the 'ought' and 'is.' In fact, anthropological and historical research shows that the reality of Polish migrations does not accord with the romantic construction of the nation-state. From the vast historical and sociological literature, a different picture emerges. Here, individuals actively pursue their dreams, social aspirations, ambitions, and individuality whether they are a 19th-century peasant or trade unionist[106] during the early 20th century, or a late 20th-century migrant. Removed from the repro-

---

[104] B. Jordan, F. Duvell 1999. *Undocumented Migrants in London. Full Research Report*; Economic and Social Research Council R000236838. http://www.esrcso cietytoday.ac.uk/esrcinfocentre/viewawardpage.aspx?awardnumber=R0002 36838

[105] E. Morawska. 1985. *For Bread with Butter: The Life-Worlds of East Central Europeans in Johnston, Pennsylvania 1890-1940*. Cambridge: Cambridge University Press.

[106] See, for instance, works of Walaszek, Morawska, Bukowczyk, Praszałowicz, and Kantor.

duction of the discourse of duty and obligations towards the national collective, these studies offer a more nuanced view of Polish migration. For instance, in a monograph about transnational social space at the local level *Między Chicago z Zaborowem* (Between Chicago and Zaborów), Ryszard Kantor shows how emigration became an integral part of inhabitants of this South Poland mountainous region and was embedded in the economic, social, and cultural life of the community, without any indication of trauma or great tragedy for it. Many other studies offer a similar picture of migration treated by social actors as a norm, a fact of life a natural phenomenon, rather than a trauma, loss, and disruption in natural order of things. Similarly, Ewa Morawska's work *For Bread with Butter* shows how family-oriented migratory movements were bound with strong culture of aspirations, status acquisition, and social mobility where the nationalistic ideologies of 'duty' and 'debt' towards the nation were not the driving factor of human actions, as nationalist historians would like to believe. In fact, Galasinska and Galasinski[107] identify a specific meta-narrative common in Polish culture presenting the following reconstruction of another hegemonic narrative of Polish emigration for economic purposes. This is a myth not only of self-reliance but also of ambition and individualism:

> ... a penniless Pole (usually a man) [who] emigrates and makes his success work in the host country where he settles down. This is the Polish version of the American Dream, except that America can be anywhere, as long as the economic system lets the individual prove his ability to 'make it', using his resourcefulness and industriousness, which, previously, were stifled in the home country. Alternatively the potential migrant brings all this money back to Poland where he is set up for life.

Similarly, Anne White's monograph on Poles living in small English towns,[108] in great ethnographic detail, describes migrants'

---

[107] D. Galasiński, D.A. Galasińska. 2007. Lost in communism, lost in migration: narratives of post-1989 Polish migrant experience. *Journal of Multicultural Discourses* 2(1):47-62 (p. 51).

[108] A. White. 2011. *Polish Families and Migration since EU Accession*. Bristol: Policy Press.

processes of settlement and life dilemmas. Most importantly, the concerns of Polish families that White studied are woven around local environments, not 'national' ones, and it seems they silently reject any framing of their lives into the grand 'national' narratives, prompting White to question the very validity of the term 'transnationalism' suggesting that 'translocalism' seems much more appropriate to reflect Polish migrants' outlook and everyday experience.

In fact, the intimate relationship between people's migration experience and everyday life, which is expressed through this demotic, bottom-up discourse, has long been part and parcel of social life in Poland. This discourse emphasises individualism, self-fulfilment, aspiration, and dignity due to performing labour which is valuable not only in terms of economics. It also encourages a down-to-earth or banal understanding of transnationalism or translocalism, as practice, resource, and a normal fact of life and national borders as a nuisance, an inconvenient feature of modern life. The level in which Polish society is in fact transnationally constructed and connected is striking but often undervalued due to the persistence and powerful political position imposed by the lenses of methodological nationalism. For example, in some localities in Poland, majority of inhabitants have relatives in the West, and it is estimated that at least a third of the total Polish population has migrant relatives.[109] An opinion poll by Ośrodek Badania Opinii Publicznej (OBOP) showed that almost two-thirds of the Polish population has a relative or a friend who worked/or works abroad. According to another national survey by Centrum Badania Opinii Publicznej (CBOS), 10% of the population (approximately 3.5 million people) has worked abroad and, in some areas of western Poland, this figure jumps to 20%.[110] In these areas, crossing the border is an everyday occurrence, and in some of

---

[109] See E. Morawska. 2001. Structuring migration: the case of Polish income-seeking travelers to the West. *Theory and Society* 30(1):47–80.

[110] CBOS (Centrum Badania Opinii Społecznej). 2006. *Praca Polaków w krajach Unii Europejskiej.* Warszawa: CBOS.

these western localities, half the population possesses dual citizenship. Probably, the most stunning blow to the dominant discourse of the nation as the locus of moral and cultural health was delivered by another CBOS survey, where respondents were asked whether it was possible to have two fatherlands (*Ojczyzna*). More than two-thirds (71%) agreed with the idea that people could have two fatherlands and only 20% disagreed.[111] Although nationalist discourse portrays the act of leaving as morally ambiguous and a threat to national loyalty, it is clear that individuals can remain strongly attached to more than one country and that they reject the state's attempts to monopolise their loyalty, identities, and sense of belonging.

Those two main meta-narratives present in Polish migration culture — one that reifies the nation, the whole, and establishes an unequal relationship between the individual and the group, and the one which is about self-fulfilment — are interdependent and also reinforce one another. These ways of understanding the nation and movement between nations are constructed in relation to each other and are dialectically interconnected, since the individual will seek to manoeuvre through sets of obligations from an imagined community as often these are tools of control devised by the elites or local structures of power. This interplay between dominant and demotic discourses shapes the ways in which Polish migrants see themselves in Britain and explains why they attach such importance to self-determination and individualism, but as we shall see also to other features, such as whiteness, social class, attitudes towards the state, law, and welfare. It also explains why they hold very ambiguous attitudes towards co-ethnics — something that seems to perplex quite a few scholars looking at Polish migrants. It seems that despite the power of nationalist ideology, they assert their own agency in contesting and resisting the hegemonic formulations of Poland's elites and their nation's

---

[111]   Centrum Badania Opinii Społecznych. 2005. *Tożsamość narodowa Polaków oraz postrzeganie mniejszośći narodowych i tnicznych w Polsce*. Komunikat z badań: CBOS.

historical legacy. In looking at the conceptual arsenal for doing this, we also need to account for another source of tensions and paradoxes that are present in Polish culture, having strong impact on migrations and their meanings: dominant and demotic understanding of social class and hierarchy.

A missing link — social class and emigration

The main argument of the book is that both aspects of social identity — class and ethnicity — form a dynamic and interconnected set of culturally constructed tools that serve individuals and groups to legitimise their actions, make sense of the social world, and pursue their goals. As Michał Buchowski notes,[112] social class in current Polish sociological literature is not a popular term and used mainly in strict mechanistic and Marxist sense as the relation of individuals to the mode of production. This approach cannot be fully satisfying for anthropological analysis, as it is rather what is perceived and constructed as 'class' that demonstrates how culturally and socially class and status are made and remade, especially in a transnational field. This is why a brief look at how social class is approached and understood in Polish society will identify the cultural framework in which Polish migrants operate.

Polish social class structure was marked by its rural, feudal, and post-feudal-based economy for centuries well and shaped by the traumatic historical events of the Second World War and its aftermath, when Polish society lost its long established Jewish population as well as underwent an internal revolution in terms of loss of status of its former elites — the gentry. Going further back, it is crucial to acknowledge that its status as the breadbasket of Europe established in the 15th century had a consolidating effect on the feudal system, enserfing previously relatively free peasants and ensuring the rise of the class of land owners, the *szlachta*, into one of the most numerous in Europe in terms of percentage of the

---

[112] M. Buchowski, E. Conte, C. Nagengast (eds.). 2001. *Poland Beyond Communism: 'Transition' in Critical Perspective*. Fribourg: Fribourg University, p. 142.

overall population.[113] Its more and more monopolised political role meant that the influence of urban centres was minimal, and commerce, banking, trade regarded as inferior and unworthy of noblemen. With exceptions, these were left to Jews or Germans whose political status after the Polish backlash against the Reformation ensured that they could be disposed of and discriminated against in case of economic problems. With the loss of independence and partitions between Russia, Prussia, and Austria, the role of the *szlachta* did not diminish, as often they become the barrier to any social and economic change, maintaining their position at the expense of the rural population.[114] At the same time, political struggles for independence from sections of that group meant that the state administrators kept an uneasy balance between the political roles of different classes. In that equation, one of the fundamental concerns of politically active noblemen, who with the industrialisation and urbanisation began to populate new emerging urban classes or *intelligentsia*, was to politically activate and mobilise rural populations. These, however, most often were not interested in political struggles of the *szlachta* and often actively participated in quashing some risings as well as supporting them.

This uneasy, turbulent relationship between the elites who, in a classical nationalist drive, saw their main task in 'enlightening', 'waking up', and educating the masses for the common national cause of resurrecting the Polish state meant that nationalism slowly became the fundamental aspect of the relations between social classes in Poland, one that in different forms still determines the shape of this society. It is also the constant problem of the Polish *intelligentsia* who in this way set its role and duty as the ones who ought to 'educate and enlighten' and hence control the masses. This process has not ceased after the partitions and during the brief period of pre-Second World War independence as Polish political life centred on the fight between emerging nationalistic

---

[113] See C. Nagengast. 1991. *Reluctant Socialists, Rural entrepreneurs: Class, Culture and the Polish State*. Boulder/San Francisco/Oxford: Westview Press, p. 216.

[114] L. Stomma. 1986. *Antropologia wsi polskiej XIX wieku*. Warszawa: Instytut Wydawniczy Pax.

and Catholic far right and liberal social urban classes with both camps fighting for support of the peasants and working-class parties. These, along with the effects of the depression, ethnic conflicts along its Eastern border, rising anti-Semitism, violently suppressed opposition and workers, and peasants riots being quashed by the police meant that in the run up to the Second World War Polish society was torn apart with strong internal social class conflicts.

The constant concern of the elites over the question—as one of the senior Polish social thinkers, Jerzy Szacki states: 'why the masses do not rise'[115] supporting the elites in their nationalist goals and the strategies to awaken them in production of national myths, meant that Polish nationalism at the very same time acquires distinct democratic and egalitarian tones. After all, the elites had to construct a common language with those who very often saw the elites as prime oppressors and the very source of their economic deprivation and social exclusion. Roman Dmowski, the father of modern Polish nationalism, stated that:

> Men are first and foremost members of a nation; only secondly are they divided into social classes within the nation … the first commandment of the citizen's catechism is solidarity, a sense of union with the entire nation.[116]

In this way, Poles defined along ethnic–religious–linguistic lines, asserted their dominance over other Polish citizens of different religion or speaking a different language. Aimed directly against the Polish Jews from middle and lower classes, this nationalistic construction of the social stratification system had powerful consequences for the rise of anti-Semitism in pre-war Poland. As Genevieve Zubrzycki notes, this was also part of the reason behind the process of how 'national identity was Catholicized and

---

[115] J. Szacki. 2007. O wieczności pytań typu: "Jedna Polska?". [in]: A. Kojder (ed.) *Jedna Polska? Dawne i nowe zróżnicowania społeczne.* Kraków: WAM, Polska Akademia Nauk, pp. 31–46.

[116] F. Millard. 1995. Nationalism in Poland. [in]: P. Latawski (ed.) *Contemporary Nationalism in East and Central Europe.* New York: St Martins Press, p. 111.

Catholicism nationalized'.[117] It also shows the 'ethnic narrowing' as Brubaker terms the process of crystallising of the nation along the primordial, essentialist, and ethno-linguistic lines.[118] What often gets lost, however, is the egalitarianism and communitarianism implicit in this nationalistic message. No wonder then that it has persisted and proven to be widely held also during the postwar communist regime. That combination of communist, egalitarian ideology with the nationalist one proved to be a powerful weapon in the hands of the communist *nomenklatura* in 1968 when the anti-semitic propaganda and repressions led to the expulsion of the remaining Polish Jews, once again stigmatised as an alien segment of Polish society.

The traumatic events of the Second World War dramatically overturned and revolutionised the fabric of Polish society. Almost all Polish Jews — from urban elites, professors, and doctors to poor craftsmen, traders, and shopkeepers — perished in the Holocaust. Both the Nazis and Stalin's political strategy designed to 'decapitate' the potential resistance to their military domination meant a continuing extermination campaign of members of the *inteligentsia*, local elites, businessmen, and anyone who could resist oppression. Also in the wake of the Second World War, the borders of the Polish state 'migrated' to the West, leaving the Eastern parts (ethnically and religiously mixed) within the Soviet Union and acquiring Eastern parts of Germany.

The imposition of the new system led to another massive social restructurisation of society along with huge industrialisation and reconstruction projects. The new Poland, the Polish People's Republic, was supposed to break with the capitalist and feudal past, and the enduring civil war right until the early 1950s was presented by the Communist Party as the swan's song of the *ancient regime*. That period was also marked by the most brutal polit-

---

[117] G. Zubrzycki. 2006. *The Crosses of Auschwitz. Nationalism and Religion in Post-Communist Poland.* Chicago/London: The University of Chicago Press, pp. 44–45 (p. 49).

[118] R. Brubaker. 1996. *Nationalism Reframed. Nationhood and the National Question in the New Europe.* Los Angeles: University of California, pp. 84–86.

ical oppressions perpetuated by the communist state and lasted until the death of Josef Stalin.

The problem of legitimacy of the new order in the eyes of the population was central to the preservation of the system, one that eventually led to its demise. Ideologically, new power holders aimed at legitimising the new order through a powerful emphasis on social justice, equality, and increased social mobility opportunities for the formerly oppressed and discriminated social classes — farmers and workers. As Buchowski notes, '*the principle of profitability was declared subordinate to that of' social justice' as implemented through the wide redistribution of income that by and large benefited the underprivileged*'[119] and despite political oppression which tended to be selective and — apart from the Stalinist era — never on massive scale a la Caucescu, the system overall developed a certain logic and achieved a degree of popular support — especially during the 1970s when, with the help of Western loans, communist regime managed to ensure a level of economic stability for large sections of Polish society. The cyclical periods of workers' strikes or students' unrest were phases of crisis of legitimacy and resulted in the state's attempts to win it back rather than aim to produce a systemic, revolutionary change. Although economically inefficient and politically oppressive, through mass employment, mass leisure programmes, and mass education and industrialisation, Polish type of socialism did develop to a certain degree a functioning welfare state. The objective of that social transformation, along with the Leninist orthodoxy, was to make all classes politically and economically dependent on the state and the state was equated with the Communist Party.

The communist system, however, needed to adjust to local circumstances, and despite the usage in common parlance of the label 'communist', there were huge variations in time and space between countries and periods. Buchowski reminds us that '*Eu-*

---

[119] M. Buchowski, E. Conte, C. Nagengast (eds.). 2001. Post-war Poland: a presentation. [in]: *Poland Beyond Communism. "Transition" in Critical Perspective*. Fribourg: Fribourg University Press, p. 17.

rope east of Elbe river was not simply red, but colourful and diversified, even if the red pigment was manifest everywhere'.[120] One of the most important aspects in case of Poland was the relative freedom of some civil, non-state institutions. First, after the Stalinist era of oppression, the Polish Catholic Church—in contrast to the Church in Czechoslovakia or East Germany—emerged as an important political actor, keeping control over some of its assets, institutions, publications, educational provision, international connections, and what's vital—peoples' minds, collective imagery, and symbols. Linked to this Polish Communists—in the face of massive opposition from rural population—quite early gave up one of the central communist ideas of collectivisation of food production. This effectively recognised a certain level of independence of the rural class from the state, although throughout the communist period, the pressure to control the rural population was considerable. The main paradox, however, as observed by Caroline Nagengast,[121] an American anthropologist conducting fieldwork over two decades in a rural community in south-eastern Poland, was that the actions of the state and relative farmers' independence and resistance led to the emergence of a specific capitalist, or proto-capitalist culture of production, recreating a specific class relationship between the rural and urban populations. She emphasises the role of the black economy which eventually led to increased inequalities within the rural class. What's crucial in her argumentation is that class divisions remained and became more entrenched during the communist period in rural areas. The vital outcome is that the anti-state, resistant, and strongly traditional outlook of Polish rural communities needs be seen in a longer term perspective and their struggle with feudal, communist, and now capitalist economic conditions as one continuous chain of struggle for survival and independence from state interference. This anti-state and anti-institutional attitude of the Polish rural

---

[120]   M. Buchowski, E. Conte, C. Nagengast (eds.). 2001. *Ibidem.* pp. 9–10.
[121]   C. Nagengast. 1991. *Reluctant Socialists, Rural Entrepreneurs. Class, Culture and the Polish State.* Boulder/San Francisco/Oxford: Westview Press.

class seems to be entrenched in long traditions and is often identified as one of obstacles to successful modernisation of its economy, seen by some prominent social thinkers as a 'hang-over' from the communist past and the persistence of the 'homo sovieticus' syndrome, characterised by anti-state attitudes, welfare dependency, lack of initiative, and mistrust or lack of social capital.[122]

If farmers were often regarded by the official Polish communist propaganda as the *bete noire* of the system, it was the working class whose status has been raised to levels unseen before. Skilled workers, especially in heavy industry, mining, mills, and shipyards were seen as the future and soul of the nation. With status went privileges, concessions, and also a strong political voice—as proved by the August 1980 Solidarity revolution. Ironically, the class mostly cherished by the communist state turned out to be not only the class that organised main anti-state strikes that led to the collapse of the system triggering the end of the Cold War, but also, the one that emerged as one of the biggest losers of the post-1989 transformation period. As Zygmunt Bauman has noted: '*The social forces which led to the downfall of the communist power* ... [were] *not those that* [would] *eventually benefit from the construction of the new system*'.[123]

One of the explanations of this phenomenon is that despite the communist purges, the role of the *intelligentsia* has not diminished. Despite the communist constitution stating that the Polish new state will: 'contain, expel and liquidate social classes that live at the expense of workers and peasants', many surviving members of the former elites managed to work through the system and actually do quite well in the process. Although now recruited not mainly from families of *szlachta* background, the reproduction of their role in society was coupled with the reproduction of specific set of myths rooted in pre-war Poland with the idea of duty to-

---

[122] P. Sztompka 1993. Civilizational incompetence: the trap of post-communist societies. *Zeitschrift für Soziologie* 22:85–95.

[123] Z. Bauman. 1994. After the patronage state: a model in search of class interests. [in]: C.G.A. Bryan, E. Mokrzycki (eds.) *The New Great Transformation? Change and Continuity in East-Central Europe*. London and New York: Routledge, pp 33.

wards the nation, its people, and the task of educating the masses the central one. Overall, the state was the only employer and in control of most aspects. The crucial aspect of the effects of Communism and its dogma on state intervention was that in terms of class, this led to levelling down wages and disassociation of earnings from social status. *'There appeared an inconsistency of status reflecting discrepancies between the social prestige attached to given professions and the salary and benefits they procured'* as Buchowski and others note,[124] which meant that the translation of economic means into social position was far from accepted; in fact, having money and conspicious consumption was regarded with disdain and suspicion—an additional element of egalitarianism strengthened by the nationalist theme of ethnic ties as binding people of all walks of life.

Social norms, however, are often negotiated and rendered void due to economic constraints and the very practical aspects of living in what was effectively a hugely ineffective and unsustainable economic system (for a long time, sustained thanks to the loans from capitalist countries). Basic economic inefficiency of the system meant that all state employees needed to compensate their earning with other means, private, independent, black market, informal activities. This—along with the black market economy that flourished in rural communities—led to the emergence of not only two-tier economics but also a set of specific cultural norms regulating informal, out-of-system, illegal activities and along with this a deep suspicion towards formal institutions and the state. Janine Wedel who conducted her fieldwork in Poland in the 1980s notes how widespread was the practice of informal dealings and networking among all groups in Poland.[125] She critically assesses the widespread practice of double standards, paradoxes in human everyday interactions forced upon people by living in fear

---

[124] M. Buchowski, E. Conte, C. Nagengast (eds.). 2001. Post-war Poland: a presentation. [in]: *Poland Beyond Communism. "Transition" in Critical Perspective*. Fribourg: Fribourg University Press, p. 17.

[125] J. Wedel. 1986. *The Private Poland: An Anthropological Look at Everyday Life*. New York: Columbia University Press.

and disjunction between the official propaganda and everyday life. Her analysis of the practice of *kombinacje* [to arrange things, to do things, to get things done] and *dojścia* [ins, connections, networks] as ways of manoeuvring through the maze of illogical and hostile laws of the socialist state has some strong moral overtones, and as we will revisit these practices among Polish migrants in London, we will attempt to link them more to the practices of working-class resistance and use of resources by the underprivileged.

This brief look at class relations in communist-time Poland shows that class and modes of distinctions have a capacity to endure despite political circumstances and economic shifts. These social constellations predominantly set power relations. The culturally ascribed role of the intelligentsia as the 'educator' of the masses, its position of the leader and power holder, the role of rural class as independent embodiment of the Polish virtues and resistance to the state, the anti-state, and anti-institutional outlook of both rural and intelligentsia classes along with a strong differentiation between economic standing and social status — are the issues to be kept in mind while we look at what role transnational migrations play in this dynamic process. These historical and cultural factors result in a quite specific set of values, norms, and embedded practices of the everyday life of Poles — whatever their class background. As a prominent Polish sociologist Ziółkowski suggests: *'In Poland, traditional authority — traditional values, religion and family — are much more important than in any other post-communist state, while the rational-legal authority of the state is not held in very high esteem. The state in Poland is not a fully legitimized institution, it is perceived mainly as a welfare state, the agent of the security net'.*[126]

---

[126] M. Ziółkowski. 2001. Changes of interests and values of Polish society. [in]: M. Buchowski, E. Conte, C. Nagengast (eds.) *Poland Beyond Communism. "Transition" in Critical Perspective.* Fribourg: Fribourg University Press, pp. 161–179 (p. 169).

In Polish sociological thought, this phenomenon had been interpreted in numerous ways. The best known is Stanisław Nowak's theory of the sociological vacuum. He argues that, in terms of fundamental societal values, Poland was a federation of families united within the nation conceived as a cultural community distinct from and opposed to the state. However, what is most vital is the enduring, constant, banal existence of a disjunction between the moral, dominant codes, and the reality of everyday life. There seems to be a constant contrast between what is the perception and idea of Poland produced by the elites and what it actually was or how people understand it. The construction of emigration as a morally dubious choice had had little impact on millions of Poles escaping poverty and oppression — and not, as many nationalists Poles would like to hear — from the occupying power, but by their own ruling class. The impression and the symbol of the Polish nation and Polish territory as essentially 'polonised' is contrasted by actual constantly shifting borders, the ethno-linguistic and religious mosaic and plurality of that land. In addition, the notion of 'freedom', so much cherished by nationalists is contrasted by the fact that this has been one of the most feudal societies in Europe, and it was often the occupying powers that have lifted the centuries-old enserfment. In nationalistic parlance, 'oppression' meant always the 'outsiders', attack on the Polish state, not the inequalities and caste-like hierarchies of the Polish feudal system with explicit political exclusion of Jewish minority and systematic anti-Semitism, leading to cyclical pogroms. That understanding of freedom in nationalistic and state-centric terms is contrasted by the fact that throughout history Poland experienced a plethora of diverse administrative state frameworks that elude a simple distinction between 'free' and 'occupied'. Although Poles were in governments in the state structures of the occupying powers, different parts had some degree of autonomy throughout the different period of partitions, and its ethnic composition was very diverse throughout history. But, when one listens to a standard account in history texts, political statements or banal nationalistic and plain ahistorical stereotypes such as the one presented earlier by Peter Stachura, the picture is simple—Poland was 'erased', was not free, and enslaved, and Poles participated in freedom fighting *en masse*. The state, nation, and individuals are thus equated and magically transformed into one.

These contrasts and ambiguities related to the process of national identity production are illustrated at all levels of society, public debates, and academic disputes. The very common theme illustrating this phenomena is the depiction of society in binary terms opposing each other and the contrast between 'two Polands', between the state and society, the society and the nation, the ruling class and the oppressed, or in the context of the transformation period after 1989, the winners and losers.[127] It is as if Polish society defines itself not through unity, but rather internal friction, dissent, and competing discourses about what it means to be. The binary perception of the collective is an interesting cultural phenomenon, and we shall encounter it also on the level of class stratification, perceptions of the state, and politics expressed by migrants themselves.

Previous studies on Poles in Great Britain and their implications

Poles have been largely ignored sociologically despite being in the UK for a substantial amount of time. Academic studies on the Poles, who settled in Britain after the Second World War (mainly war refugees and members of the Polish armed forces), was until recently confined to the work of Jerzy Zubrzycki, Keith Sword, and several articles by Sheila Patterson. This in its own right

---

[127] See, for instance, an edited volume entitled: *One Poland? Past and New Social Differences*. Wydawnictwo WAM, PAN 2007; published by Polish Academy of Science in which some prominent Polish sociologists aimed at summarising social changes after the collapse of Communism. Jerzy Szacki's article in this volume is entitled: *About the Eternal Importance of the Question: One Poland?*

should tell us something significant. Anthropologists know well that omission or avoidance of a specific topic by an informer in an interview is an important piece of information in itself. If the history of research on different minority groups in Britain was treated like an interview, we would definitely want to know why researchers have been much more eager to look at 'black and Asian' communities rather than white Christians.

In his monograph on Poles as an emerging ethnic community in post-war Britain, Jerzy Zubrzycki followed in the Chicago school tradition where immigrant communities were seen as following a well-trodden path from segregation, to integration and then on to assimilation. Invaluable as a work on a community still in its early stages of formation, his monograph *Polish migrant in Great Britain* draws a conclusion which in later developments have been confirmed — that the specific political ideology would keep the community together and separate from the British majority. As a later historian, Jan Lencznarowicz, writes, a particular set of narratives and symbols were established, which acted as founding political myths.[128] These myths claimed that a true, patriotic, free, and authentic Poland had had to be removed from the territory and had been preserved among the soldiers and refugees scattered around the world after 1945. The myth was politically articulated through the idea of *legalizm*, that is that the Polish political system and state legitimacy was represented only by the government-in-exile in London. The Warsaw regime was, therefore, illegal, illegitimate, and — in essence — un-Polish. Bearing in mind what was described earlier about the role of political transnationalism plays in Polish culture, it is not surprising that Polish community in the post-war Britain found themselves on familiar symbolic territory; they were doing precisely what their cultural imaginary ancestors did 100 years ago in Paris.

The second major monograph, written by Keith Sword, looks at Poles when, in his own words, the community was in

---

[128] J. Lencznarowicz. 2000. Wyobraźnia polityczna polskiej emigracji niepodległościowej po II wojnie światowej. Zarys tematu. [in:] J.E. Zamojski (ed.) *Migracje polityczne XX wieku. Migracje i społeczeństwo* 4. Warszawa: Neriton, pp. 65–85.

'decline' in late 1980s and mid-1990s. His detailed study of community institutions, social life, and identity problems, especially among the second generation, offers a valuable insight into how a relatively small group of refugees managed to maintain a distinct ethos and political ideology and, despite the odds, preserve the traditions of pre-war Poland—mainly through rituals, symbols, and commemorative events. This achievement required, however, considerable suspicion towards any novelty, and what Zubrzycki identified as their political ethos proved also to be the force that conserved and immobilised that group in terms of cultural reproduction, a feature that led Sword to claim the inevitable decline of the group. Furthermore, it supported a rigid hierarchical order and a narrow range of diasporic institutions. High external and internal barriers had to be maintained in order to exclude outsiders and control insiders. The exiled elite with strong male dominance sustained its power by controlling financial assets, political and cultural symbols, and community institutions.[129]

Paradoxically, the threat to its power did not emanate from the British majority—in educational, financial, and social terms, British Poles integrated rather smoothly achieving high degrees of social mobility. The threat of polluting and distorting the static ideological foundations of this elite group came from other Poles—those who shared similar cultural traits, language, and heritage, but who held different beliefs about what it meant to be Polish in Britain. As the Polish anthropologist Zygmunt Benedyktowicz notes, in the relational construction of social identities, it is not simply any 'Other' that we define ourselves against.[130] The most threatening is the 'close Other'—someone who shares the same or almost the same social and cultural features. We do not need to differentiate ourselves too firmly from those who are perceived as very 'distant', but when these are absent, we need to

[129] This tendency of formalism, that is, seeing community only through formal life of the institutions, was strongly criticised by Bogusia Temple; see: B. Temple. 1994. *Polish Identity and Community*. University of Manchester Occasional Papers in Sociology no 38.
[130] Z. Benedyktowicz. 2000. *Portrety "Obcego"*. Kraków: Wydawnictwo UJ.

draw on other mechanisms from cultural and symbolic domains. We begin to look for other ways to differentiate, be it at the local, regional, gender, or axiological level. Crucially, we need to communicate these differences in much stronger and recognisable ways, so those who are constructing *external definitions* understand us and recognise our distinct features, especially if these are factors in our place in the hierarchy of power, specific resources, and perception among others. Benedyktowicz's explanation of how people differentiate between close and distant Others explains an issue which Sword fails to explore — how new migrants from Poland were treated by the established, political émigrés during the 1990s. In other words, how are ethnicity, class, and power negotiated between people, who are part of British society but share a historical identity with Polish newcomers? In years up to the Poland's accession into the EU in 2004, established British Poles often did not want to associate with migrants, who were often seen as low-skilled, working-class, and undocumented workers. Gender also played a part. Sword discusses, for example, the stereotypical situation frequently depicted in diasporic press warnings of Polish 'passport hunters' — women in search of wealthy British Poles able to secure them a future and British passport. This situation was often expressed by the established British Poles as epitomising that 'Poles from Poland' are a different group, one that does not share the same values, norms, and ideological views and one that one should be wary about. One of the modalities of this tension were the conflicts between the émigré combatant groups and the Polish Church, whose priests that are supposed to cater to that group are sometimes rejected as being 'sovietised' in Poland and, therefore, unsuitable to perform their pastoral role.

On an empirical level as Patterson, Sword, Burrell,[131] Irek, and myself[132] note, this ideological construction of a distinct group

[131] K. Burell. 2003. Small-scale transnationalism: homeland connections and the Polish 'community' in Leister. *International Journal of Population Geography* 9(4):323–335.

[132] M. Garapich. 2008. Odyssean refugees, migrants and power: construction of the "other" within the Polish community in the United Kingdom. [in]: D. Reed-Danahay, C. Brettell (red.) *Citizenship, Political Engagement and Belonging. Immi-*

is paradoxically accompanied by strong family, occupational and personal connections which link émigrés to other Poles in both Poland. In other words, these groups are linked together in the same migration chain through family networks, economic activity, and lifestyles—after all Polish émigrés also needed a plumber, builder, or carer. However, these links do not weaken the old émigrés' ideology—on the contrary, it seems that the closer the contacts, the more the need to maintain and communicate the boundary, even within one family. Boundary-making mechanisms within these groups seemed to acquire much more important meaning since they communicated to what social class people belong to and what position of power they aspire to. Paradoxically, one may say that the community Sword was predicting would decline has been revived by the need for that boundary revival, this time between migrants who communicate their class position through nationalistic discourse—something I explore in more detail in Chapter 7. From the migrants' perspective, this complex relationship between internal discourses of difference and similarity acquires specific meanings shaped by class and ethnicity. In the next chapter, I will focus on the role played by class in the migration from Poland to the UK during the last decade.

Understandably, last years brought an important expansion of scholarship on Polish migration in Britain, and some crucial research has been carried out by scholars, both from Poland and the UK. Kathy Burrell after her monograph on older generations of emigrants from various European countries, including Poland living in Leicester, edited an important collection of articles[133] which documents settlement, pattern of mobility, discourses, network creation, gender dimensions, and labour market outcomes of post-Accession Poles. Louise Ryan and her team have, in particular, published a series of important articles on the value and nature of networks among Polish migrants and also on the experi-

grants in Europe and the United States. New Brunswick/New Jersey/London: Rutgers University Press, pp. 124–144.

[133] K. Burrell. 2009. Polish migration to the UK in the 'new' European Union: after 2004. [in]: K. Burrell (ed.) *Studies in Migration and Diaspora.* Aldershot: Ashgate.

ences of schooling among Polish parents.[134] Anne White, besides numerous articles, has published an important monograph analysing complex pattern of settlement and adaptation to small-scale towns in England.[135] Marta Kempny[136] has written a book documenting Polish migrants' identity formation and negotiations in Belfast and Agnieszka Bielewska[137] looked at similar processes in Manchester. There are also fascinating studies looking at Polish women converting to Islam,[138] Polish Roma,[139] political participation,[140] gender relations,[141] social class and work,[142] and migration

---

[134] L. Ryan. 2010. Becoming Polish in London: negotiating ethnicity through migration. *Social Identities: Journal for the Study of Race, Nation and Culture* 16(3):359–376; L. Ryan, R. Sales, M. Tilki, B. Siara. 2009, Family strategies and transnational migration: recent Polish migrants in London. *Journal of Ethnic and Migration Studies* 35(1):61–77; L. Ryan, A. D'Angelo. 2011. Sites of socialisation—Polish parents and children in London schools. *Przegląd Polonijny*. Rok XXXVII z. 1/2011.

[135] A. White. 2011a. *Polish families and Migration in Poland since EU Accession,* Bristol: Policy Press; A. White. 2011b. The mobility of Polish families in the West of England. Translocalism and attitudes to return. *Przegląd Polonijny*. Rok XXXVII z. 1/2011.

[136] M. Kempny. 2010. *Polish Migrants in Belfast: Border Crossing and Identity Construction.* Newcastle upon Tyne: Cambridge Scholars Press.

[137] A. Bielewska. 2012. *Changing Polish Identities. Post-War and Post-Accession Polish Migrants in Manchester.* Oxford, Bern, Berlin, Bruxelles, Frankfurt am Main, New York, Wien: Peter Lang.

[138] J. Krotofil. 2011. 'If I am to be a Muslim, I have to be a good one'. Polish migrant women embracing Islam and reconstructing identity in dialogue with self and others. [in]: K. Górak-Sosnowska (ed.) *Muslims in Poland and Eastern Europe. Widening the European Discourse on Islam.* Warsaw: University of Warsaw.

[139] T. Staniewicz. 2011. Negotiating space and contesting boundaries. The case of Polish Roma and Polish migrants. *Przegląd Polonijny*. Rok XXXVII z. 1/2011.

[140] S. Driver, M. Garapich. 2012, 'Everyone for themselves'? Non-national EU citizens from eastern and central Europe and the 2012 London elections. http://www.sociology.ox.ac.uk/documents/epop/papers/EPOP_article_garapichdriver_SEPTEMBER_07_mg.pdf
See also, J. Kucharczyk. 2013. Nic o nas bez nas. [in]: W. Brytanii (red.) *Partycypacja obywatelska Polaków.* Warszawa: Instytut Spraw Publicznych.

[141] M. Garapich. 2011. 'It's a jungle out there. You need to stick together': anti-institutionalism, alcohol and performed masculinities among Polish homeless men in London. *Liminalities: A Journal of Performance Studies* 7(3):Autumn 2011; K. Burrell. 2008. Male and female polishness in post-war Leicester: gender and its intersections in a refugee community. [in]: L. Ryan, W. Webster (eds.) *Gendering Migration: Masculinity, Femininity and Ethnicity in Post-war Britain.* Aldershot:

strategies.[143] Many themes present in these studies will also be brought up in this book, and I will draw on these studies where appropriate. Looking at Polish migration from an anthropological perspective and then focusing on its development over the last decade in London, one of the most crucial sites of transnational connections will necessarily bring forward the transnational or translocal nature of social identity formation over time. In fact, there is — as we shall see — no clear boundry dividing Polish society and London, which is captured bythe metaphor of this city's 'Polish borders'.

Ashgate, pp. 71–87; B. Siara. 2013. Construction of gender in the migration space: Polish women in the UK, *GENDER. Zeitschrift für Geschlecht, Kultur und Gesellschaft [GENDER. Journal of Gender, Culture and Society]* 1:105–120; B. Siara. 2011. Body, gender and sexuality in recent migration of Poles to the United Kingdom. *Migration Studies: Polish Review* 1:111–128; A. Datta. 2009. 'This is special humour': visual narratives of polish masculinities on London's building sites. [in]: K. Burrell. *Polish Migration to the UK in the 'New' European Union.* Surrey: Ashgate.

[142] P. Trevena. 2011. Divided by class, connected by work. Class divisions among the new wave of Polish migrants in the UK. *Przegląd Polonijny* Rok XXXVII z. 1/2011.

[143] M. Garapich, S. Drinkwater. 2015. Migration strategies of Polish migrants: do they have any at all? *Journal of Ethnic and Migration Studies* 41(12):1909–1931.

Chapter 3

From 'illegals' to EU citizens.
The collapse of the communist system and rise of migration as adaptation

Grand historical narratives are connected to vital political events that radically change the social and economic structures and peoples' perception of the past and present. Individuals and groups are aware of the political narratives that nation-state discourses construct around mobility, territory, and identities, partially through being affected by the consequences of the vast socio-economic upheavals, which makes these symbolic legitimisations all the more necessary. In Poland, the most dramatic change has been the collapse of the communist system and the relative opening up of its borders to the West after 1989. And although already since the 1970s the harsh restriction of travel of the previous era has been eased,[144] the freedom that the collapse of the Iron Curtain brought for millions of individuals meant precisely the freedom to move across their national borders and the ability to 'domesticate' their passports.[145]

Polish migration of the last three decades needs to be understood, therefore, in the context of the transformation from a socialist, post-rural, industrial but highly inefficient economy dependent in later stages on Western loans[146] and adaptation to a free market economy — something that has never been seen as easy

---

[144] D. Stola. 2001. Międzynarodowa mobilność w PRL. [in]: E. Jaźwińska, M. Okólski (eds.) *Ludzie na huśtawce*. Warszawa: Scholar, pp. 62–97.

[145] E. Morawska. 2001. Structuring migration: the case of Polish income-seeking travelers to the West. *Theory and Society* 30(1):47–80.

[146] J. Staniszkis. 1991. *The Dynamics of the Breakthrough in Eastern Europe: The Polish Experience* (Society and Culture in East-Central Europe). California: University of California Press.

or without severe social costs. The verdict on the costs and benefits is a paradoxical one. Here, on the one hand, there is the success story—one that would surely satisfy the gurus of economic
liberalism from Freedman to Hayek. The inadequacies of the
communist-run economy have been clearly demonstrated—not
just to intellectuals but also to millions whose experience as consumers was daily proof of the weaknesses and systemic fallacy of
a centrally planned economy. In the early stage of transformation,
it was widely believed that the free market would remedy the ills
inflicted by the disastrous economic policies of the socialist system. In the early 1990s, Poland changed rapidly and a new class of
entrepreneurs, managers, and traders emerged to provide the
infant market economy with an aura of pioneering optimism.[147]
Government statistics and reports from the Organisation for Economic Cooperation and Development (OECD) and the World
Bank encouraged this optimistic mood—the economy was growing far more rapidly than in the West, cities were rebuilt, and lifestyles acquired the gloss of Western modernity. Entry into the
North Atlantic Treaty Organisation (NATO) and then the EU in
2004 seemed to seal the gap between the East and West, between
the underdeveloped European periphery and the centre.

Yet, beneath the ideal and the happy story of Polish transformation lies another one—a story of bitter new social divisions,
rising inequalities, shocking levels of poverty, and degradation[148]
appearing together with revitalised old frictions, which were
sometimes shaped by ethnic and religious loyalties—especially
the uneasy and still traumatic fact of the loss of almost all Polish
Jews.[149] In the face of rapid social change, many Poles anxiously
explored their identity in the face of a dynamic, globalising world.
The economic transformations in Poland, especially the downscal-

[147] H. Domański. 2000. *On the Verge of Convergence. Social Stratification in Eastern
Europe.* Budapest: CEU Press.
[148] T. Rakowski. 2009. *Łowcy, zbieracze, praktycy niemocy. Etnografia człowieka
zdegradowanego.* Słowo/obraz/terytoria: Gdańsk.
[149] G. Zubrzycki. 2006. *The Crosses of Auschwitz: Nationalism and Religion in Post-
Communist Poland.* Chicago: University of Chicago Press.

ing of heavy industry, led to high unemployment and a deep re-structuring of the labour market. For many people, the change from a poor but predictable environment to a wealthy but free-for-all wild capitalism was a traumatic experience[150] throwing people into destitution, systemic unemployment, and poverty.[151] As Zygmunt Bauman noted,[152] the irony that workers in shipyards and coal mines were losing their jobs, because of the political pro-cesses they themselves had initiated through the Solidarity revolts of the 1980s, did not go unnoticed.

The collapse of Communism also brought more subtle, cul-tural changes, which could not be explained simply by old, Cold War rhetoric. For those among the elites in the opposition and anti-communist movement, the former struggles against the re-gime offered a world view structured along a simple dichotomy between the communists and Solidarity, the state and society, oppression, and freedom. The enemy seemed well defined hence struggle straightforward, nurtured by powerful nationalist narra-tives where 'Poles' were always confronted by 'enemies' and community of suffering for national cause was unified by the hos-tile world outside—the partitioning powers, the communists, 'the system', the unfortunate geopolitical environment or in more con-spiratory but popular scenarios by liberals, Jewish financiers, or morally corrupt Western elites. The times of struggle offered a conceptually clear world view where 'we' the Poles, were fighting 'them'.

Yet, the waters became little more murky during the politi-cal negotiations between the regime and the opposition in the late

---

[150] P. Sztompka. 2000. *Trauma wielkiej zmiany: społeczne koszty transformacji.* Warszawa.

[151] T. Rakowski. 2009. *Łowcy, zbieracze, praktycy niemocy.* Warszawa: Słowo/obraz/terytoria; H. Domański. 2002. *Ubóstwo w społeczeństwach postkomunistycznych.* Warszawa: Wyd. Instytut Spraw Publicznych.

[152] Z. Bauman. 1994. After the patronage state: a model in search of class interests. [in]: C.G.A. Bryan, E. Mokrzycki (eds.) *The New Great Transformation? Change and Continuity in East-Central Europe.* London/New York: Routledge, pp. 33.

[152] M. Buchowski, , E. Conte, C. Nagengast (eds.). 2001. *Poland Beyond Communism: 'Transition' in Critical Perspective.* Fribourg: Fribourg University Press, p. 17.

1980s and early 1990s—negotiations which brought about something quite unparalleled in Polish history—a bloodless change of
power, a systemic change without a shot fired.[153] But those outside
the world of political activism began to question the previous 'us'
and 'them' dichotomy, especially when they suffered from the
new economic reforms. In the face of wild invasive world of capitalism, the communist period began to appear as a time if not of
prosperity, then certainly stability, relative security but also moral
clarity when it was obvious who is on which side of history. Suddenly, the system of lifetime employment, generous welfare system, free health care, education, the straight path from school to
work, the clear and predictable life strategies to be pursued in
order to lead a stable life, and the neat division between the communists and the opposition had disappeared. People could lose
their jobs because of foreign takeovers, financial turmoil around
the globe, or simply because the employer decided to do so. Private ownership, free market, and individualism—the mantra of
the new economics in Poland—became a double-edged sword
since it offered wealth for some and misery, uncertainty, and loss
to many others.[154] In the 1990s, it became increasingly and alarm-
ingly clear that the growth of inequality in Poland was one of the
fastest across the eastern region,[155] despite the rosy picture por-
trayed by the government and Western foreign capital.

---

[153] The most typical example of that never-ending search for answers on 'who was
who' are the accusations about the Solidarity icon, the Nobel Peace Prize winner, and ex-Polish president Lech Walesa. He is accused by some of his former
colleagues and some historians of being a communist police informant during
the 1970s and then, as president, destroying the evidence.

[154] H. Świda-Ziemba. 1994. Mentalność postkomunistyczna. *Kultura i
Społeczeństwo* 1(3):35–50.

[155] J. Hausner, et al. 1999. *Trzy Polski. Potencjał i bariery integracji z Unią Europejską.*
Warszawa: EU-Monitoring; K. Frieske. 1997. *Ofiary sukcesu. Zjawiska
marginalizacji społecznej w Polsce.* Warszawa: Instytut Socjologii UW.

The biggest social change arose from people being forced to radically rethink their plans,[156] life strategies, meaning-making practices, and understandings of the market economy. Moreover, the realities of the transformation led people to question more and more the ideological underpinning of the new Polish capitalism, which in line with the neo-liberal mantra insisted that people's energies flourished only in a meritocratic, free market system and that Poland was now a society where individual capabilities and skills determined a person's social mobility rather than the right connections with the communist *nomenklatura*, an omnipresent cronyism and ability to dodge the system.[157]

However, despite the majority of the political elite's claim that anyone could now join the new middle class of entrepreneurs and wealth was accessible for all with the right individualistic, liberal, and modern mind set, it became increasingly clear that the structural and cultural frameworks of the former regime had ingeniously adapted itself to the new economy. A form of 'political capitalism' emerged — according to some, a corrupted and distorted version of what 'real' capitalism was supposed to look like.[158] As several observers pointed out,[159] former communist state officials used their social and cultural capital to set up and run the institutions of the newly formed capitalist economy. Banks, trusts, state-run companies, media, public relations, and big business recruited many of these former state officials. Paradoxically, to be a good capitalist, it helped to be member of a Communist party or

---

[156] P. Sztompka. 2000. The trauma of change: a case of post-communist society. [in]: J. Alexander, et al. (eds.) *Cultural Trauma*. Berkeley: University of California Press.

[157] J. Wedel. 1986. *The Private Poland: An Anthropological Look at Everyday Life*. New York: Columbia University Press

[158] J. Staniszkis. 1998. Polityka postkomunistycznej instytucjonalizacji w perspektywie historycznej. *Studia Polityczne* 4(5):39–60.

[159] M. Los, A. Zybertowicz. 2000. *Privatizing the Police-State: The Case of Poland*. London: Palgrave; A. Zybertowicz. 2002. Demokracja jako fasada: przypadek III RP. [in]: E. Mokrzycki, A. Rychard, A. Zybertowicz (eds.) *Utracona dynamika? O niedojrzałości polskiej demokracji*. Warszawa: Wydawn.

at least to have good connections in circles of the former *nomenkla-tura*.

This 'privatisation of the state'[160] created a clientelist culture, and corruption rapidly grew[161] to peak during the 2001–2005 post-Communist party Solusz Lewicy Demokratycznej (SLD)-led government. It is in this environment that the rise of the nationalistic right in Poland after the elections in 2005 needs to be seen. The electoral successes of the identical twins (the Kaczyński brothers), who led the right-wing Law and Justice party (Prawo i Sprawiedliwość — PiS), can be partially explained by the dissatisfaction of those excluded from the benefits of Polish transformation a promise of reform of the system and accomplishment of 'true' freedom and democracy, not stained by previous negotiations with the *ancient regime* figures. As before,[162] this movement had a specific Polish flavour of previous resistance social movements of being mainly anti-capitalist, anti-state, at times nationalistic, and cherishing the virtues and traditions of rural Poland and its Catholic heritage.

Here, we witness a powerful tension and internal disconnection between the ideal and social practice, which in turn generates long-established traditional responses and specific social and cultural practices — a phenomenon familiar in Polish history. Just as the egalitarianism of official propaganda was disconnected from everyday life under Communism, so did the neo-liberal discourse of individualism, equal opportunities, meritocracy, entrepreneurship, and creativity fail to counter the growing perception among large sections of society that Poland was increasingly becoming a banana republic with corrupt, nepotistic elites, informal

---

[160] A. Kamiński. 1988. The privatization of the state. Trends in the evolution of "real" socialist political systems. *The Asian Journal of Public Administration* 10(1):27–47.

[161] K. Gadowska. 2005. Clientelism in the Silesian Coal Mining Industry. [in]: *Political Corruption in Poland*. Forschungsstelle Osteuropa Bremen: Arbeitspapiere und Materialien, 65/2005, pp. 21–48.

[162] C. Nagengast. 1991. *Reluctant Socialists, Rural entrepreneurs: Class, Culture and the Polish State*. Boulder/San Francisco/Oxford: Westview Press, p. 199.

networks, and shadowy cliques driving the political agenda and foreign capital aggressively undermining Polish economic and political sovereignty. Not delving into the empirical base of these perceptions—what is crucial is the role and function of the discrepancy, contradictions, and mismatch between what is preached and what is being done, what is the discursive underpinning, ideological justification, and practical application; in other words, between the dominant norms imposed by the elites as 'just' and their impact on the lower classes, between the world as it should be and as it is. These internal contradictions are sources of both individual and social tensions, and as I elaborate further in detailing Polish migrants' ethnic myth-making, peoples' agency, and discursive, meaning-making practices aim to intelectually and emotionally contain these contradictions. As the previous chapter demonstrated, these tensions produce particular narratives and myths, which compete for an explanation of the world people live in. As in the dominant discourse of emigration, here we encounter one of the powerful features of Polish society—its internal contradictions, frictions, tensions, and disjunctions between ideals, norms, and social practices.

Post-1989 migrations as tested survival strategies

The massive social and economic changes meant that people needed to learn quickly how to survive in the world of new capitalism. One tried and tested strategy was to emigrate and, not surprisingly, the numbers of migrants dramatically increased after the collapse of Communism[163] and indeed, Poles became one of the most mobile populations in Europe. Initially, they went to the traditional destinations, such as Germany and the USA, but then began to seek out entirely new places, for example, Italy or Greece. In this period of the early-to-late 1990s, unemployment peaked in some regions to 30–40%. Mobility enabled many to keep

---

[163]   M. Okólski, E. Jazwinska. 2001. *Ludzie na huśtawce*. Warszawa: Scholar.

pace with rising costs, consumption needs, and the global inter-dependence of different economies. These migrants came predom-inantly from the countryside and former industrial towns. A par-ticular form of international mobility developed, which Ewa Jaźwińska and Marek Okólski refer to as 'incomplete migration' — largely seasonal and designed to support family income back in Poland.[164] As they argue in their seminal collection of studies un-dertaken by the Centre of Migration Research at the University of Warsaw, this strategy of shuttle, short-term, largely undocument-ed migration developed in response to the under-urbanisation of the communist period and an extension of the 'worker-peasant' system of the communist period, where factory workers lived in temporary, hostel-like accommodation and returned to their vil-lages for the harvest season.

However, Britain's emergence as the prime destination for Poles in the aftermath of the EU enlargement in 2004 has per-plexed social scientists and public commentators in both Poland and the UK.[165] In reports published a year earlier, the government predicted much lower net migration flows,[166] and because this proved a gross underestimate,[167] the Labour government found itself under even more fire in a debate, which overlapped with

---

[164]   M. Okolski, E. Jazwinska. 2001. *Ibidem.*
[165]   P. Kaczmarczyk, M. Okólski 2008. Demographic and labour market impacts of migration on Poland. *Oxford Review of Economic Policy* 24(3):600.
[166]   Department of Work and Pensions report by J. Portes, S. French. 2005. The impact of free movement of workers from central and eastern Europe on the UK labour market: early evidence, pp. 6–7. http://www.dwp.gov.uk/asd/asd5/WP18.pdf.
[167]   The number of citizens from Accession countries, who registered in the Work-ers Registration Scheme at the Home Office, stood at one moment at over a million, of which the Poles formed over 60%. However, as the Home Office emphasises: *'The number of applicants to the WRS does not represent a measurement of net migration to the UK (inflows minus outflows). Rather, it is a gross (cumulative) figure for the number of workers applying to the WRS. The figures are not current: an individual who has registered to work and who leaves employment is not required to de-register, so some of those counted will have left the employment for which they reg-istered and indeed some are likely to have left the UK'* (Accession Monitoring Report page   3,4).   http://www.ind.homeoffice.gov.uk/aboutus/reports/acce ssion_monitoring_report.

concern about social cohesion, multiculturalism, and relations with Europe.[168] However, what the debate failed to realise was that Polish migration did not suddenly begin on 1 May 2004. The new arrivals were helped by well-established, complex migration system that already linked the two countries for more than a decade. Hence, the media and academic interest in Polish migration, both in Poland and Britain, reflects changing perceptions rather than radically different empirical realities on the ground. Academic explanations have to be sought in the strength of transnational networks and the ways in which those networks were shaped by the migrants' own decision-making in the context of post-1989 Poland and European integration. If we look at these flows closely, it becomes clear that the opening of the labour market by the Labour government simply regularised existing flows rather than ushering in a new chapter of migration history.

Of course, while May 2004 may be regarded as a 'watershed moment in history',[169] the question would be how far Polish migration has changed through the legal right to reside and work in the old EU Member States. This debate—in my view— overemphasises 'change' over 'continuity' dimension as the evidence points that it puts too much weight on structural factors shaping flows over human agency. Poles act upon meanings, myths, and narratives that reflect deeper tensions and conflicts within their society, which in the *longue duree* perspective have not changed drastically and to which one way of dealing was to migrate, opt out, move, and enter into a highly functional— regardless of the structural conditions—transnational social field woven over generations. Today, they may have legal entitlements as EU citizens, but the meanings attached to notions of emigration, class, and ethnic identity may not differ that much.

---

[168]   That debate led effectively to the introduction of restrictions on entry from Romania and Bulgaria when they joined in 2007.

[169]   K. Burrell. 2009. Introduction: Migration to the UK from Poland: Continuity and change in east-west European mobility. [in]: K. Burrell (ed.) *Polish Migration to the UK in the 'New' European Union.* Aldershot: Ashgate, p. 6.

In order to understand the cultural dimension of this migration process, which involved the creation of transnational migration networks and numerous transnational social fields, it is crucial to realise that the door to the UK was partly open well before May 2004. Polish nationals were able to enter Britain after 1993 without acquiring a visa prior to leaving. They were normally granted a six-month tourist visa at the port of entry as long as they were able to present a justification for stay and indicate the means of supporting themselves—a practice, which was notoriously stretched and negotiated with a 'beat the system' attitude positively valuing an ability to outmanoeuvre the British immigration authorities. In theory, it was enough to have a kin, friend, family member whose name was given to the immigration authorities or a formal invitation from a language school. In practice, it meant that entering Britain was relatively easy, at least for those with right 'connections' or knowledge of the system. And Poles used these avenues big time. In 2002, according to immigration statistics, around 298,000 Poles were allowed entry,[170] and although 147,000 said that they were coming as visitors, it is highly likely that the vast majority worked as undocumented workers. In the year just before the accession, 2003, the Polish influx further increased, rising to 360,000.[171] Whatever their real intention for coming, the scale of migration is striking when compared with other countries, which had a more established link with Britain. In 2002, their numbers were not much smaller than those coming from Australia (827,000), Canada (784,000), India (540,000), the USA (422,000), and South Africa (403,000).[172]

Home Office officials acknowledged that Poles were the most determined in their attempts to come to Britain for employment purposes despite the formal restrictions based on tourist visas and limited employment and social rights.[173] In 2002, Poles

---

170   Home Office. 2002. *Control of Immigration Statistics*, p. 53.
171   Home Office. 2003. *Control of Immigration Statistics*, p. 30.
172   Home Office. 2002. *Ibidem*, pp. 53–56.
173   As Frank Duvell notes: '*Polish nationals currently have either been identified by the Immigration Service Enforcement Directorate for its illegal strategies […]. In 1996,*

constituted the largest group of foreign national, who were refused entry at British ports — 11,670 compared with Jamaicans
(6,285) and Filipinos (3,960).[174] These statistics show not only their
tremendous stubbornness and innovation[175] but also that, in practice, the British government adopted a laissez-faire attitude towards these flows prior to enlargement. This is why the decision
to open the labour market after May 2004 amounted to a *de facto*
regularisation of previously clandestine movements. Migrants
with experiences of coming to the UK prior to 2004 frequently
spoke about the ways in which they circumvented official regulations, sometimes through illegal means. Resistance to state control
clearly built on people's experience of the communist system back
in Poland where 'beat the system' attitude was moraly justified as
not just necessary skill of survival but a proof of ones' worth and
position in society.[176] Crucially, then Polish migrants saw nothing
wrong in breaking immigration laws and regarded movement as
their fundamental right. Bill Jordan noted:

> *Poles seek to earn, to pay for cars or deposit on flats. They assert their eco-*
> *nomic value to the host society and justify their undocumented, informal and*
> *shadow activities as legitimate labour market behavior. On their accounts, the*
> *immigration restrictions that they violate by working when on 'tourist' visits*
> *should not exist; there should be free movement for them all over Europe.*
> *Their actions could, therefore, be taken as a kind of protest or resistance*
> *against present border controls and regulations.[177]*

Polish nationals came third amongst those being identified for illegal entry'. F. Duvell.
2001. *Highly Skilled, Self-Employed and Illegal Immigrants from Poland in United
Kingdom*. Warsaw: Working Papers, Centre of Migration Research Working
Papers. http://www.migracje.uw.edu.pl/obm/pix/054.pdf.

[174] Home Office. 2002. *Control of Immigration Statistics*, p. 53.

[175] B. Jordan. 2002. Migrant Polish workers in London. Mobility, labour market
and the prospects for democratic development. Paper given at the conference:
Beyond Transition. Development Perspectives and Dilemmas. Warsaw, 12–13 April
2002, p. 2.

[176] J. Wedel. 1986. *The Private Poland: An Anthropological Look at Everyday Life*. New
York: Columbia University Press.

[177] B. Jordan. 2002. Migrant Polish Workers in London. Mobility, labour market
and the prospects for democratic development. Paper given at the conference:
Beyond Transition. Development Perspectives and Dilemmas. Warsaw, 12–13 April
2002, p. 2.

From the perspective of how individual social actors shape state policies and are a driving force of innovation, this attitude of Polish migrants is of vital importance and needs to be decoded further. For if we treat citizenship as something more than just membership of one-state system, but rather as the tool by which people negotiate their place in contemporary Europe in using their rights and pushing for the rights they believe they *should* have, the evasion of border controls and restrictions in the labour market can be treated as a form of civil disobedience and strategy to make the set of rights removed from the specific nation-state framework.

A good example of this uneasy relationship between state dominance and individual agency is Bogdan, who when interviewed in 2006 was living in London after migrating from Sokółka, a town in the north-eastern part of Poland close to Białystok. Sokółka retained elements of its pre-Second World War multiethnic and multireligious society as well as experiencing mass unemployment and poverty in the aftermath of the collapse of the socialist command economy. Like many others from this area, Bogdan had been a migrant for a long time. During the 1970s and 1980s, he had travelled to Germany where he was employed as an undocumented worker in farms and factories. Then, in the 1990s, he spent several years as an undocumented worker in Brussels. He had unpleasant memories of police controls, immigration officials, harassment, and restrictions, and these elaborate disciplining and policing of what he saw as his basic right—to work in order to sustain his family—he often dressed in historical narrative of continuing inequality between parts of Europe and saw himself as being at the front of that injustice. Bogdan was very often full of bitter remarks about how the East–West divide was maintained through policing him despite the hype about a unified Europe. He spoke forcefully about being forced to board a plane from Brussels to Warsaw in handcuffs—*'just because I wanted to work there'*. Eventually, through his friends, he migrated to Britain in late 1990s and, at the time of interview in 2007, ran a successful construction company.

Adam, a carpenter from Piwniczna region, a mountainous area in South East of Poland—about whom more will be told in the next chapter—had been coming to London for over a decade and described the strategies which his clients had pursued in order to avoid the questioning of immigration officers. Between 1993 and 2004, the most common practice was to cite a family visit and his clients usually 'adopted' him for this purpose. A letter from a relative or a telephone number from someone, who could confirm the invitation, was a crucial and well-known tool to facilitate entry into the UK. It is impossible to overestimate the scale of social capital involved in these practices, the number of strong networks established and the way in which having someone 'out there' was an important source of not only prestige and power but also potential employment. In the following chapters, we will find plenty of evidence that the post-enlargement migrations were, in fact, dependent on these transnational social networks which were frequently developed in order to breach British immigration and labour restrictions. The network of support facilitating entry involved both British citizens, Polish migrants from previous cohorts, businesses, employers, and so on.

Migrants' agency changing structures of power

The myriad dodgy and shadowy practices, which Polish migrants undertook before 2004, have become the stuff of urban legends frequently recalled during interviews, most often with a sense of pride. Information about the strategies of British immigration controls towards different groups spread quite quickly among migrants and their communities back in Poland. At one stage in the early 2000s, for instance, someone discovered that it was fairly easy to enter Britain through pre-paid package tours by bus to London. Rumours spread fast that immigration officers waved these buses through without asking questions. According to one story, the strategy was so established and well known that, after entering Britain the tour guides announced through the loud speaker: *'Ok, so who is really going to the National Gallery tomorrow?'* and the tour usually returned half-empty. Another strategy took advantage of religious officials not being questioned on entry. This resulted in one grotesque occasion when a nun was stopped after immigration officers discovered that she was seven months pregnant.[178] These stories and anecdotes are now treated with a historical nostalgia, but they were very often recalled on various occasions — Poles passing for Polish Roma (in order to get entry as an asylum seeker), Poles passing for Danish, French, German citizens in order to get work without any questions being asked, migrants paying for a facilitator of entry (someone who would confirm that he or she is a close family member), forging documents facilitating employment, sale of British passports,[179] entry through lesser known ports in the north of England, false language schools, non-existent employers, fake cousins, family members, spouses, and so on. Looking at individuals' migration experiences in following chapters, it is important to keep these practices in mind precisely because, by migrants themselves, they were treated as commonplace, a norm, an accepted way of finding one's way in London and — most importantly, as Duvell points out[180] — as an assertion of their own individual rights.

In a fascinating example of the power of individuals over state hostile mobility regimes, this strong assertion followed by individual actions led to a shift in institutional structures. As mentioned, these flows were also noticed by British policy makers and were crucial in their decision-making in the run up to the EU expansion. According to Jonathan Portes, the then Chief Economist at the Department of Work and Pensions, who advised the British

[178] An anecdote recalled in 2004 by then Polish Consul General; fieldwork notes.
[179] In 2003, an advert on the corner shop in West London proclaimed: *'British passport for sale. Photo can be changed'.*
180 F. Duvell. 2001. *Highly Skilled, Self-Employed and Illegal Immigrants from Poland in United Kingdom.* Warsaw: Working Papers, Centre of Migration Research Working Papers. http://www.migracje.uw.edu.pl/obm/pix/054.pdf.

government on the decision about whether to open the labour market fully in May 2004, or impose temporal restrictions, the decision was based on the policy makers' understanding that Poles would come (using the business visa scheme or illegally) anyway, so there was no point in any barriers, as they would be breached. As Portes notes:

> Because Polish nationals would, under any circumstances, have been entitled to move to the UK on 1 May 2004, we could not stop them coming: we could only stop them working legally. Had we imposed transitional controls, some, would have come and worked as "self-employed' notionally or otherwise; some would have simply come here and worked illegally. Since the capacity of the UK authorities to prevent illegal working, or to check up on whether people were genuinely self-employed, was minimal, many UK officials, including me, thought that one of the main impacts of imposing transitional controls would simply be to increase illegal working. This was clearly undesirable.[181]

So, what Portes admitted is in fact a victory for Polish migrants breaking the law that seemed unfair to them and unmanageable to the British state. In other words, *en masse*, Polish migrants managed to shape the institutional framework they were operating in to their advantage. If one needs a proof of ability of migrants' agency to influence state actions, we need to look no further. Anti-state resistance not only worked but also clearly paid out.

These skills, resources, and forms of capital, which Polish migrants displayed when circumventing British immigration restrictions and regulations, have usually been explained in terms of values developed during the communist period and the 'beat the system' attitude which did help people to be not only innovative but also ready to break the law. Many social scientists refer to this set of attitudes towards the law as the *homo sovieticus* syndrome. People preferred backstage dealings and encouraged a 'Robin Hood' ethos of gaining fame by successfully beating the system through shady deals or *kombinacje* (surviving, being smart, cheating, getting to know the system, and how to beat it).

---

[181] Personal correspondence with Jonathan Portes, March 2015.

This cultural practice and its meaning and consequence will resurface in this book in few places: hence, it is interesting to note that many scholars have implicitly or explicitly valued this practice very negatively. For many, it was seen as impeding Polish modernisation and as an obstacle in post-socialist transition. It was treated as a factor undermining trust in institutions, which many scholars in Poland claim to be the lowest in all Europe. Janine Wedel, for example, accounts with a degree of irony that her friends and colleagues noticed her higher tendency to lie and deceive after her return from fieldwork in Poland during the early 1980s. The term *homo sovieticus,* used first by the Russian dissident writer Aleksander Zinowiev, became a *bete noire* for such prominent Polish sociologists as Piotr Sztompka, who regards this residue of 'socialist mentality' as the main burden of historical legacy, one without which transition would be much smoother. Besides the tendency to see law and government as inherently hostile, the syndrome also involves the application of double standards in public and private life, disrespect for others, an unwillingness to work for the common good. Morawska, on the other hand, takes a less normative approach, linking it with migratory practices of the post-transition Polish working class and argues that: *'Capitalism based on transnational, decentralized, flexible production of consumer services in areas/sectors of the economy unregulated by legal-institutional frameworks renders some features of the accustomed homo-sovieticus syndrome into effective strategies of economic action in the new situation'.* Similarly, we may argue that, if we look at the normalisation of disparity between ethical guidance and social praxis, as in the example of migration dominant discourse discussed in the previous chapter and people's attempts to contest it, the *syndrome* looks more like an attempt to reconcile these disparities, to mentally survive in that schizophrenic situation of having to say one thing in public and do another one—a common feature in socialist times.

The stories told with pride about 'beating the system' tell us then much more. If we interpret them as meaning-making practices, attempts of making sense of structural upheavals of the social world, we can uncover something much more crucial and important — a culturally meaningful assertion that, despite the turbulent history of their society and their powerless position, people develop their own agency and have control over their destiny in adverse circumstances — be it Communist Poland or neo-liberal transition. In fact, as the example of manoeuvring through immigration restrictions shows, this syndrome should not only be seen in the context of transnational migration as a successful use of cultural resources but also as a mode of resistance, where individuals cope with a hostile state regime and their own unprivileged position in local as well as global power relations and rejection by discriminatory labour policies. The syndrome is not something 'inherent' in an Eastern European psyche, something that people 'have' and cannot dispose of, unless they internalise the 'Western' values of respect for law and formal social relations governing work, mobility and citizen–state relations. It is the way people respond to structural position of subordination carving their own sphere of cultural, social, and economic autonomy.

Both Duvell and Jordan and as well as my numerous respondents pointed out the hypocrisy and unfairness of pre-enlargement immigration restrictions, which were also marked from the West by strong logical disparity between the ideal and practice. On the one hand, the official glorious story cherished the 'unification' of Europe and a definite end of the Cold War East–West divide; on the other hand, migrants saw borders suddenly reemerging through restrictive immigration laws, employment restrictions that forced people into clandestine and shadowy existence on the margins of European capitals. These controls prevented them from working, which were not only an economic activity and an expression of personal worth for the migrants but also their rights as economic actors. The strong value placed on work — a feature discussed at length in Chapter 5 — does not match, therefore, with the *homo sovieticus* syndrome and its association with laziness, inefficiency, and a passive attitude towards reality — what Polish sociologists called 'learned helplessness',[182] a feature associated with the marginalised sections of Polish society losing out on modernity. The story of how people had made it, using methods to circumvent state control, has powerful significance for individuals. It not only renders contradictions between the ideal (unified Europe) and real (restrictions) easier to deal with and conceptually containable. Crucially, it validates the individual's power as a transnational agent.

The part played by pre-accession ties in helping migrants to look for work and improve their position is clearly illustrated in migrants' accounts. The evidence of chain migration points to the importance which these ties played in the later development of flows. In dozens of interviews, focus groups, and casual encounters throughout the last decade of research among Polish migrants, I continually meet cases where people, who came to Britain before accession, facilitated the arrival of countless friends, cousins, and acquaintances. A typical example is this person who, during a visit in Poland, encouraged friends to follow suit: *'Yes, we came here together .... One of my friends was here with her boyfriend* [in London, before 2004]. *She came to our town and she said: "Listen, girls, let's go to London, we can make it. There is plenty of work we can make it, there is nothing to do in Poland, who is going to work for 800* [zlotys] *per month* [120 pounds]*". She made it here* [in London] *so we believed her .... And she said: "Get packing and let's go". So we packed and off we went'.*

Sometimes, the networks bridging the post-accession with pre-accessions had a much longer history. Once again I refer to Sokółka, where part of fieldwork within the ESRC study was carried out in 2006. According to several informants, the links between the area and London span more than 60 years, since some Polish war veterans, who stayed in Britain after 1945, had strong family connections there. These were revived in the late 1970s and early 1980s when some people from Sokółka came to London and

---

[182]   J. Koralewicz, M. Ziółkowski. 2003. *Mentalność Polaków. Sposoby myślenia o polityce, gospodarce i życiu społecznym 1988-2000*. Warszawa: Scholar.

then developed into full-blown migration chain during the late 1990s and early 2000s. Other authors, like Burrell, Irek, Bielewska also point to the continuity of these links,[183] and despite the strong rhetoric of boundary between the 'old' and 'new' Polish migrants, the politics of which I will discuss in the last chapter, it is clear that family connections survived throughout the Cold War and beyond. In 2008, during an interview with Jan Mokrzycki, the then president of the Federation of Poles in Great Britain — a Pole born in UK in the 1940s — I asked whether from his friends among older Poles living in Britain since the war he knows someone who, at some stage, was not contacted by his/her family or friends from Poland with the intention of coming to the UK: *No* — was the answer.

The role of the migration industry

The role of pre-accession networks is emphasised by a rapid growth of a sector of commercial activity, which in scholarship is often referred to as the 'migration industry'.[184] When accession states and EU Members signed the Associate Members Agreement in 1993, nationals from the Associate Members acquired the right to establish businesses in EU states. The right was interpreted differently in each country; but in Britain, it helped Polish migrants to enter the labour market relatively easily from the late

---

[183] K. Burell. 2003. Small-scale transnationalism: homeland connections and the Polish 'community' in Leicester. *International Journal of Population Geography* 9(4):323–335; M. Irek. 2011. The myth of 'weak ties'. [in]: B. Jałowiecki, M. Szczepański. 2008. *Dziedzictwo polskich regionów. Jedna Polska? Dawne i nowe zróżnicowania społeczne*. PAN 2007. Wroclaw: Wydawnictwo WAM; A. Bielewska. 2012. *Changing Polish Identities. Post-War and Post-Accession Polish Migrants in Manchester*. Oxford: Peter Lang.

[184] M. Garapich. 2008. The migration industry and civil society: Polish immigrants in the United Kingdom before and after EU enlargement. *Journal of Ethnic and Migration Studies* 34(5):735–752.

1990s.[185] Since the process of establishing a business took a considerable amount of time and bureaucratic obstacles had to be overcome, a group of immigration advisors emerged responding to a need for specific services to would-be migrants or migrants in need of prolonging their stay. Between 2000 and 2004, this group, to some extent, transformed the behaviour of migrants in their ethnic economic niche. Most of these advisors began as low key, back-door, one-person businesses, and they often used a single telephone number and relied on private visits. They were not really professional immigration lawyers but people who had seized an opportunity by helping others to fill out the forms and follow the procedures—for a fee, of course. Within a couple of years, some of them emerged as very important social brokers, employers, and leaders active in the local Polish public sphere.

Research on Poles in London during this period predicted correctly that the self-employment schemes would contribute to the 'deepening of the infrastructure of Polish social relations in London'.[186] Indeed, during these years, around 40 immigration advice offices sprang up in the metropolis. The process had its drawbacks, however, since the migration industry could also exploit newcomers, since the whole sector was based on an unequal relationship between experts in law and those in need.[187] Some of the Polish advisors quickly developed respectable businesses, but others were involved in human smuggling or provided migrants with false documents, broken promises, and exploitated them. Clients were often cheated, and a significant number of advisors were investigated by New Scotland Yard or the Office of Immigration Service Commission. Some advisors changed venues and

---

[185] F. Duvell. 2004. *Highly skilled, self-employed and illegal immigrants from Poland in United Kingdom.* Working Papers, Warsaw: Centre for Migration Studies. http://www.migracje.uw.edu.pl/obm/pix/054.pdf

[186] F. Duvell. 2004. *Ibidem*, p. 25.

[187] M. Miller, S. Castles. 1993. *The Age of Migration: International Population Movements in the Contemporary World.* London: Macmillan, p. 26.

business names in order to attract new customers when things went wrong.[188]

Between 2001 and 2004, tens of thousands of Polish migrants obtained the so-called 'self-employed visa', which allowed them to legalise their presence, work, pay taxes, take out mortgages, and be freer to participate in Britain's social and economic life. The popularity of this avenue for migration is reflected in the Home Office 2003 Immigration Statistics report stating: '*2003 saw an increase of 151 per cent in the number of persons granted an extension as a person of independent means or as businessmen to 24.800 .... Significant increases occurred in nationals from Poland (up 156 per cent to 9,410)*'.[189]

This mixture of informal ties and formal business practices in economies occupied by a foreign labour force is not new, of course. Here, however, advisors were easing the passage from a grey economy into the formal one. From the ambiguous position of being tourists/illegal immigrants/visitors, migrants were entering the legal status of self-employed entrepreneurs. Stretching the rules, negotiating the law, and creating precedents were integral to this process. For instance, thousands of identical business plans were produced; the occupations were often fictitious, and advisors explicitly shared with the clients the fiction behind the whole scheme, winking every time the Home Office was mentioned.[190]

This system was eventually attacked by the right-wing press and Conservative politicians as various scams were uncovered in March 2004, which led to the downfall of the then Minister for Immigration, Beverly Hughes. The scams, described in the press, concerned the practice of acquiring the same visa in Bulgar-

---

[188] In late 2003, for example, the Home Office asked the Polish Consulate to accept around 3,000 Polish passports that had been submitted with an application for a self-employment visa but could not be processed because the advisor did not have a licence or had disappeared — fieldwork notes.

[189] Home Office. 2003. p. 15.

[190] For example, my own business plan for self-employment visa application was made from a template of a construction worker, and the sole change consisted of changing the category of 'builder' into 'journalist'.

ia, but essentially the technicalities of bending the rules was the same. The situation was not helped by some Polish advisors boasting about doing the things that were technically impossible under British law. One of them advertised his ability to 'legalise illegals' in the local Polish press — a sure shock for any Home Office official who may have read it.

Despite this high degree of informality and rule bending, for this group of immigrant entrepreneurs, the system worked rather well. Millions of pounds were generated through a £500 charge for the visa, together with such extras as arranging National Insurance enrolment, setting up a bank account, and registering with the Inland Revenue — things that were free for those in the know of course. Yet, as May 2004 approached, these entrepreneurs began to realise that they would have to adapt to the new circumstances, where Poles were able to come and work in the UK without previous restrictions. Some moved into the highly competitive and expanding media sector, which now sustains four weekly magazines, each with a circulation of up to 50,000 readers. There are also at least a dozen different websites and numerous radio stations attracting visitors in both Poland and UK. These advisors were able, therefore, to turn themselves into business consultants and create a richly informative media sector. Other advisors moved into personnel recruitment or tax consultancy. However, all these different occupations were closely connected with the media — a sector that quickly emerged as a place where things could be discussed, news digested, and community identities constructed.

In his classic study of 'institutional completeness' of ethnic communities, Raymond Breton emphasises that ethnic publications are a powerful tool in creating and developing interpersonal ties.[191] Newspapers disseminate information which had been previously restricted to informal networks. The effect of this development was to make people more secure, since they no longer

---

[191]   R. Breton. 1964. Institutional completeness of ethnic communities and the personal relations of immigrants. *American Journal of Sociology* 70(2):193–205.

relied on those who dominated these networks. They helped to give voice to those who were previously silent and excluded. Polish migrants can now learn from the newspapers not only how to get a National Insurance card and jobs but also how to mini-mise the risks associated with migration by claiming benefits, using trade union membership, suing a dishonest employer, and lobbying local politicians. They can also learn what British people think about them, what the British media writes, and various nitty gritty issues of London life. The public sphere provided by the media made migrants more reflexive, more aware of differences, similarities, and the peculiarities of British society.

The above-mentioned developments meant that informali-ty, small networks, strong suspicion towards co-ethnics and au-thorities—these features, which strongly characterised the world of Polish migrants in London according to the limited sociological research done among them prior to enlargement,[192] began to be slowly redefined and evolving into a more public, formalised, and participatory structure of immigrants' social space. Due to new market initiatives and opportunities, informal networks began to emerge from the shadows of the informal economy or under-ground life and become formalised. However, the construction of a new set of institutionalised networks, commercial advocacies, and mutual connectedness developed not due to some abstract sense of common heritage, duty towards extended kinship group, cultural affiliation, or essentialist definitions of national identity or shared common set of values but because migrants were structur-ally included into the labour market, which created a niche for agents to ease incorporation and spread of information. In the case of Polish migrants, no voluntary NGO would facilitate migrants' entry into host society better than the media did. As will be ex-plained in more detail later on in Chapter 7, participation in for-mal ethnic associations is generally small, with migrants display-

---

[192]   F. Duvell. 2004. *Highly skilled, self-employed and illegal immigrants from Poland in United Kingdom*. Working Papers, Warsaw: Centre for Migration Studies. http://www.migracje.uw.edu.pl/obm/pix/054.pdf.

ing low levels of trust towards these. However, the economic networks sustained by the migration industry compensate for these low levels of participation, and it seems that polish migrants simply prefer less formal and individualized forms of participation.

Since, by definition, the market-driven role of the new media was to enlarge the circle of participants, it enabled the migration industry to generate bridging social capital beyond the closed circle of co-ethnics. The best example is probably the massive display of common religious identity after the death of John Paul II when around 30,000 people marched to the Palace of Westminster in an ad hoc organised march. This march had been organised within a few days, mainly using highly popular Internet chat rooms and websites and attracted not only Poles but Catholics in general. Another important event organised by the papers are the regular job fairs, where around 5,000–8,000 people turn up and meet recruitment company representatives, trade union officials, local government members, language teachers, and organising of CV-writing training courses. The fairs often transcend ethnic ties with many migrants from other countries turning up. The owner of one of the magazines, who has also a business consultancy, recruitment company, and property maintenance company and has a turnover of £3,000,000 a year, is actively marketing his business among other migrant groups, such as Ukrainians, Bulgarians, and Slovaks.

The conclusion from these developments—and we are not at the end of it yet, since, for instance, some Polish publishing businesses are moving to the English language market[193]—is that the growth of the entrepreneurial and business class in Poland due to the collapse of the communist system in Poland is paralleled and accompanied by a rise of a similar class of Polish immigrant entrepreneurs in the countries of destinations. As we shall see later on, perceived lack of business opportunities, red-tape,

---

[193]   The niche has been also recognised by the English press—both *The Guardian Media Group* and *The Sun* have at some point experimented with Polish language publications for Polish migrants in the UK.

and structural domination of old cliques has prevented many Poles not only in the Polish labour market but also expanding their businesses. The fact that these businesses in the UK operate in a niche facilitating mobility and adaptation to the local environment—the migration industry—means that additional pull factor has been created, one that has paved the way for subsequent waves of migrants to London well before the accession in 2004. The fact that all owners of the four weeklies printed for Poles in London and most of owners of the biggest commercial advice offices are immigrants who came in the 1980s or 1990s is another proof that the post-accession migrations were strongly facilitated by the previous waves. As we shall see in Chapter 7, this has some important consequences in ethnic community formation, internal power relations, and issues of representation.

Economic and demographic picture—problems and predicaments

It is crucial here to pause and discuss—who are we actually talking about? This book is not about one of many 'ethnic groups in Britain' since as we shall see it is hard to pinpoint and geographically delineate these people according to national borders. 'Post-EU enlargement migration' is an artificial construct, and as the rise of the migration industry shows that, in order to understand this process, we need to see it in the larger perspective of transformation in Poland and social and economic developments in Britain before and after May 2004. What about those Poles who arrived in the 1980s or 1970s? Should we include them in the analysis? My answer is yes, as long as they participated in the construction of the transnational social space between Poland and Great Britain. As noted in Chapter 2, migrations not only involve physical movement—migrants also reflect on this movement through informal discussion among themselves and in public debate in both Poland and Britain; in fact, discourses around migrations form such a powerful avenue with which national identity is demonstrated—or contested—that Poles may be described as culturally and socially embedded in transnational social fields which consist of political, economic, and religious fields, each affecting individual identities and agency in its own way. They do cross-cut each other but sometimes operate completely independently, reflecting the earlier discussed division between the transnationalism as a way of being and belonging.

So far, I have not considered the issue of large-scale databases and the demographic and economic profile of Polish migrants in Britain, particularly London. My reluctance is due to some reservations about the ways in which we sometimes interpret the data. Officials usually assume that there is a neat divide between the 'sending' and receiving society—an assumption which is not borned out in real life and is rather superficial from the migrants' perspective, it reproduces methodological nationalism and the container model of society omitting transnational social fields. It misses the fact that societies overlap one another and that, at some point, the distinction between Polish and British society becomes rather blurred.

One of the reasons for the complexity and chaos of the British debate about migration has been the unrealistic joggling with numbers. The very idea that, at one given moment, one can count exactly how many Polish nationals are living in the UK is not only unrealistic but employs a static and methodologically flawed notion of 'living', which is defined as residing, more or less permanently, in one place only and belonging solely to one country. The methodological nationalism at work here does not account for all those, who are 'in-between', who are frequently changing places, and crucially whose life interests and plans embed them in more than one country. In fact, some Polish scholars question the very usefulness of counting how many Polish nationals emigrate or migrate, since it often obscures more than it reveals.[194] Between 2004 and 2011, British authorities attempted to monitor the num-

---

[194]   P. Kaczmarczyk, M. Okólski. 2008. Demographic and labour market impacts of migration on Poland. *Oxford Review of Economic Policy* 24(3): 601.

bers of A8 migrants, through the Worker Registration Scheme, a highly controversial statistical tool, but one that gave some indication of numbers coming in (without giving the numbers of those who left). The Worker Registration Scheme (WRS) did not capture all people, who took up employment, however. For example, according to the survey carried out for the BBC in July 2006 and the smaller study undertaken in Hammersmith and Fulham, roughly a third of newcomers were not registered with the WRS — because they were not obliged to since they were self-employed, did not want to because the costs were high, or simply because they were working off the books. At some point, WRS estimated an approximate figure of 800,000 Poles who had come to Britain by mid-2008 which seems to add cumulatively figures of people coming in without taking into consideration the circularity, temporality, and transnationality of this migrant flow.[195] In 2008 and 2009, the WRS's figures were the source of much controversy and misunderstanding, since they did not reveal how many have gone back to Poland. The Institute of Public Policy Research, using data from the Labour Force Survey, the WRS, and their own survey, concluded in mid-2008 that at least 50% of those who came after 2004 had already returned.[196] This estimate looked statistically probable but still assumed that migration is a linear process where people either arrive intending to stay permanently or return for good. On the other hand, this account was disputed by Polish migration scholars, most notably Krystyna Iglicka, who argued that, if these people left UK, then they must have gone somewhere else, since they are not being picked up by Polish data. In her own words, it

---

[195] For more on the discussion flows, see: M. Okólski, J. Salt. 2014. Polish Emigration to the UK after 2004; Why did So Many Come? *Central and Eastern European Migration Review* December 2014:1–27.

[196] N. Pollard, M. Latorre, D. Sriskandarajah. 2008. *Floodgates or Turnstiles? Post-EU Enlargement Migration Flows to (and from) the UK*. London: IPPR. http://www.ippr.org/files/images/media/files/publication/2011/05/floodgates_or_turnstiles_1637.pdf?noredirect=1

is simply not true to say that 'half of Poles' have gone back to Poland.[197]

This discussion took another turn in the aftermath of the economic crash of the 2008 and consequent crisis across the EU. Poland, as opposed to its neighbours and other post-socialist economies managed to avoid falling into recession, registering a slower but still relatively significant growth, prompting speculations that since UK and other economies were doing so badly, the migration wave will reverse and migrants will begin to head back. There was a huge media expectation in the UK, as well as some on the policy-making level, prompting the Polish government to set up a special programme for returnees.[198] Again, it proved an overestimate, as very little evidence of return migration due to the economic crisis has been reported.

On the contrary, it seemed that, despite poor economic condition of the British economy since 2008, migrants continue to come to the UK. Many accounts from my respondents who have gone back to Poland indicate that London is still on the agenda even if someone made the trip back at some stage. Marian, whom we will meet again on the pages of this book, after five years in London decided to go back, since he fell in love and his new girlfriend wanted to live in Warsaw. He states, however: *'Well, if this won't work out* [his relationship with his girlfriend] *I will probably be back ... you know you can always go back to London'.*

So, how many are there? The 2011 census came to the rescue to some extent showing that Poles are now the second largest ethnic group in the UK with 579,121 people born in Poland and 853,000 Polish citizens living in England and Wales. The dynamic in this last decade is substantial. As the Office of National Statistics notes: *'Between the year ending December 2003 and the year ending December 2010 the Polish-born population of the UK increased from 75,000 to 532,000. More recently immigration of Polish people has declined. Immigration was highest in 2007 at 96,000 Polish citizens, but*

---

[197] http://news.bbc.co.uk/today/hi/today/newsid_8472000/8472980.stm
[198] http://zielonalinia.gov.pl/default.aspx?docId=13119

this declined to 39,000 in 2009. Emigration has also decreased from 54,000 to 29,000 over the same time period'.[199] According to the ONS, 23% of the total of Poles live in London—around 130,000.

Despite the limitations of the quantitative data, it is important, nevertheless, and it is possible to establish some distinctive demographic characteristics of the post-enlargement migrants. In 2010, WRS data were pointing to a relatively young cohort with over 80% below the age of 34 years and almost half below the age of 24 years. There seems to be slightly more men than women and very little numbers of migrants coming with dependents, although recent data on births of children with one parent from Poland indicate to a significant baby boom among that group. As the Office of National Statistics noted in 2012, Polish mothers overtook those from Pakistan as the single largest group of foreign-born mothers in 2010 and 2011, accounting for more than 10% of births within this group.[200] This confirms some scholarly prediction that, although this was migration of young people, they were also at a stage of their lives most likely to have children.

It is harder to get a picture of educational level, but surveys carried out indicate that around 20% come with a higher education degree and another 20% are students. Okólski and Kaczmarczyk point out that, because, on the large demographic scale, the post-accession migrations from Poland constitute the 'crowding-out' effect of adjustment to the labour market, there is a higher tendency of people with tertiary education to migrate.[201] In terms of economic activity, this is a cohort that marks higher employment levels than the British born. The vast majority of migrants are employed in the service sector—construction, health, domestic, and social service, as well as hospitality and catering. A study

[199]   ONS 2012. Polish People in the UK—Half a million Polish Residents. http://www.ons.gov.uk/ons/rel/migration1/migration-statistics-quarterly-report/august-2011/polish-people-in-the-uk.html

[200]   http://www.ft.com/cms/s/0/bf1c1d7c-1465-11e2-8ef2-00144feabdc0.html

[201]   R. Kaczmarczyk, M. Okólski. 2008. Demographic and labour market impacts of migration on Poland. *Oxford Review of Economic Policy* 24(3):600.

in 2007 showed that Poles worked the most hours for the least pay.[202] An analysis by Lionel Fulton for the Labour Research Department in 2015 shows that, statistically, Polish migrants tend to be concentrated in low-paid sectors, confirming the IPPR data.[203]

So, the statistical picture shows a cohort of young but poorly paid individuals, who were generally well educated and filled the typical sectors of service industry associated with immigration and the secondary labour market. The construction industry is a sector where Poles were particularly concentrated. At the same time, it is important to bear in mind that Poles can be found in many financial institutions, in arts, design, education, public sector occupations, and business. This wide variety of jobs in a range of sectors will be a recurring theme in our analysis. The continuum, which ranged from the former Polish prime minister working in one of the city's financial corporations to the substantial number of homeless Poles on London streets, shows that the very notion of a typical 'Polish migrant' becomes questionable to say the least. Moreover, the view on people through their current occupation at the moment of the study does not and cannot offer an answer to what life strategies they employ—long-term, seasonal migrant, taking a wait-and-see approach, etc.—and how they justify them in current economic condition and how they operate in various transnational social fields. It is simplistic and too generalising to summarise the statistical picture under common categories of 'economic migration', 'cheap labour', and so forth—categories cherished by the media, that through their symbolic violence tend to subordinate and create a class exclusionary discursive practice. As I trace individuals' lives and perceptions of changes, it will become clear that to 'fix' them conceptually under a particular category is to their agency and their capacity to be able to consciously choose, shift, and change a particular course of

---

[202] J. Rutter. 2007. *Britain's Immigrants: An economic profile*. 2007. London: IPPR. http://www.ippr.org.uk/research/teams/?id=3571&tID=3571

[203] M. Garapich. 2008. *Between the Local and the Transnational. A8 migrants in Hammersmith and Fulham*.

action. This agency is thus not just a matter of concrete consequences but also mental ability to make sense and reflect upon the
social world, which in turn informs action.

Consequently, we need to look at the migrants' perceptions,
attitudes towards social stratification, social class, social mobility,
and their own understanding of dynamics of inequalities and life
chances in a global city. The increase in mobility between Poland
and Britain in the last decade has profoundly influenced how
people structure their life plans, redefine their relationship with
space, community, and social networks, and what cultural and
social meanings they attach to the places they call homes. They are
confronted by new ethnic 'Others', giving them a new insight and
meanings into what it means to be Polish. They are led to reflect
on their class identity since mobility has become a key factor in
social stratification. Their personal strategies and the meanings,
which they employ, will become clearer in the next chapter where
I consider migrants' patterns of mobility, their strategies and
transnational orientations, and lifestyles.

Chapter 4

Migration strategies and the making of transnational social fields

Being here and there

As we have seen in previous chapter, the development of a transnational social field, where individuals, goods, values, and meanings are continually moving back and forth between Poland and Britain, was a proces, which preceded EU enlargement due to the development of migration networks, labour demands in Britain, and the economic situation in Poland. Most of my interviewees, in one way or another, operated in social environments that connected both countries. Some have become seasonal, pendulum commuters, or maintain relations through participation in migration chains, while others regularly visit their localities of origin several times a year. All are consumers of Polish media, websites, food, and cultural events, thereby stimulating the rapid growth of ethnic shops, entertainment, media, accounting advice, remittances offices — the migration industry.

This attachment to two social settings is not simply confined to the 'myth of return' and the construction of ideological diaspora. It is expressed in everyday life through physical contact and constant communication. These transnational social fields cut across and connect various social groups in both societies, to some extent merging them and making distinctions between Poles 'here' and Poles 'there' arbitrary and difficult to pin down. For example, in 2007, around 50,000 people voted in Britain during parliamentary elections in Poland, which saw the removal of the right-wing Law and Justice party from power, and a similar number took part in the elections in 2010 and then in presidential elections in 2015. The London club scene sees Polish music groups performing every week and for Polish musicians London has become a constant fixture—a place treated just like any other large Polish town.

Transnational way of being is a matter of daily rhythm of social life. From the 50 sample in the ESRC study,[204] 80% visited Poland between three to ten times a year; 70% maintained direct economic and life interests in their home community through buying land, investing in property, businesses, education, job seeking, voting in Polish elections, and expressing a general interest in what was happening 'back home'. Twenty-four per cent had also bought or were intending to buy a flat or a house from money earned in London. A larger MIGPOL survey,[205] conducted in 2007, produced a similar picture. Twenty per cent went to Poland four times a year and 40% twice a year; 25% had daily contact with their families/friends in Poland via email, phone, and text while, 43% got in touch several times a week. Fifty-two per cent of this poll's respondents used the Polish Internet everyday or several times a week and 28% regularly watched Polish satellite TV channels. Yet, if the transnational flows above describe a certain social morphology, it is clear, as Vertovec points out, that transnationalism may be also treated as a mode of consciousness[206] going even deeper into the very perception of place and belonging people may exhibit. For example, a common practice in Internet discussion forums on British–Polish websites is to use a double-orientation identification. The participants' signatures read, for instance: Darek, London/Wroclaw, Jurek, Nottingham/Poznan or Magda, London/Gorzow. This self-identification speaks more than any survey. Being *from* somewhere and being *somewhere now*

---

[204] J. Eade, M. Garapich, S. Drinkwater 2006. *Class and Ethnicity: Polish Migrants in London*. Economic and Social Research Council End of Award Report, RES-000-22-1294.

[205] M. Garapich, D. Osipovic. 2007. Badanie sondażowe wśród obywateli polskich zamieszkałych w Wielkiej Brytanii i Irlandii. http://www.polishpsycholo gists.org/wp-content/uploads/2012/12/Raport_migpol.pdf

[206] S. Vertovec. 1999. Conceiving and researching transnationalism. *Ethnic and Racial Studies* 22(2):447–462.

can be combined and merged to define what it means to be a Polish migrant in Britain.

Having said that, it is important to explore the diversity of actual 'being' somewhere, what lies behind these practices. The dual attachment has many different outcomes, and these, in turn, are interdependent forming a specific functional migratory system of networks — the transnational social field, referred to sometimes by Glick–Schiller as the *network of networks*. In exploring different migration strategies employed by Poles, we can construct a specific typology of movements and ways of 'being' and 'belonging' of these migrants. As we shall see, they include a variety of ways of living within this field, which partly explain the dynamics of movements between London and Poland. The surveys undertaken by myself between 2006 and 2009, although in different locations and with different samples, demonstrated that, if we take respondents' declarations about their intentions of stay at face value, there is little difference across the years despite the hardening of economic conditions. Although there is some evidence that Polish migrants were moving back to Poland in the aftermath of the economic crisis, over the years, the general patterns remained the same. In some way — as we shall see — some Poles were always coming back and forth.

Short-term migrants — *storks* and *hamsters*

This immersion in the world which resembles social realities back home — shopping in Polish supermarkets, eating Polish food, consuming Polish media, and operating within ethnic social networks, leads to the question whether in a sociological sense these people actually left Poland? It does not appear so if we look at the composition of their social networks. Opportunities in London and how people viewed them are strikingly similar to those which traditionally circulate between Poland's rural/urban social divide — a process which has provided the rural class a chance of employment and rising living standards. In fact, short-term or circular migrants reveal an inseparable connection between their migration strategies and social class.

Again, I would hesitate to put a specific figure on how many of thousands of Poles can be put into the classic category of 'target migrants' or as I call them storks and hamsters. Both the BBC survey in 2006 and the one undertaken in Hammersmith and Fulham in 2007 show that around 15% made frequent, short visits, but it is clear that this group is the hardest to reach through street surveys, because of their high mobility and focus on work. If we include students coming for summer to supplement their income, seasonal carers, or older family members coming over to assist with childcare, it would be safe to say that at least 25% are seasonal, temporal migrants. Furthermore, this strategy of seasonal work is much more predominant in rural areas of England with agricultural work available during specific months. Whatever the proportions, however, it is clear that short-term migratory movements are an important outcome of both Polish class stratification, its uneasy path to modern capitalism and British structure of the labour market. At the same time, because these movements are so similar in outcome and characteristics with some traditional mobility patterns within Poland, it seems that we encounter here a powerful, stable social pattern of behaviour.

This is where I should introduce Adam, a carpenter from southern Poland, who has been visiting Britain since the mid-1990s. He represents not only the social aspects of rural/urban divide in todays' Poland but also a longer historical tradition linking the Polish migration culture of socialist Poland and the mobility exhibited by the rural class described in the classic work of Thomas Williams and Florian Znaniecki, *The Polish Peasant in Europe and America*. The incredible stubbornness of certain cultural and social pattern of behaviour here is worth emphasising. Adam was invited to London to work for people who belong to a network of pre-1989 émigrés and had facilitated his entry on a tourist visa, introducing him to the authorities as a relative. He usually lived with his employers as a kind of live-in builder and decorator. He does not speak English, goes out mainly on Sundays to the Polish church, and devotes his time to work. Being a short-term migrant, his main goal was to save as much money as possible in the shortest period of time. He and his family seemed well prepared to undertake such an employment pattern. His London trips were just an extension of his previous employment strategy of going to Warsaw, where he had spent some time in the army back in the 1980s.

> ... three weeks there and a week home ... that's how I was going to Warsaw ... and then I made it to come to England. So I am coming here ... for a bit longer. But now one can do it for shorter periods, since there is the [European] Union now so more often one can go home.

Going to London instead of Warsaw had its advantages in the mid-1990s, since the Polish economy began to slow down after the boom of the early 1990s. The situation reversed, however, in recent years, and Adam in early years of this decade took advantage of the construction boom in Warsaw undertaking jobs also there. His options widened further when, through his friends, he secured also some contracts in Holland and since 2011 had made his main work place there. So, in a space of several years, he operated between his small village in the southern mountains, Warsaw, London, and Amsterdam. When probed, his choice of location depended on both the availability of jobs, which are abundant in all three cities, according to him, his financial needs, lengths of separation from his family, and agricultural work he has to do on his plot of land. When he needs a larger cash injection, he chooses London but while work in Warsaw may be less financially rewarding, he does not have to spend as much time away from his wife and four children. At the same time, this pan-EU schedule is determined by agricultural seasons since Adam has to be at home during certain times of the year due to unchangeable pattern of agricultural labour: 'In winter I come here to work, and in the summer, for the harvest season and haymaking I got to be home'. As numerous migration scholars note,[207] this ability to manoeuvre between economic needs, work opportunities, and taking care of land, for rural migrants is a challenge, but in the right sets of circumstances possible to maintain without permanent migration to the city.

So why does this person, like thousands of other seasonal, temporal Polish migrants, not take advantage of his skills and move to Warsaw, London, or a town closer to his native village? This question also raises the issue of spatiality and temporality, the tensions between the centre and periphery, land and the city. It also offers an answer to the limits of modernity and development and those who may regard this strong attachment to land and rural life as a proof of backwardness, an inability to reform and evolve in accordance with modernisation theories. However, this question would miss the fact that, for Adam, modernisation — as in the case of the collapse of Communism — had already happened and it simply did not work. His village is close to a ski resort which, after 1989, saw increased unemployment and insecurity associated with the new capitalist labour market:

> ... you know there is big unemployment in Poland now ... there are a lot of people in poverty now. You see it around the villages, so the scale of unemployment is big .... The state companies were closed. In Piwniczna there are only two companies now. Before there were so many tourist venues – that was the place's industry ....

State-funded vacations, resorts, and the general acceptance that some labour groups have a right to free holidays was quite an important propaganda tool with which the government asserted legitimacy, a tool which was economically not viable in times of constant shortage. When this socialist modernity project collapsed, it reinforced the belief held by Adam and many of the Polish rural class that what offers security is not industry, capital, education, and modernity, but land tenure and traditional modes of subsistence, and migration is precisely that. The only source of certainty was the land and, however small, it enabled people to survive in

---

[207]   M. Miller, S. Castles. 1999. *The Age of Migrations. International Population Movements in the Contemporary World*. London: Macmillan.

new circumstances. Even if people could not rely solely on the land, Adam does not want to move to the town; the very idea sounded abstract and not worth the effort:

> *Well, to live in a town ... no ... I was there when I was in the army in War-saw ... it is good in a town ... but too cramped .... No space, no freedom ... too big these towns .... But it also depends what towns; some are like the ones in Śląsk [Silesia] where the state companies got closed and unemployment is there ....*

In the modern, globalised world of a capitalist labour market Adam makes a trade-off between security of land tenure and a relative security of the new urban class. This trade-off reveals the strong sense of class among rural Poles who, despite Communism, wars, and a feudal stratification system, have shown extraordinary survival abilities and resilience as a social group. Shifting between cutting hay and milking cows in his rural and remote village and renovating houses in Chelsea requires not only skills but a strong sense of righteous order — that *this* is how things should be if life on the land is to be maintained, that *this* is the price to pay for keeping the lifestyle of a part-time farmer with its 'space' and 'freedom'. Adam's association of freedom and space with rural life does not, then, refer only to a sense of belonging but to an individual choice in negotiating modern labour conditions. Adam knows that if he is able to combine life in both rural and urban society he can break away from the shackles of the former communist state economy. The strong sense of rural/urban divide in Polish society is a divide between safety and insecurity, familiarity and chaos, communal life, and wild capitalism. Unsurprisingly, asked what divisions in Poland he sees, Adam is clear: *'There are classes ... town and village divide – this is class'*.

Polish migration scholars have recognised that the so-called 'people on the swing', involved in seasonal movement between rural and urban worlds, were a typical feature of Polish post-transformation migration but that this pattern developed much earlier. It has been argued that, because Poland was a predominantly rural society with fast-developing heavy industries, there emerged a semi-industrialised migration pattern where people commuted daily from the countryside to towns and factories to earn a living.[208] This has created a distinct category of socialist workers termed 'peasant workers', or *chłopo-robotnicy*. These were usually males, who either commuted daily to large factories in towns or remained there for extended periods of time in specific, provisional accommodation, not unlike today's migrants' hostels or overcrowded flats. Today's system is different in terms of spatial context, but the pattern remains relatively the same—the Polish industrial urban destination centre is simply replaced by a Western European one associated with the construction or service industry. Adam can shift from being an internal to an international migrant with relative ease, depending on his immediate needs and farming calendar. In his case, lack of restrictions on mobility renders the distinction between 'internal' and international migration meaningless and analytically invalid.

Hence, it is crucial to state that the ongoing question on nature of settlement of migration from Poland does miss the point that 'Polish migrant' is an elusive and very general category encompassing very different life strategies, migration patterns, class situation, and so on. One of these differences is exemplified by the case of Adam, but other patterns will be explored here. *Hamsters*, in my terminology, are individuals with short-term plans and the intention to accumulate capital on a one-off basis. However, upon their return the option of repeating the trip to London is still on the table. Sixteen per cent from my ESRC 2006 sample said that they were going back soon—as Miller and Castles calls them, these were target migrants,[209] people with specific plans, who do not wish to perpetuate their migratory behaviour for longer. In later surveys, the figure varies, but roughly between 12% and 20% could be classified in this way. Irena offers a perfect illustration of

[208] E. Jaźwińska, M. Okólski (eds.). 2001. *Ludzie na huśtawce. Migracje między peryferiami Polski a Zachodu*. Warszawa: Scholar. R. Jenkins. 1997. *Rethinking Ethnicity. Arguments and Explorations*. London: Sage Publications.

[209] S. Castles, M. Miller. 1999. *The Age of Migrations. International Population Movements in the Contemporary World*. London: Macmillan, p. 28.

that category. She 'came here as a tourist and in a way is a tourist' in her own words. Her main aim is to earn some money to pay her student fees in Poland, and she does not envisage repeating the trip any more:

> I knew I will come back to Poland. I never wanted to come here for good and I don't want to .... I knew I will come back .... I have my family there and I miss them.

People like Irena usually have a property to look after or pay off, some business venture, debts, or precise plans for the future. For instance, Krzysztof is a young graduate from Kraków. He emphasises his desire to live there and start up a business; his reason for coming to London is to simply earn enough money and then return:

> I have lived almost 2 years in London, but do not want to stay here forever .... I am from Krakow and I like it there so much that I want to go back. My idea was to come for a while to earn a bit and then go back. I was living for a while in Germany so I have a kind of comparison .... I graduated in Krakow and to be honest I came here to earn some cash. I want to save it for opening some business .... As for my plans here, I want to be here no more than two years and then I will go back.

Another, extreme example is that of a taxi driver I met, who manages to live in Łódź during weekends and flies to London between Monday and Friday to work, usually 12-hour shifts. This is exhausting but, because he manages to stay with his relatives, he cuts costs of this 1,000-mile weekly commute. In a sense, *hamsters* and *storks* such as those described earlier form a distinct group of migrants. Their strongly economic and target-driven attitudes towards their stay explain a lot about their London lifestyles. Krzysztof, for instance, works almost 70 hours per week in catering; some weeks he even works 80 hours. His drive to accumulate enough capital is also an asset in the eyes of his employers. It may be argued that the reputation of Polish migrants for hard work is due to the desire a substantial number of them to work as hard as possible in as little time as possible in order to accumulate enough savings. Expenses are kept to the minimum, free time is almost non-existent, and the main focus of their attention is their bank balance. The secret of the good reputation of Polish builders, plumbers, and workers stems partly from the very fact that their work ethic is time bound and geographically oriented — periods of work are condensed into a few months in order to raise its status and well-being in their home settings, free time is perceived as a waste, and consumption is associated with being 'there' rather than 'here'. This spatial distinction between the spaces of work and the spaces of consumption is what transnational fields enable, with sometimes — as we have seen in case of Adam — astonishing functionality.

Yet, there still remain subtle differences between those whose life stretches between London and rural Poland in equilibrium and those, who regard the period in London as a one-off, important but hard, experience. Krzysztof wants to move up the social ladder by becoming a self-sufficient businessman. Unlike Adam, who went to great lengths to preserve his traditional social world order by maintaining his base in rural Poland, Krzysztof intends to enter the capitalist labour market in order to climb up the Polish strata with capital accumulated abroad. While it may be said one looks back, the other looks forward, although both aim to bolster their economic power and position back in Poland. One organised his migrations into a sustainable and rationally planned pattern that does not differentiate between states but operates within the urban/rural divide (the village on one side and Warsaw/London/Amsterdam on the other); the other sees them as a necessary but one-off step to accumulate enough capital. But on the other hand, one is equipped with generations-long, security-oriented tradition of combining rural life with work in the city, off-setting risks of the modern life, fluctuations of the capitalist market, crisis, and the whole unpredictability of urban condition; the other risks all and takes the modernity promises as the only way forwards.

The question of proportions and numbers need to be put here, even if this may be difficult and politically charged. With a health warning, as these are not representative figures, across my surveys, if we add the typical seasonal migrants or *storks* to the figure of around 15% intent to return within a year, it could be argued that around 35% of Polish migrants come to Britain with the definite intention of staying only for a short time—from a few months up to few years. This figure is supported by other estimates, which have tried to ascertain how many Poles have actually gone back to Poland. The Department of Work and Pensions has analysed the cumulative figures from the WRS against the stock of migrants recorded by the Labour Force Survey and estimated that about 40% had returned.[210] The Institute of Public Policy Research (IPPR) has used similar data sets and has put the return rate at 50%.[211] Since these studies have been undertaken by independent bodies, it looks as though only half of those referred to in the newspaper headlines, have left Britain. However, as mentioned earlier, this does not necessarily mean that these migrants are at any given moment in Poland. In fact, the IPPR's findings came under strong criticism from a leading Polish demographer, Krystyna Iglicka. She argued that the figure of half a million return migrants is inaccurate. She questioned the methodology being used and mentioned that, as for 2008, the official figures of returnees in the Polish Office of Statistics stands at 22,000.[212]

Yet, these debates demonstrate something else since the question—'have the Poles gone home?'—is a highly politicised one, especially at a time of economic downturn and public spending cuts, and in particular with the migration from enlarged EU impacting on the British debates over its place in the EU and the 'Brexit' referendum. It is understandable that for the Labour gov-

---

[210] S. Lemos, J. Portes. 2008. The impact of migration from the new European Union Member States on native workers. Department for Work and Pensions. June 2008. http://www.dwp.gov.uk/asd/asd5/wp52.pdf

[211] N. Pollard, M. Lattore, D. Sriskandarajah. 2008. Floodgates or turnstiles Post-EU enlargement migration flows to (and from) the UK. IPPR. http://www.ippr.org/files/images/media/files/publication/2011/05/floodg ates_or_turnstiles_1637.pdf?noredirect=1

[212] http://news.bbc.co.uk/today/hi/today/newsid_8472000/8472980.stm

ernment, an ideal scenario would be for some migrants to return, leaving space for local labour force. From my data, it seems that, as in 2010, the return is a trickle rather than a returning flood, and data from later years until 2013 show a continuous, but smaller, number of Poles coming to Britain, despite the gloom of economic figures, and in 2014 and 2015 figures rose again. This, however, means that general migration strategies have not changed drastically. Despite the drop of the value of the pound, it is still profitable for a Polish student or seasonal agriculture worker to come for a few months or a year to accumulate enough capital to pay student fees or invest in business. In fact, it is very likely that the *stork* and *hamster* migration strategy will remain a practical one, as long as disparities in earning power remain. Adam is clearly happy with that arrangement, as the very nature of his world view assumes the need to get capital outside his village. Krzysztof and Irena have already returned to Poland to fulfill their plans. The taxi driver may still shuttle back and forth between London and Łódź. What is crucial, however, is that if these goals were not accomplished, they have one option — they can always make the trip again. It is most likely that they have and nurture social networks in London 'just in case', hence reserving an escape route in any case something goes wrong with the economy. Again, as generations ago, migration remains an available opportunity and is always there just in case the uncertainty of life in Poland will become unbearable.

Stayers

What about the other half? Another group which I have identified in terms of their migration strategy are *stayers*. They state firmly that their future is in Britain and they make highly effective use of the long-established community networks and resources we described in Chapter 3. One-fifth from the ESRC study sample emphasised that they came with the intention of staying permanently and the larger surveys show roughly a similar proportion — between 15% and 30%. Yet, because Polish migration to this country began long before May 2004, we need to distinguish between two different types of stayers — those who have lived here for years prior to 2004 and those arriving after accession. In what ways are they different? The first is exemplified by Andrzej, who came to London in the mid-1990s. When the Polish economy rapidly declined in the mid-1990s and his business collapsed, he decided to leave and move permanently to the UK. It was not easy to move:

> *After 1992 I had that big company that imported electronics from Far East ... and there came the hyperinflation of the early nineties ... In that period a lot of companies went bust ... so we thought that either we start again or leave ... so we decided to leave. ... These were tough times in the UK as well. Because we were coming as tourists, we decided that the only thing we can do is to start our own business. I did not want to start with manual work .... These were again the electronics businesses.*

After some ups and downs, Andrzej managed to move into construction and is now operating a successful company. His children were in local London schools and even if he invests in property back in Poland, Andrzej insists that his determination to stay here has helped him to cope with difficult times in his business and adapting to London life. But — and this is a crucial but — his business depends and operates within a strictly transnational field, since he employs mainly Poles ('I know how they think, so from a managerial perspective this is good') and relies in turn on their networks of friends and acquaintances to produce a steady stream of labour. In brief, here is a stayer who relies on storks or hamsters.

Clearly, having a family in London makes a crucial difference. Karolina and her husband, Maciek, came from Sokółka a year before EU enlargement and so far declare that they are happy to remain in London, where he runs a construction company and she does the books. As yet, they do not want to abandon the notion that they will eventually return. They mention that they might go back when their child reaches secondary school level, but they also acknowledge that their roots here may be too deep by that time. Bogdan, who runs another construction business, also recognises that he will be in London for a long time despite his desire to return:

> Q. Are you planning to come back to Poland?
>
> A. Not at the moment.
>
> Q. What will make you come back?
>
> A. I think [in] a normal economic situation in Poland, I would maybe come back then but I don't see it in next ten or twenty years … for now I see myself here.

In the narratives of migrants, the decision not to return is linked to negative experiences in Poland, such as poor pay, a disrespectful boss, discrimination, or the country's 'backwardness' and conservatism, combined with an appreciation of London's diversity and manifold opportunities. These stayers are highly individualistic and aspirational—returning to Poland is seen as a backward step. Izabela Grabowska-Lusińska in her book[213] on the relationship between structure and agency in the case of migrants' occupational careers, refers to that process of increased individuality and sense of worth, as one of main social outcomes of migrants' agency, having a strong impact on overall structural conditions—labour market, the economy, and so on. In this sense, moving up the social ladder and creating a favourable opportunity structure,

---

[213]   I. Grabowska. 2016. *Movers and Stayers: Sociaal Mobility, Migration and Skills.* Frankfurt Am Main: Peter Lang.

means embarking upon spatial mobility. The freedom to assert one's individuality depends, therefore, on leaving one's native land. Dariusz, who is gay, began to feel increasingly uncomfortable during the times of right-wing government of the Kaczynski brothers between 2005 and 2007:

Q. You had some plans or something?

A. No, no plans; there is always that curiosity to for a new culture, new people, how you live there … because if you just stay a month that not enough … I've been here few times and was quite taken by the city, I liked it – the openness of its people, the rush. And then I thought that it would be cool to come one day here to live … but I suppose also that I wanted to leave Poland as well ….

Q. Why?

A. A lack of prospects. In Poland you have this feeling that at one stage you stop developing … your connections aren't enough … and you just don't develop. Because, as I said, in my business the prospects … especially after the last elections, these prospects have got much weaker.

Q. Why?

A. I had a case some time ago during a party on a boat … where we make shows …. And one of directors of one of the biggest electronics groups in Poland … had a drink … and made a scene that at the party, gays [pedał – a derogatory word is being used] *are being promoted. So where does it comes from? He made a fuss about the drag queen show, where a guy is dressed as a woman. This guy didn't think about it, that it is art in some way …. So … from every part the government and everybody keeps talking that these gays and all that; the Church also starts to bark; the media also …. All this, taken together, makes you feel that there is a powerful enemy out there … and you know human mentality, people began to attack when they feel they can.*

While Dariusz does not want to go back, this does not mean that he wants to stay in Britain. Ironically, some stayers are hoping to move on eventually to another country. Like many British people they saw the USA, Australia, and Canada as attractive destinations. In a very similar way, the perception of Poland by Polish Roma determines their perception of return. Polish Roma have a quite distinct migration history from Poland, having started to move within small family networks immediately after 1989, seeking asylum. Several Roma encountered during my research were clear that there is nothing that awaits them in Poland and that they will not be considering going back. Their negative experience stretches back to the early 1990s, which saw a considerable rise in anti-Roma activity by far-right groups. Being already marginalised,[214] the Roma — as in other former communist states — were one of the most affected by the emergence of the market economy. As one woman in her 50s says:

> There was nothing for us ... no jobs, no future, nothing ... and in addition, Polish people started to be hostile .... It's not nice when you go through your town and graffiti that say: 'Gypsy out!' We had to go.

These important negative meanings ascribed to the situation in Poland will be further explored elsewhere. Here, the main conclusion is that stayers are a clearly distinguishable group, but crucially they are linked by family, occupational, interest links with migrants characterised by other forms of migration strategies.

The meaning of not knowing

Surveys obviously operate on the assumption that people have a more or less clear idea about their plans and lives. As White and Ryan rightly point out in their analysis of the development of transnational social networks among Polish migrants, their statements of intentions in surveys should be treated with care, since these change according to various factors — family situation, changes in the economy, and the acquisition of new social networks.[215] As they note, it is striking that so many respondents state that they have no firm plans. Surprisingly but probably frustratingly for statisticians and demographers, it seems a strong feature of contemporary migrations that migrants' plans are often

---

[214] E. Nowicka. 1999. *U nas dole i niedole — sytuacja Romów w Polsce*. Warszawa: Wyd Nomas; A. Mirga, N. Gheorghe. 1999. *Romowie w XXI wieku: studium polityczne*. Kraków: Universitas.

[215] A. White, L. Ryan. 2008. Polish "temporary" migration: the formation and significance of social networks. *Europe-Asia Studies* 60(9):1467–1502.

deliberately open ended, flexible, difficult to predict and highly opportunistic, adaptable to dynamic conditions. This is probably the most fascinating aspect of many Polish migrants' attitudes towards their mobility and adaptation to EU enlargement. Those who are the most vague about their plans I term the *searchers*. The figures from surveys demonstrate that this is quite a large section of people — 42%, almost half of those interviewed in the ESRC study in 2006, did not know what their plans were in an immediate future. The most typical answers to the question 'How long you intend to stay in Britain?' were:

> *I don't know. No clue. Maybe yes, maybe not, maybe in three months, maybe in ten years. I don't know.*

> *I don't know ... I'm not able to say now.*

> *I want to come back ... but don't know when*

> *Maybe I would prefer to come back, but my husband not ... I can say that 50% I would like to go back and 50% to stay, because I think that we have a good life here, and we are not sure what is in Poland.*

These answers may reflect the time, which individuals enjoyed during qualitative interviews to reflect on and qualify their responses. However, the quantitative data show a similar picture. In the BBC survey in 2006, around 30% did not know how long they were going to remain and 32% in Hammersmith and Fulham responded in the same way. The WRS also asked the same question and in 2006 around 43% stated that they intend to stay less than three months, while 48% left the question unanswered or ticked the 'I don't know' box. In 2007, the 'I don't knows' had dropped to 26% but 57% stated that they intend to come for less than three months only. The 2007 MIGPOL survey offers even more revealing data. The table below cross-tabulates intentions of stay with actual time spent in the UK:

Declarations of intentions of stay depending on length of stay

		Length of stay						
		Less than 6 months (%)	Between 6 and 12 months (%)	Between 1 and 2 years (%)	Between 2 and 5 years (%)	Between 5 and 10 years (%)	Between 10 and 18 years (%)	Total (%)
How long intends to stay in the UK/Ireland	Less than 6 months	34.8	4.1	10.8	7.8	3.3	8.3	**13.4**
	Between 6 and 24 months (2 years)	13.4	21.5	11.2	11.4	9.8	4.2	**12.6**
	Between 2 and 5 years	11.2	19.0	23.4	15.9	14.1	4.2	**16.9**
	More than 5 years	5.8	11.6	10.8	16.5	14.1	4.2	**11.7**
	Permanently	8.9	14.0	11.9	17.7	25.0	50.0	**15.2**
	I don't know/hard to say	25.9	29.8	31.9	30.8	33.7	29.2	**30.2**
Total		100.0	100.0	100.0	100.0	100.0	100.0	100.0

Source: Garapich, Osipovic 2007.

As we see, a third of these respondents answered that they did not know how long their stay would last. Yet, even more interestingly, this percentage does not change dramatically with the length of time a person has stayed in Britain, nor is it affected by education, income, gender, or age.

To understand what is going on the assumptions behind the question and various meanings, which people ascribe to the 'don't know' answer needs to be explored. First, there is something of a rationality bias present here, the question assumes that we are dealing with rational, strategically thinking individuals, who knowingly undertake risks to improve their situation and know very precisely what they are migrating for. The second assumption is that these individuals know how long their stay will take and regard unpredictability as a source of insecurity and stress. Although these two assumptions may be correct in some cases, they do not always apply. In fact, people frequently deliberately refuse to confine themselves or their long-term plans to one country. Respondents, who emphasise that they do not know what they are going to do, pursue a strategy of what I call, 'intentional unpredictability' — that is, a tendency to keeping options open, taking a 'wait-and-see approach', and adapting to circumstances as life goes on. They do not exclude the possibility of going back, bringing their families to the UK, travelling the world, or moving on to the USA or Australia.

There are clear methodological problems with the question, of course. When migrants are asked how long they want to stay, they are forced into a position of defining themselves, in terms of not only time but also social integration and their willingness to be accepted. 'How long you here for?' is laden with emotional and symbolic meanings, since the question exposes the migrant's liminal state of being at the entry point, of being new, a mere guest, and alien. We do not know of any survey run by Gallup or Mori that asks British citizens about how long they intend to stay in Britain, despite emigration from Britain being as substantial as immigration. A question about intentions to stay thus sets up a symbolic hierarchy where time equals commitment, where the length of stay implies the need to accept the norms of those who are asking the question. An answer, then, is more than a simple declaration about the time a person wants to stay in a particular place—it is a statement about belonging and the self-definition of a stranger. This may explain higher percentage of the 'don't knows' given on the Home Office form compared with those given to a native language interviewer. It can be argued—taking into account an anti-institutional outlook of many Poles—that presented with an intimidating question from a state institution a larger number of respondents were keener to present themselves as mere guests, since—in their perception—declaring the intention to settle could evoke hostility.

It is clear that the symbolic violence implicit in this question stems from an assumption that people *have to* know where they want to live and the temporal dimension of their stay—for how long? Yet, this does not have to be so. Intentional unpredictability refers to people's growing realisation that, in a risky society, carefully watching two or more social environments may bring more benefits than committing oneself to one particular place. This may sound obvious[216] but by being too close to our noses obvious things often remain underestimated. Intentional unpredictability highlights one of the most important aspects of migrations in modern Europe—its fluidity, open-endedness, and nonlinearity, as well as the growing importance of transnational fields, where territorialisation and fixed settings becomes an obstacle for social, economic, and cultural activities. In these fields, a person's chances of expanding networks, finding opportunities and building social capital are increased by being on the move. As Robert, an IT technician in his early 30s says:

> *I'm ok here actually. ... I spend my money here ... either having fun or investing in my computer .... I don't see a reason why I should send* [money] *there .... I have a house there—my grandma's house—with a garden ....*

---

[216] We must not forget that one of the demographic factors shaping that strategy is the overall age of migrants to the UK—80% were in 2007 below 34 years of age, according to the 2011 census 67% are between 16 and 34 years of age.

Well, maybe soon I would need to look at it, it may need some restoration. But I don't tie my future with England. What I actually look for is to be <u>independent from both countries ... not to have one base</u> [emphasis added] ... not to be stuck in one place .... After all I don't have a family so I don't need to think of it yet .... That's why it's easy now ... I may have some plans – business plans – but that's the future.

This 'independence from two states' was, interestingly, something that was highlighted by many other respondents. For Maciek, who owns one of the websites active in the 'migration industry', the ideal would be to live in Poland but remotely control his business and generate funds in London. Taking advantage of differences in prices, he tries to arrange his life in such a way, as to have the best of both worlds. Bartek, on the other hand, who runs a car parts sale business in North London, seeks to spend as much time in his native Kraków as possible and tries to be with his friends at least once a month. This is made possible only because he actually imports the car parts from Poland.

In the case of migration from Poland, intentional unpredictability is shaped by the changes taking place within the country. The refusal to strictly plan ahead when moving across the EU is the individual equivalent of the shift from a centrally planned socialist economy to the contemporary capitalist free market. It is the move from a familiar, centrally planned, secure, and collective environment[217] to a risky but potentially rewarding world where entrepreneurship and individual innovation pay dividends. In a high-risk capitalist labour market accepting unpredictability enables people to respond to quickly changing demands and to anticipate new opportunities. This acceptance not only reflects the ways in which individuals cope with increasing uncertainty of the postmodern world,[218] but it is also a way to multiply their social and cultural capital, expand networks, gain experience, and increase their pool of available options. In this way, migrants not only follow the requirements of a deregulated modern capitalist

---

[217] Many respondents stress that one of the main motivations to migrate was the will to move out from the family home.

[218] A. Giddens. 1991. *Modernity and Self-Identity*. Cambridge: Polity Press.

labour market but also are actively engaged in shaping its out-comes and outreach. In that sense, as Grabowska-Lusińska notes,[219] their agency actively shapes structures they operate in — the migration industry, for example being one of its manifesta-tions.

The 'I don't know' answer also implies that the individual *has* somewhere to go back to, that returning is always possible, and that social capital, networks, and resources 'back home' can still be mobilised. Given Poland's recent economic growth, those who are flexible about where they live have a clear advantage over those who commit themselves to one place only. In other words, by keeping their options open and not excluding the pos-sibility of going back, migrants insure themselves against the pre-carious condition of the modern capitalist world — high property prices, flexible employment arrangements, shaky markets, and economic downturns. If something happens, they can always go back, and this is not an option for a British-born worker. Participa-tion in a transnational social field and making it a meaningful act is a risk-reducing strategy in which migrants nurture the possibil-ity of going back in case of bad luck, and things going not accord-ing to plan.

This acceptance of unpredictability is reflected in one of the striking themes in migrant narratives — the role of luck, of fortune, of that near-impossible event which, in fact, does happen and does change people's lives. Stefan was interviewed as he was looking for work around the notorious informal labour market at the so-called 'wailing wall' in Hammersmith. He was unemployed at the time and in distress and in danger of sleeping rough. However, he still did not exclude that, with luck, he could get a job and eventu-ally bring his family over:

> *Here you can climb fast really fast. You just have to be in the right place at the right time .... For example, myself ... when only luck will be with me, I*

---

[219] I. Grabowska. 2016. *Movers and Stayers: Sociaal Mobility, Migration and Skills.* Frankfurt Am Main: Peter Lang.

believe that putting my shoe in the door ... I will be able to climb up ... I am this type that when allowed to, I will climb up.

The role of luck was one of the most interesting aspects of migrants' narratives about their understanding of London life. Magda, for instance, as a young woman from Wrocław, arrived in 2005 and worked in Camden Market. She had made quite a good life for herself, was happy and considered herself middle class compared with her lifestyle back in Poland. However, due to misfortune and a dishonest friend, she lost that job and found herself out of work and having to start from scratch. She confronted her misfortune unflinchingly:

now it looks different – I need to watch what I spend. Goodbye restaurants, cinemas and the like, you know ... Now it's time to count the money, make dinner at home ... but in London you know it's like that you can be very high at one point and then fall so quickly [emphasis added].

Luck is everywhere, especially when a migrant lacks crucial social networks and resources. It keeps hopes alive among those who have just arrived and are looking for work, as well as those who have lost their job for some reason or struggle with their addictions. During one of the many evenings spent at a charitable centre, which catered for the homeless and unemployed people in a West London Methodist church, the following scene occurred among those that were not sure whether they would eat or have a bed that evening:

A group of men, unshaven in their 40s stood in front of the free meals charity. Smoking and casually exchanging rather pessimistic remarks, they all reflected on difficulties of finding work, having to put up with dishonest employers, police, attacks by other homeless. The mood was grim, especially on two of my informants' faces – two brothers in their late 40s, who had been unsuccessfully looking for work for some time. The sense of despair and misery was all too obvious until another man approached. He quickly told a story, that he had spent the morning at the 'wailing wall', the notorious informal labour market in Hammersmith where people wait in the morning for casual labour. The story the man told electrified everyone. He basically claimed that while he stood there, a man approached him and offered employment. It turned out that the job is relatively long term – at least three months (a lot for casual labour in construction industry). Suddenly, the mood among men changed drastical-

ly – they were clearly excited, smiling, full of hope and were talking enthusi-astically about the fate of being a migrant in London, a fate that is so strongly. determined by strokes of luck such this one. Gone was the mood of pessimism, in the excitement of availability of opportunities and the unpredictability of what the next day had to offer. These things do happen and London is full of stories like this one. 'We just wait for our turn' – said the men. (Fieldwork notes)

Luck, unpredictability, fate, and a perception that some things are beyond control of individual actors strongly contrasts with the parallel strong assertion by many Polish migrants interviewed over the years that it is the individual capabilities and work ethic that counts and decides about one's fate in the meritocratic London labour market. Described more in detail in following chapters, this strong individualism and pull-yourself-up attitude and hard work ethic rests on the belief that human actions have specific consequences and that there is a linear cause and effect connection between work, honesty, efficiency and career, status and economic gains – something, as we saw, that has been doubted in new, post-Communist Poland and is a constant reference point for people in London.

In this world view, a stroke of luck seems the opposite to the sense of agency that Polish migrants demonstrate and articulate. Nevertheless, these attitudes and perception do coexist since they offer both a strong motivation factor and a sense of righteous causation behind what happens to an individual in a new, hostile, and unpredictable environment. Luck and the skills to capture an opportunity are, in fact, two sides of a set of cultural perceptions of the social world, which is both determined by uncontrollable structures and prone to influence by human behaviour. The meta-narrative of hard work and luck form a logical and practical legitimacy for individuals' actions – they offer both explanations for success and failure and give the social world some sort of stability, rationality, and sense.

It is not a coincidence, then, that luck plays such an important part in the narratives collected during the study among Polish homeless men in London. These men had experienced extreme hardship and most commonly came from impoverished areas of Poland, where the direct outcome of economic transformation of the socialist state was poverty, exclusion, and mass unemployment.[220] Most of them had worked in London prior or during falling into homelessness but their narratives of migratory trajectory are full of accounts of strokes of fortune, incredible coincidences, and 'things happening' beyond their control. For instance, many homeless men interviewed during the study had no paperwork or IDs and the most common explanation was that they had been stolen, lost during a drinking binge, or had been accidentally damaged beyond repair. Another similar story concerns the discovery of items — a gold ring, an expensive mobile phone, a Rolex, a pair of shoes, musical instruments, or finding small sums of money, especially during Friday nights when the local Brits go out and drink. The importance of these anecdotes for the migrants is obvious, they seem to be uniform and people tell them very eagerly — they *want* the researcher to hear this.

The fieldwork note with homeless men below demonstrates the crucial role played by 'treasures' found on the London pavements:

> *After brief greetings between me and R. he pulled me aside and showed me something which he was quite excited about. In a small plastic bag he held a watch. 'A Rolex', he said proudly. 'I already have a buyer, but he gives just 700 quid so I told him to piss off. I'll sell it for 3 grand. Look it has a number, look this is a real Rolex. Haven't I told you, streets are paved with gold here!' I asked carefully if it was not a fake. 'No way, the Jew* [the dealer who offered the money] *told me it is genuine.'*

In fact, the question about whether the found Rolex was fake or not missed the point. The point R. was making is that *it is* possible to survive in London the way he does and that in a rich city like this, even a homeless person without a penny can have his day. This brief sense of power and ability — tuned also with collective consumption of alcohol where these stories circulate — shows how Polish migrants conceptualise luck and unpredictability. It does

---

[220]   T. Rakowski. 2009. *Łowcy, zbieracze, praktycy niemocy*. Słowo/obraz/terytoria.

not render their agency invalid; indeed, it may actually reinforce a belief that anything can happen and hope should always be there in the struggle for survival. These stories legitimise their perception of life in London as continually unpredictable and unstable; anything — good or bad — can happen. Living in London is not only the source of potential reward but also pain. The agency of individuals manifests itself in *being* here and the structural conditions of London will render that *being* — whether a homeless migrant, builder, a banker — beneficial.

Interdependence of migration strategies

For some Polish scholars, the strategy, which favours cyclical, temporal movements back and forth, and the strategy of keeping 'a foot in each place' by refusing to set spatial and timely limits to ones' actions, results in social marginalisation and social exclusion, in both the sending and receiving countries.[221] Although very diverse local communities have been studied with different migratory histories and destination countries, this 'double marginalisation' hypothesis should be treated with care. The assumption at work here is that individuals are seen as functioning fully only in one national setting. It projects a sort of state monopoly over the concept of integration. Furthermore, social class and social mobility is limited to a particular nation and so the whole transnational and temporal dimension is left out. There is also a romantic assumption that integration into the 'community' results in individuals not being marginalised or excluded. Finally, it treats migration as a zero-sum game where people need to decide once for all where they will stay, since they can only be integrated once they have stopped migrating.

The inadequacies of the 'double marginalisation' perspective are revealed by the migrants' accounts. They see migration as

---

[221] M. Okólski. 2006. Costs and benefits of migration for Central European countries. Center of Migration Research Working Papers. http://www.migracje.u w.edu.pl/site_media/files/007_65.pdf. p. 7.

an act of social mobility and a biographical move across space, which does not rupture family and other ties with their home communities. From the interviews conducted for the ESRC study, more than half saw their social class position in Britain as higher than in Poland — in other words, in their eyes, they have climbed socially through being physically mobile. Only seven interviewees from 50, said that they had lost their place in social class hierarchy by migrating, while a dozen stated that they are on the same level as in Poland or do not see themselves as part of British society. Hence, for these migrants, their participation in the transnational social field constitutes a form of social mobility. Individuals are establishing themselves in the most convenient economic niches in order to maximise their profits and expand their opportunities, by simultaneously improving their social position and accumulating social and economic capital in both localities. This is done in various ways which I will explore in the next chapter.

The most important evidence against the 'double marginalisation' hypothesis comes from the interdependence between different types of migration strategies. The majority of *storks* and *hamsters* relied on those, who were much more established in the country. The typical case is the above-mentioned long-term settler, whose construction business relies on a steady flow of short-term migrants. Bogdan, who came from Sokółka in the mid-1990s and runs a building company, receives a constant turnover of cousins and his friends' sons and daughters. Even Adam, the seasonal migrant from southern Poland, could not move back and forth without the support of those who had come to Britain during the 1980s or just after the Second World War.

By providing assistance to newcomers, seasonal workers, or just participating in Internet debates about Polish migration, the stayers form a crucial link in the migration chain. So, Poles with different patterns of mobility participate in the same transnational social field, reinforcing and facilitating transnational mobility between two localities. This mobility system is simple — the more people embed themselves in the British labour market and acquire crucial networks here, the more they create opportunities for those looking to accumulate funds quickly through seasonal and short-term work. Modern communications means that people like Adam can recruit workers for their London construction sites within a few days. Care-work operates with similar speed. Relatives or friends are often invited over for a few weeks when the carer goes on holiday to Poland. Maria and her sisters, who were visited in western Poland in the course of the ESRC study, frequently came to London to cover for her aunt, who cares for an elderly Englishman. In another case, a migrant lives in his sister's flat when in London and, in return for keeping him for couple of months when the work is around, he redecorates her bathroom or repairs the plumbing. Having a free, 'live-in' decorator or plumber is an important asset, which not many British households enjoy. As he acknowledges: *'You know, this is good* układ [arrangement] *for everyone. I don't bother much, take kids to school sometimes; when plumbing goes, I can fix it ... I work a bit and then go home'*.

This has important consequences for my further argument—the successful accumulation of capital and position on the local labour market heavily depends on transnational flows of short-term migrants, who treat their trips as a supplement income, whether they are students during the summer or rural farm owners, who work on construction sites during the winter. Thus, these different migration strategies are linked together in a mutually functional and reinforcing system, which facilitates further diversification of migration strategies. Probably nowhere is this more obvious than in the growth of the 'migration industry' catering to Poles in London, which was described in the previous chapter. All the owners and editors of Polish magazines based in London, who had built up commercial advice offices helping people to set up a bank account or a business, seek compensation, engage in litigation to providing accountancy and social benefits claims, had come during the 1980s and 1990s and are long-term settlers, most often British citizens. Their business—both media and advice—relies on selling information, which is crucial for newcomers—

those who have been around for some time, have adequate language skills do not have to pay for information they know may be free elsewhere.

The 'migration industry' outlets also frequently employ those who are in London for a short time. The quick turnover of staff in the ethnic media has clear advantages for the owners, since they do not have to pay high wages to permanent staff, or even rely on volunteers and students on placements. On the other hand, their employees also have a chance to use their Polish qualifications and experience and are not disadvantaged by their poor English. Most of the ethnic press use the services of short-term apprentices and volunteers eager to gain experience in the media or simply willing to compensate for having to work manually. This interconnection goes even further. As many scholars on transnational movements have noted, the field includes those left behind as well. Families, friends, and acquaintances back in Polish towns and villages form a crucial part of these migration networks by negotiating terms of their relative's stay, shaping consumption patterns, etc.

Continuity in place of rapture — boundary redefined

The social construction of the transnational field is a constant and enduring act. One of the numerous discursive and behavioural ways it is maintained is by treating mobility as a normal, mundane activity and using the Polish verb *emigrować*, which is laden with symbolic and historical references, in a detached way. People talked very casually about the decision to move:

> Q. Ok, you are in London now, why did you come here?
>
> A. It's quite funny actually, because one day I was sitting on the internet and just by curiosity looked for flight prices to London and saw these tickets for five zlotys …. So I called Marcin and told him: 'Hey, there are tickets for a fiver, shall we book?' 'Ok!' So we booked, it was totally spontaneous.

Or in this fascinating case, when a short Christmas visit to see a brother turned into a longer stay:

Q. How did that happen that you came?

A. My brother was here. He came six months before me with his girlfriend and .... I was supposed to come just for Christmas, just to get some job maybe for two weeks .... So I got that leaflets distribution [job] *and my brother later asked if I won't stay. And yes,* [I thought] *life is easy here, I like it here. So I say to my mum: 'Mum, you are coming back on your own'. And my mum said: 'That's fine son. Do as you wish'.*

Or in another case, where coping with post-communist reality in new capitalist Poland ends with a friend returning from London and helping the person to simply pack and go:

My mum worked at the post office and my father was a builder, a manual worker .... So I finished that school and in that same company where I worked as a plumber, I got that job as a construction worker. In that company I worked ten years. During that time – military service, wife, kids ... and the changes in Poland. My company, suddenly from being state owned, turned private but without all the good sides of it. ... Just before I left to London I had a permanent job, I was a welder ... I was earning 700 złotych [120 pounds] *a month .... I lived on an estate block .... So simply my decision was to sell the flat and try to build a house ... my own house.*

So what I did: I arranged all the paperwork, sold the flat and started to build the house. I left my job also, because my boss started to pay me in three installments a month, and it wasn't simply enough. So I resigned and started to build a house. On my own. ... So one day I started to dig. Money ran out quickly – I barely finished digging the foundations. Meanwhile, a friend of mine, who was in London at that time, came to visit me – I still stayed at that flat on the estate, we lived nearby. He came, sat on a bench and said: 'I will find you a job in London. But I needed an invitation still [this being 2003] *.... It was in the summer and that was* [the job in London] *for the winter.*

The snap-shot decision-making process may be typical for younger people, eager to know the grand world of the big city, and certainly, in many responses, it is a dominant theme — people move because it is part of the modern lifestyles they aspire to. Yet, it also seems that quite a lot of people, whom we met, were strongly socialised in the specific culture of migration. Our respondents from Sokółka are an example. For them leaving at a particular stage is a standard phase in human life — a typical characteristic of certain regions of Poland with strong traditions of international mobility.[222] In this town of north-east Poland, leaving is a cultural-ly embedded social practice for grown-ups; it is a rite of passage into adult life for anyone wanting to move on.

Again, the casual nature of decision-making is strongly affected by the existence of support networks. Although the vast majority of Polish migrants had these resources, there were some who clearly did not and who decided to come with funds to sustain themselves independently. Nevertheless, once in Britain, the task of crossing appears much easier. They are changing places in a way which involves continuity rather than rupture. As Kathy Burrell notes in case of Polish migrants, '[m]igration is not so much a disruption in space, as a continuation in time.'[223]

Through physical travel or virtual communication with Polish localities, migrants negotiate and resist the symbolic power of the boundary of the imagined community. This is not to say that the boundary does not exist—rather Poles abroad redefine it. The constant connection with Poland, the uncertainty of intentional unpredictability and frequent border crossing renders the exclusive boundary between Poland and the outside world defunct, banal and hence unimportant, losing its previous (linked so strongly with national identity making) cultural meaning. The reproduction of the transnational field by occupying a social space as a *way of being* means that there is no either–or as it was in the dominant discourse, there is no way of being out of the imagined community or inside it. The symbolic boundary, which defined it, loses its power to define the specific traits that Poles abroad are supposed to have. In a way, the discursive force of the banality of leaving, its normality and treatment as standard practice is aimed at weakening the power of the symbolic boundary defining the

---

[222] M. Okólski. 2001. The transformation of spatial mobility and new forms of international population movements: incomplete migration in central and eastern Europe. [in]: W.J. Dacyl (ed.) *Challenges of Cultural Diversity in Europe.* Stockholm: CEIFO, pp. 57–109.

[223] K. Burrell. 2008. Time matters: temporal contexts of Polish transnationalism. [in]: M.P. Smith, J. Eade (eds.), *Transnational Ties: Cities, Migrations and Identities.* New Brunswick: Transaction Publishers.

mental and cultural space of Poland versus 'out there'. It is an individual, demotic strategy in which the association of boundary with territory is replaced by an association with the self, individual aspirations, and plans.

Sokołka, at the micro-level, offers something more—a fascinating proof of the conflicting and competing discourses around migration that shape today's Polish society. Most of the respondents from that town, as well as local government officials and NGO leaders, were of the opinion that, while clearly depopulating the town, emigration has been a traditional practice and will remain so. The activist of one NGOs helping families with alcohol abuse problems even strongly endorsed the view that migration actually helps to mitigate or ease these. She quoted an example of an alcoholic father who, only when separated from his family while working in Germany, managed to fulfil his duties as a breadwinner. Another example consisted of siblings, who were able to escape an abusive father only by securing work and accommodation with their family in London.

However, this discourse was countered by two priests, who gave their views about their migrating 'flock'. The younger one was critical and, in accordance with the nationalist view, saw migration as essentially threatening the fabric of society. Nevertheless, he did show some sympathy towards people who simply wanted to better themselves. The second, elderly priest was less understanding. When asked, he kept silent, then slammed his hand on the table and said in a tone that left no space for argumentation: *'Their place is here ... they should stay!'*

This embodiment of competing discourses, which we have discussed previously, involves fundamental questions, dilemmas, and contradictions in the relationship between the individual and the group, the member and the collective. It also assists in the personification and performing these discourses, as the conversation with the priests in Sokółka indicates. The notion of duty, sacrifice, and obligation dominates in the case of the discourses employed by the elites, the Church and those institutions whose interest is related to state legitimacy and social control over an increasingly mobile and assertive population.

On the other hand, people in pursuit of their individual goals and aims employ a pragmatic and rational calculation of gains and losses when thinking about migration. Moving for various reasons, broadly described as economic, Polish migrants make decisions in a specific cultural climate that forces them to react to dominant narratives and myths through various strategies. These involve strong emphasis on cultural meanings of self-determination, luck, stubbornness, the will to work, material advancement, individualism, and an egalitarian myth of meritocracy which I will describe in depth in next chapter. This is not to say that they are 'individualistic' whatever it may mean. In fact, their reliance on social networks, migratory social capital, the symbolic role of the collective, the function of the family, indicates that migrating Poles are most successful while operating in a social grouping — be it a transnational chain migration, the migration industry, or the penetration of the local labour market through informal connections. They however resist and treat with deep suspicion any attempts to collectivise their experience by the elites.

Hence, the emphasis on self-determination is a message intended to describe to whom the individual is not in debt, to whom the migrant does not hold any relation of service, sacrifice or duty, and whose power is contested. It is, then, an anti-collectivistic discursive act of resistance. In response to the hegemonic, uncritically treated, and despotic impositions, such as the one expressed by the priest in Sokółka, individual social actors offer their response, their world-view, where dominant discourses concerning the nation and the social collective are resisted and contested. In the following chapters, we will see more examples of these relationally constructed, cultural attitudes of migrating Poles.

Chapter 5

Class, work, and the meaning of transnational social mobility

Diverse migration strategies and the role of maintaining ties, networks, and connections 'back home' leads us to one of the central questions of this book — how in this transnational social field between Poland and the UK is social class experienced, understood, and practised? Transient migrants, established *stayers,* those left behind, and those adapting an intentional unpredictability strategy, use and reformulate their own understanding of stratification in the new transnational fields in which they find themselves. How does this reformulation take place, in what form and in what context?

In anthropological tradition, I explore these questions through an exploration of differentiations between groups, beliefs about status, the meanings given to work, labour, and money, and how classifications are marked on the body and expressed through discourses and daily practices. People position themselves within a social hierarchy shaped by social and economic resources; however, these positionings are always articulated in a cultural form embedded in specific, contextualised experiences of modern Poland and social memory about the country's past and also by interactions with new Others. It is impossible to understand how social class is made and remade outside the cultural meanings dynamically constructed in different contexts. In his ethnography of rural community in post-socialist Poland, Buchowski stresses this dynamic and functional relationship between culture and class:

> *Social status shapes individual behaviour rooted in customs as well as perception of group interrelations; human actions and views constitute class identity and at the same time are constituted by it. Classification parameters are*

culturally constructed and reproduction of class identity takes on specific historical form, also in the post-socialist era. Socially determined individuals' cultural competence helps them to develop new strategies for survival in which 'models are made and remade through use.[224]

Culture, therefore, is a medium through which social relations and interactions makes differentiating people meaningful. It does not 'freeze differences' but rather is an arena where values, norms, and patterns of meanings are permanently negotiated and social groups contest for influence.[225]

Class is 'made' through social actors' everyday interactions, practices, behaviour, and discursive modes that take place in transnational fields — no matter if the focus is a narrative of a *stork*, a *searcher*, or someone whose direct transnational networks are not extensive at all, who is a *stayer* or even — as we will see in case of British Poles in Chapter 7 — forms part of established British society. In fact, due to its relational nature, the class perceptions developed by Polish migrants seems to be peculiarly de-territorialised — they are located within practices, discourses, norms, and policies that cross-cut two societies. Yet, at the same time, these reformulations are shaped by national traditions — those produced by the Polish class system with its post-communist, rural and proto-capitalist legacy and contradictions, as well as those generated by — as John Eade[226] or Saskia Sassen[227] demonstrate in their texts on the global city — a de-industrialised global, service economy, which is heavily dependent on migrant workers.

---

[224] M. Buchowski. 2004. Redefining work in a local community in Poland. Transformation and class, culture and work. [in]: A. Procoli (ed.) *Workers and Narratives of Survival in Europe. The Management of Precariousness at the end of the Twentieth Century.* New York: State Univrsity of New York Press, p. 174.

[225] M. Buchowski. 2004. *Ibidem.* p. 175.

[226] J. Eade. 2004. Living the globalizing city: globalization in the context of European Urban development. [in]: F. Eckardt, D. Hassenpflug (eds). *Urbanism and Globalization.* Frankfurt: Peter Lang, pp. 191–202.

[227] S. Sassen. 1991. *The Global City: New York, London, Tokyo.* Princeton: Princeton University Press.

The myth of meritocracy

There are several contradictions that we encounter comparing statistical data and peoples' understanding of social class and social mobility. At first glance, for instance, it seems paradoxical that, despite being statistically close to the bottom of the British labour market[228] and although taken as an ethnic category, Polish migrants are paid the least per hour while working the most nonetheless most of my interviewees and people taking part in surveys I carried out seem rather positive about their economic situation in London — most of them equate physical mobility with social one. There are, of course, counter-examples and nuances, but throughout accounts, the belief in individual achievement and meritocracy prevails. In general, respondents constructed Britain and Poland as two extremes in a continuum of righteous economic order — Britain in this picture is an example of how modernisation, capitalism, and worker–employer relations should look like while Poland is associated with a dysfunctional economic order. After five years of living in London, Damian, who owned a small construction company generating an average of £60,000 profit a year, was clear about this:

> In Poland we did not have money to invest. And as for these [last] five years we have … something − not a lot, but I think we made it …. Of course, it was hard work all the time but it paid off …. In Poland we would not have any money to invest, or open a business, and working somewhere we would never have had opportunity to save.

Like many other entrepreneurs, Damian was excited by the emergence of a market economy in Poland during the early 1990s. Initially, he explored several avenues in Sokółka, where he came under increasing pressure to move out with his wife from his parents' house. He then decided to take another option, which seemed natural in a town with a vast transnational network, and

---

[228] See the IPPR study where Poles are identified as the ethnic group working most hours but being paid the least: J. Rutter. 2007. *Britain's Immigrants: An Economic Profile.* IPPR. http://www.ippr.org.uk/research/teams/ ?id=3571&tID=3571.

went to London. The move was, according to him, a good choice, and when I met him, his business was thriving. He was helped by his wife, who did the accounts and collected rents from tenants, enabling them to pay off the mortgage on a house in south-west London. For this family, Poland had failed to deliver what the market economy ideology after the collapse of the communist system promised.

Not that this experience is new to Polish society overall. The conceptual tension between the state or dominant discourse and reality runs deep through historical tradition. During 50 years of Communism, state discourse and the totally unmatched reality made Poles resilient and cynical about the alternative. Moreover, one may argue that the contradictions implicit in Catholic Church preaching, with its easy acceptance and forgiveness of rule-breaking, have additionally encouraged Poles to accept the contradictions between the ethical prescriptions of normative order and the reality of everyday life. This perception of social world as inherently in a state of contradiction between the 'is' and the 'ought' fits with a suspicion towards institutions, based on a particular moral code—the state, the Church, the nation—and gives additional strength to anti-establishment views.

This tension, which eventually brought down the communist system, did not pass with its demise. The tension between the unfulfilled promises of a dominant market and state ideology and the stark reality of a post-Communist Poland encourages people to look for new opportunities or created grief. Physical movement in that context becomes the vehicle for class mobility and principally entails establishing not only which way the financial winds are blowing, but also what advantages can be gained by maintaining links in both places simultaneously.

During many informal conversations, formal interviews, and web chat forums, this comparison between the two places—Poland and the UK—is a dominant feature, always implicit but usually made explicit. Permanent comparison is the understandable product of the 'intentional unpredictable' strategy, since this strategy requires the constant assessment of the pros and cons of staying in Britain, returning to Poland, or keeping options open. This transnational reflexivity, has a sort of, we can argue, clear therapeutic and motivational dimension. Britain is seen as a place — in contrast to Poland — where you can do things, achieve your dreams, be yourself: it is the meritocratic model where hard work and ambitions bring dividends and rewards — exactly what was promised to that generation with the collapse of the communist regime. Following comments from migrants' quotes are very common:

> *Over here there is so many work, everyone works, everyone has things and can make it ….*

> *Especially for young people because young people in Poland did not have a chance to show what they can and here they can do lots of things*

> *You can do so many things here, unlike in Poland. And this is why I would not like to go back there. During these three months where I had no job, I didn't think of going back. There are endless possibilities and you just need to give a lot from yourself.*

This construction runs deep in studies on Polish migrants, especially research which discusses the theme of normality and perception of the 'normal' in the UK. On this theme, Marta Rabikowska argues that taken from a constructivist point of view, 'normalcy' has a delicate, transnational, and paradoxical nature: As she argues:

> *'Migrants refer to 'normality' in a symbolic sense to signify any kind of stabilisation in their lives, but also they see it as a practical measure of success which can be discriminated against what has been missing in their lives. A state of normalcy in the case of migrants can be called a new version of normality, different from what they had known at home, but at the same time imitating home to a high extent'.*[229]

The comparative nature of 'normalcy' discourse is clear, for example, in Magdalena Lopez Rodrigues' study on Polish mothers'

---

[229] M. Rabikowska. 2010. Introduction: negotiation of normality and identity among migrants from eastern Europe to the United Kingdom after 2004. *Social Identities: Journal for the Study of Race, Nation and Culture* 16(3):285–296.

perception of state assistance,[230] Internet debates over what is 'normal life' in Galasińska and Kozłowska's research,[231] or discursive tools migrants use to position themselves in what McGhee, Heath, and Trevena, call 'transnational autobiographical field'. In that last argument, authors claim that the *'articulations of individuals' pasts, presents and anticipated futures are also significant factors shaping their migration, settlement, and re-migration'*.[232] But making comparisons has additional function: the perceived lack of opportunities in Poland reinforces the myth of meritocratic London and experiences in London validate negative views of Poland. Praising the range of opportunities in Britain is both a message about Poland and their new place. It is a constant reminder that, potentially, one needs to be open to any opportunity that arises in the future. Intentional unpredictability is about potentiality and risk awareness in an increasingly economically fragile world but also about the ability to transplant some cultural practices from one place to another. This relational perspective is expressed in different ways according to who one talks to. In my fieldwork, this may refer to a cleaner who prefers her job to an office position back in her rural town, since it frees her from family controls; it gives her a feeling of self-respect, because she now relies on her own initiative and agency rather than local nepotism. A businessman cites the huge tax burdens which strangle his initiative. Another respondent says that local cliques constrain development and he prefers to be a no-one in London than someone in his little town. Another left a job as a journalist in Warsaw, and although she recognises that she may have lost some social status, she stresses that her job as an estate agent in London is better, because it can

---

[230] M. Lopez Rodriguez. 2010. Migration and a quest for 'normalcy'. Polish migrant mothers and the capitalisation of meritocratic opportunities in the UK. *Social Identities: Journal for the Study of Race, Nation and Culture.* 16(3):339–358.

[231] A. Galasińska, O. Kozłowska. 2009. Discourses of a 'normal life' among postaccession migrants from Poland to Britain. [in]: K. Burrell (ed.) *Polish Migration in the UK in the 'New' European Union.* Farnham: Ashgate.

[232] D. McGhee, S. Heath, P. Trevena. 2012. Dignity, happiness, and being able to live a 'normal life' in the UK — an examination of post-accession Polish migrants' transnational autobiographical fields. *Social Identities* 18(6):711–727.

assure her child a proper education—something she could not afford in Poland.

During a focus group with finance sector workers, this contrast was presented as one between a Polish hierarchical work environment, dominated by older men, and the horizontal, more informal, and easier relations between employees in a British workplace. These comments reflect the general attitude of many Poles, even if they were expressed by those employed in the highly competitive setting of British financial institutions:

> I worked in these banks in Poland [Krakow], in Citibank and Millennium and I observed that the higher up you went, people were less educated ... and those on the bottom were discriminated because of that .... The best thing was when foreign guests were coming—then the management was hiding and they were pushing the younger ones—you know, junior staff, the lowest in the hierarchy, who could speak English to deal with the guests.

> [Here in UK] I like the professionalism—people just take responsibility for the jobs they do .... For example, if someone's actions have contributed to the success of the project then the person would stress the team effort and the words would be: 'Ok, I did something but you—the team—did it really great'. I think in Poland the tendency would be to take the credit by people high up, not recognising the role of people lower in the hierarchy ... As far as I know, here companies are much more willing to invest in their employees than in Poland .... Training, the very attitude of the manager who wants to train you rather than keep the knowledge to himself, because he thinks that you will replace him; all that attitude is different from Poland.

From a banker to a plumber and journalist to cleaner, the theme of the easier life and greater opportunities dominate. We can view this as an old version of the strong ideological appeal of the West, the new version of the meta-narrative Galasińska and Horolets are writing about[233]—where the West is a land of the free and abundant material wealth—but I would argue that there is something much more culturally complex at play here. When people compare Polish and British labour markets, they develop a narrative of an ideal meritocracy and a neo-liberal mindset, which sees a clear

---

[233] A. Galasińska, A. Horolets. 2012. The (pro)long(ed) life of a 'grand narrative': The case of internet forum discussions on post-2004 Polish migration to the UK. *Text and Talk* 32(2):125–143.

progression from merit to rewards—something promised but yet unfulfilled in both Communist as well as early post-Communist Poland.

This myth of British meritocracy, by which I do not mean a false misconception or kind of Marxian false-consciousness, but a narrative legitimising individuals' actions, is a powerful theme in most migrants' attitudes towards their migration decisions. From a relational perspective, we can see that they are telling us more about their beliefs concerning the constraints on Polish social mobility and meanings of class hierarchy than what British society looks like. In fact, those who had recently arrived had a rather vague understanding of British social class distinctions and peculiarities. Meritocracy largely meant the apparent lack of favouritism at work, more egalitarian relationships between employer and employee, decent, 'normal' salary recognising the value of labour, and a 'nice' boss who did not yell at his employees.

Why people construct these narratives is a matter of interpretation and attention to who is the listener. In various articles on recent migration from Poland, the practice of contrast making is a common feature but its use may be diverse. Maruska Svasek, for example, in her description of focus groups among Polish migrants taking part in a Shared History project in Belfast, stresses that self-presentation as 'victims of poverty' was an active claim, which justified their presence in Northern Ireland.[234] The focus on economic factors was, therefore, a strategic choice, informed by a collective wish to induce empathy in the viewers. Galasińska and Kozłowska, on the other hand, in an analysis of Internet forum debates between migrants, emphasise that, through constructing narratives of 'normality' and 'normal life' in Britain in opposition to 'back home,' migrants recreate a positive image of transnational

---

[234] M. Svasek. 2009. Shared history? Polish migrant experiences and the politics of display in Northern Ireland. [in]: K. Burrell (ed.) *Polish Migration to the UK in the 'New' European Union*. Surrey: Ashgate.

movement. The grand narrative of the West-bound, active individual, who is making it, indicates what is wrong in Poland.[235]

These very pessimistic views about social mobility in Poland are a dominant feature in the majority of Polish migrants' narratives. Poland is seen as a country torn apart and dominated by a tiny elite, where the middle class is virtually absent. The rigid and impenetrable system of elite recruitment during the socialist period seems to have survived despite the new, capitalist discourse of individual merit and skills. Moreover, this system has become more visible and hence less acceptable normatively. After all, neo-liberal philosophy in its crude, popular form meant that everyone should fend for themselves and that everyone is an individualistic and opportunistic actor. If inequality, ostentatious wealth, economic entrepreneurship, and trade were regarded with suspicion during communist times, post-socialism is marked by an enthusiastic endorsement of consumerism and wealth creation practices where 'anything goes'. In a way—as in the small rural community Buchowski studied—post-socialism made 'social hierarchy transparent'[236] and social differences—to large extent present during Communism[237]—brushed under the carpet of official communist propaganda, were laid bare.

One of the key criticisms of relations in Poland is the role played by informal connections in structuring social class divisions. This is a fascinating case of continuity through the communist system of informal favours and the practices of *dojścia* and *kombinacje*, as well as the pre-war role of the gentry which, through family connections and intermarriage endogamy rules, maintained its dominant position within society. Connections are

---

[235] A. Galasińska, O. Kozłowska. 2009. Discourses of 'normal life' among post-acceession migrants from Poland to Britain. [in]: K. Burrell (ed.) *Polish Migration to the UK in the 'New' European Union.* Surrey: Ashgate 2009.

[236] M. Buchowski. 2004. Redefining work in a local community in Poland. Transformation and class, culture and work. [in]: Angela Procoli (ed.) *Workers and Narratives of Survival in Europe. The Management of Precariousness at the End of the Twentieth Century.* New York: State University of New York Press, p. 179.

[237] C. Nagengast. 1991. *Reluctant Socialists, Rural entrepreneurs: Class, Culture and the Polish State.* Boulder/San Francisco/Oxford: Westview Press.

crucial, through having rich parents, family members, friends, being able to pay bribes and perpetuating an informal, corrupt system of social advancement. Connections are the only game in town, and if you do not play it, you impede your own capability to deal with life. As one migrant, from Jasło, SE Poland, a *stork*, building a house in his home town puts it:

> *Putting it simply* [Poland] *this is just a society where deal-making…*[238], *without them there is no chance … I am a sign of it myself. I am getting some things done in the administration and I need a document from the local court. To push the whole thing I need it now. So what I do? I haven't lived in Poland for two years now but old habits are there. I pick up the phone, dial a number for the office of local government where my cousin works. And I tell her: 'Please find me someone in the courts!' So she calls back: 'Go there and there, that's my friend' … and I have the thing done in the same day. You need connections, contacts … you need to know people ….*

A typical attitude is represented by this woman, who came in 2002 and in 2008, studied art, and worked in catering at the same time:

> *Classes?* [in Poland] *I don't know … maybe the poorest one … then a bit richer people … then nothing for long time and then the richest ones, who know which way the wind blows – those that no matter what happen are always on top.*
>
> *Q: And where would you see yourself?*
>
> *A: Above a bit over those that are very, very poor …*
>
> *Q: And why is it like this in Poland?*
>
> *A: I don't know really … You know I think Poland was always partitioned, torn apart … People only think about themselves, about the benefits for them only … not about the country but about the party or their position or just own interest … Poland was always full of thieves ….*
>
> *Q: So how do you get to the top?*
>
> *A: You have to sell yourself, be corrupted ….* [laughs]

---

[238] *państwo układów; układ* – this is generally a description of the importance of shadowy, informal, backstage arrangement, deal-making, that drives Polish social, political, and economic life; *układ* is sometimes synonymous with mafia, that is, a blurred division between politics and business in the post-socialist political capitalism.

It is worth stressing the long historical perspective this interviewee takes — Poland was *always* full of thieves, who knew *which way the wind blows* is a relatively common reference to corrupt elites, not just now, during communist times, but even during the partition era of the 19th century where the wealthy land-owning gentry was notoriously accused of selling out the national cause. In a *long duree* perspective, the theme of internal rupture along class lines, which seems the Polish fate, is simply a reminiscence of deep class division between the gentry and peasant class developed over the last couple of centuries.

Push and pull or simply go?

The question of human motivations has always been a problematic one in migration literature, balancing between the deterministic and individualistic view. In the case of Polish migrants in London, it would be wrong to assume that people's decisions to migrate are determined solely by changing social and economic conditions in Poland. In fact, they were keen to stress that they left Poland in order to go to London rather than went to London in order to leave Poland. This means that the neat division between pull and push factors needs to be questioned. People do not distinguish between these and often see their motives as complex and multidimensional.

Why is this so? First of all, the myth of a meritocratic Britain is a motivational tool. People do not have to dwell too much on class divisions, difficulties in the British labour market, the complex system of getting onto the occupational ladder, or the fact that most find work only in the low paid, uncertain secondary labour market. One needs to believe in a meritocratic Britain in order to go there and work, even if this proves to be far from reality when they encounter exploitation, destitution, and poverty. In other words, believing that things in Poland are so bad helps people maintain the vision of Britain as a meritocracy, which, in turn, underpins the belief that merit and skills are what really count.

Many are, of course, well aware of the precariousness of the capitalist labour market and that they perform jobs that no British workers are willing to do. This does not stop many Polish migrants I interviewed believing that they can be successful here and that their effort will have much more chance of being recognised than in Poland. As one respondent explained:

> I'm the cheap labour … English wouldn't do this job for that money …. I accept this because it gives me … well … it is fine for me now in terms of what my demands are now to be able to realise my plans [emphasis added] …. Of course, I'm not the kind of person that lives from eating pasta for 35p and saves everything … I just live normally.

I found that most respondents refuse to dwell too much on how their life chances are determined by their socio-economic position in Britain. What they are primarily concerned about are Poland's inadequacies — the baleful effect of 'connections' and state bureaucracy, which are independent of class. Migration enables them to escape these inadequacies. Yet, are conditions in Poland really so bad? It is important to understand that social actors tell stories, which go beyond stating basic facts. They construct a culturally dependent and normative framework, which underpins human agency and offers a world-view that is consistent with their acts — what anthropologists also call simply part of myth-making strategies that legitimise their actions.

When we look at empirical evidence, the picture is of course much more nuanced. As a leading Polish scholar on social stratification, Henryk Domański, notes, intergenerational social mobility in Poland compares quite well with West European countries, even during the socialist period of a command economy. Moreover, after 1989, the expanding business sector was more open than the myth claims. Although members of the socialist *nomenklatura* class also entered business classes, they were outnumbered by those outside this elite.[239] In other words, it helped to be a com-

---

[239] H. Domański. 1995. Rekompozycja stratyfikacji społecznej i reorientacja wartości. [in]: A. Sułek, J. Styk (eds.) *Ludzie i instytucje. Stawanie się ładu*

munist if one wanted to become a capitalist, but not being one was not an impediment. Obviously, these data may differ from what people know from their own experiences. The omnipresent picture of a local clique, which impedes social mobility and opportunities for others, points to very conflicting pictures of what the market economy has produced. It is yet another contradiction and yet another source of tension and contestation of the dominant narratives about the Polish modernisation project.

The cultural meaning of moaning

There is one crucial characteristic of everyday interaction between many Poles that reproduce, revive, and negotiate the themes discussed earlier — the practice of moaning, of being overtly pessimistic about work, society, and what the future may bring. The fact that respondents are eager to elaborate on negative aspects of Polish society and economy should remind us that besides the factual significance of what people say, we must be sensitive to the meanings of messages behind what is being expressed. Narratives need to be understood in their situational contexts — who is the audience — and the specific cultural functions which certain rhetorical practices fulfil. Moaning, like hate-speech, gossip, political manifestos, and religious sermons, are not just textual narratives — they are also performed social rituals through which people channel their perceptions of social life.

Informal conversations with Poles, as well as during the interviews, frequently brought up a deep sense of pessimism, uncertainty, and limited achievement — a feature which recurs in my and others' scholars interviews with migrants from Poland and which is also a frequent subject of media debates. It would be regarded as impolite, artificial, and probably false to boast about one's successes at work or to be overoptimistic about the state of Polish politics. Hence, the moaning has a strong integrative func-

---

społecznego. Wyd. U MCS, 1995; see also, H. Domański 2000. *On the Verge of Convergence: Social Stratification in Eastern Europe*, Budapest: CEU Press, p. 5.

tion of creating a common bond across classes and backgrounds. Through these exchanges intimate ties and a collective fate are created. Failure, loss, and tragedy pull people together, while success has the potential to be divisive and hierarchical. A following casual conversation overheard many times and present in mundane interactions expresses this ritualisation of moaning very well:

> *'Hi, what's up?'*
>
> *'Well, fucked up as usual, work and all that'* [jak zwykle przejebane, praca i w ogóle].

In this ritual exchange, what people are communicating are not feelings about work but a casual agreement about what they have in common. The 'all that' assumes that the interlocutor understands very well what is going on. Indeed, the whole exchange is actually very difficult to translate into English. A similar ritualised exchange is the reply to the 'how are you?' question which the reply is: *stara bida*[240] — a phrase evoking poverty, pessimism, or fatalism but one that is predictable, constant, known, and accepted. This agreement over cultural meanings reaches its peak when the subject of conversation is politics, the state, politicians, or elites. Here, Poles seem to indulge in elaborate arguments about their place in modern Polish history, which are shot through with bitter regret and pessimism.

Although there may be factual reasons for such negativity, the practice of moaning tells us something deeper about the relations between the individual and the collective, the state and the ideological legitimisation of the social order. 'Polish moaning' reproduces the clear, black and white social divisions so omnipresent in Polish social history, but also reproduced through various discursive practices on different levels of society. The boundaries between 'us' and 'them', 'society' and the state, *naród* [nation] and *rząd*, [the government] are through this practice reproduced

---

[240] Literally, it translates into: 'old poverty'. It is the equivalent of 'old stuff', 'same shit'.

and reinforced. Through moaning, people can express their dislike of the structural constraints and economic inequalities of an emerging capitalist Poland and create horizontal ties with those who are participating in the exchange. Its omnipresence in Polish ethnography[241] suggests that it can be identified as what James Scott calls the 'hidden transcript',[242] a form of banal, everyday resistance to the Polish class hierarchy, power relations, and also the essence of the modernisation project.

There is thus a strong discursive link between the myth of Britain as a place 'one can make it' and the practice of moaning. The myth of British meritocracy reveals a fresh attitude of optimism, which would be difficult to explain in the light of the frequently harsh working conditions endured by Polish migrants. As we saw in the previous chapter, this optimism is often 'optimism on credit', since people frame their presence in London in temporal terms—they look to see what the future may bring rather than their current situation.

Hence, Polish migrants express their class identity through the relationship between optimism and pessimism, the future and the past, as well as the desire for social mobility. They draw on deeply entrenched, culturally specific notions of social order, which refer to relations between elites and the working masses which seek independence, self-affirmation, and development, but outside the system, voicing what Hirshman calls the 'exit' option,[243] seeking freedom from social constraints. The transnational field provides the comparative perspective through which they are able to reflect on these relations in different national contexts. In other words, symbolically they need the construction of Poland

---

[241] M. Rakowski. 2009. *Łowcy, zbieracze, praktycy niemocy.* Warszawa: Słowo/obraz/terytoria

[242] J.C. Scott. 1990. *Domination and the Art of Resistance: Hidden Transcripts.* New Haven: Yale University Press.

[243] A.O. Hirschman. 1970. Exit, Voice, and Loyalty: Responses to Decline in Firms, Organizations, and States. Cambridge: Harvard University Press.

as a negative example in order to believe in their chances in London.

The rural/urban divide and the endurance of the rural class

Only two generations ago, over two-thirds of Poland's population lived off the agricultural sector dominated by small farms. The country is thus deeply influenced by the legacies of a peasant society. Despite the economic changes unleashed after 1989, the proportion of people living in rural areas still hovers around 20%, and in some areas of the country, this percentage is much higher. The importance of this rural heritage and the intelligentsia's roots in the land-owning gentry has led some commentators to describe Poland as a 'post-peasant' society.[244]

Polish peasants are a far from a homogeneous group.[245] Rural communities are rigidly stratified through differential access to land, machinery, transnational networks, and political power. These structures of hierarchies are reproduced through endogamy, modes of consumption, and political patronage.[246] As Nagengast reveals in her extensive anthropological study of rural south-east Poland, the revival of capitalism in Poland did not signal the inevitable victory of a superior economic system but rather reflects continuities in earlier, class-based social relations which masqueraded as socialist relations for five decades.[247] Polish agriculture was never collectivised and private ownership of rural land became one of the contradictions which led to the implosion

[244] C. Nagengast. 1991. *Reluctant Socialists, Rural entrepreneurs: Class, Culture and the Polish State*. Boulder/San Francisco/Oxford: Westview Press.

[245] M. Buchowski. 2004. Redefining work in a local community in Poland. Transformation and class, culture and work. [in]: A. Procoli (ed.) *Workers and Narratives of Survival in Europe. The Management of Precariousness at the End of the Twentieth Century*. New York: State University of New York Press

[246] M. Buchowski. 2004. *Ibidem*.

[247] C. Nagengast. 1991. *Reluctant Socialists, Rural entrepreneurs: Class, Culture and the Polish State*. Boulder/San Francisco/Oxford: Westview Press, p. 3.

of the system. Small farmers pursued proto-capitalist practices through a huge and highly influential black economy and a rural underclass was created through the pressure of rising prices and the inefficiencies of the command economy. So, in spite of neo-liberal criticisms, Polish farmers are pursuing their own capitalist path—a path which emerges from their strategies of dealing with the economic inefficiencies of Communism.[248]

As we have seen, those taking this path were not equal. After 1989, the numbers of rural poor increased, particularly those who commuted daily to factories but still held on to their small rural plots (*chłopo-robotnicy*). These 'people on the swing' saw emigration as a way out of their economic plight during the turbulent transition after 1989. Jerzy and Józef, two brothers who migrated in their late 40s from a village near Rzeszów, met and interviewed at a homeless shelter in London in 2010, illustrate this process well. After the closure of a state-owned factory where they both worked in the early 1990s, some very tough choices had to be made:

> [Jerzy] *Well, you can't really say there are class divisions; our society is divided between an elite* [and the rest] *... and that elite partially belongs to a mafia ... because that* [is] *how it should be called. These are people that have taken over the whole industry. These communists have arranged things for themselves very well ... have set up companies and become businessmen in a few years, while in the* [United] *States you need generations to get that ... So they live like kings ... and the rest is as you see*
>
> Q. *Which are?*
>
> [Józef] *Around 50% of society lives in poverty ....*
>
> [Jerzy] *There was that huge textile industry where there was a massive investment in the '70s and it was deliberately destroyed, the machinery was neglected, broken and all that ... Machinery was expensive and after 1989 they were dismantling them down for scrap, for nothing ... and the bosses were taking money for it ... It was daylight robbery.*

A familiar theme here—a story of loss, robbery, elites taking advantage of the working class, and thieving of Poland's assets. But

---

[248] M. Buchowski. 2001. *Rethinking Transformation...*, p. 164.

the brothers needed to adapt. They began to work in Germany on a seasonal basis in the early 1990s and then also found jobs in Norway. Transnational migration became a family strategy, since their sisters went to Italy to work as carers—a feature of survival for thousands of Polish families coping with new system. The village became both a point of departure and a place of reunion for the whole family, who would occasionally return for holidays or Christmas. It would be wrong, however, to depict their itinerant lives, disrupted by grand historical events, in bleak terms. Both brothers proudly point out that, despite all the disadvantages and poverty, their transnational migration had led to educational opportunities for their children.

> You need to educate your kids, because these days they need it ... but the situation again is similar to the one we had [in the 1960s] ... It's hard to send them anywhere up when there is no money to do that ... it is inheriting poverty. Our oldest brother's son went and got a language degree at the university ... but the brother had a decent job then ... But us ... because ... all our family were going abroad ... I built a house [and] my brother helped me ... and my brother, after that, put the money in the bank and it gave him an opportunity to educate his son.

Jerzy and Jozef agreed that education was the way to get round the stifling system of connections (dojścia). However, Adam—the typical *stork* presented in previous chapter—from rural south-east Poland, placed far more emphasis on land and traditional lifestyles. He and his brothers were in their 40s so their work experience was shaped by the communist period and the early transition phase deeply affecting farming and the relation with the state (in his case, collapse of the internal tourist industry in Piwniczna region). They were skilled at adapting to economic change, but at the same time, they sought to maintain traditional rural lifestyles, hierarchy of statuses, and ideas of self-worth for which land tenure was fundamental. For them, education was still a luxury—something that required huge sacrifices and do not necessarily translate into social mobility. In these uncertain times, land tenure was something solid and predictable.

Persistent in Polish culture and noted by Znaniecki and Thomas in their *magnum opus* on Polish peasants in America, land is more than tenure—it is a status, a connection with ancestors, and a source of security. Hence, pride (made even more meaningful since Jerzy and Józef were interviewed in a shelter for homeless people) was not an attempt to rationalise harsh choices but a message that land tenure has been secured and their place in society acknowledged—no matter that their migration history was full of disappointment, exploitation, homelessness, ill health, and a high level of insecurity. As a farmer, one does not sell land in order to better oneself and move elsewhere—one moves elsewhere on a temporary basis in order to keep the land. In fact, most of farmers I interviewed valued land tenure and the building of a house, as one of their main life goals. From other research in Poland, it is clear that migrants invest their migration money in real estate mainly, either building a house or buying land.[249]

It would be wrong to assume that this is a universal value for Polish peasantry. The younger generation viewed education rather differently. Przemysław works in a hotel in London as a cleaner and comes from a rural town near Rzeszów. He is a prime example of how educational aspirations were permeating rural society and, for many people, upsetting the traditional structure of values of the land. His family was not well educated, but he decided to join his best friends and do the *matura* (Polish A-levels). He also wanted to go to university but lacked the funds, and, therefore, chose to join his brother in London. Not surprisingly, he is very negative about his prospects in Poland:

> *Q. What are the chances for young people like you in Poland?*
>
> *A. Like shit. Some people make it … by scams, connections …. We are an educated nation but they don't give us a chance.*
>
> *Q. Does this say something about social divisions?*

---

[249] E. Jaźwińska, M. Okólski. 2001. *Ludzie na huśtawce. Migracje między peryferiami Polski a Zachodu.* Warszawa: Scholar. R. Jenkins. 1997. *Rethinking Ethnicity. Arguments and Explorations.* London: Sage Publications.

> A. … *You know we are a nation that* [is] … *corrupted* … *We are divided by private egoism* … *If you want to make something, you need to have connections and all that.*

Przemysław frames these 'connections' within the division between rural and urban society. Going to school in big cities gave people a big advantage. After two years of manual work in London, during 2008, Przemysław decided to enrol at one of the London's universities , since 'it is much easier here'. It would help him overcome the barrier between the 'English' and the 'foreigners' and offer the chance of some solid prospects:

> *My chances will get better* … *I won't be like the English but I will surely have more chances* … *when they will accept me* [at the university] *and I will get an occupation* … *For me it does not make any sense to live like that — just to survive* … *For a few months, fine, but if you want to stay longer you need to make a decision* … *or you* [will just] *work, work and work.*

For Przemysław, then, acquiring education is not only about overcoming the barrier, which prevented him from studying in Poland, but also about moving up the English class system through the path of incorporation into the labour market via education. A number of people revealed this aspect of class aspirations and showed how two separate processes were reinforcing each other — the increasing emphasis in Polish rural society on educational achievement and an engagement with the values of the neo-liberal market economy where education was presented as the path to earnings through individual effort.

The links between these two processes go a long way to explaining both the Polish migrants' reputation for hard work in London and how rural elites were changing and adopting the proto-capitalists modes of exchange and production well before the collapse of Communism.[250] Rafał is a 28-year-old psychology graduate who, by 2008, had been in London for over a year. His parents came from a village in one of the poorest regions of Poland (near Suwałki, in the north-east) and had received only a

---

[250]   See C. Nagengast. 1991. *Reluctant Socialists, Rural entrepreneurs: Class, Culture and the Polish State*. Boulder/San Francisco/Oxford: Westview Press.

basic vocational education. Rafał initially thought that he would only do his A-levels, since he frequently had to work on his parents' and grandparents' farms. When he mentioned that he was the only one in his family who went to university and moved to Warsaw, I asked him what was so special about that. He responded slightly irritated—*'Well, don't tell me it's special ... [it] should be normal!'* For Rafał, educational achievement was the prime feature of his class identity but he also recognises the uneasy legacy of being brought up in a rural environment, where manual labour and hard work are deeply respected but individual ambition is not facilitated:

> *My family comes from* [a rural area] *... and they work hard, of course, but in today's times it is not enough to work hard — you need also to have a vision or something ... a kind of flexibility, an ability to adapt to changing conditions, to the market really. Because it is about something else than just to kill a piglet or milk a cow these days ... And, unfortunately, a lot of people today think that way still ... because it's hard to get a job and ... it's hard to sustain oneself ... To compare,* [there are] *... two groups of family.* [First], *people who got stuck in a kind of* [traditional] *life and they don't risk too much ... although they work really very, very hard. They try but they don't have anything in return ... They are closed over there* [points his head]; *in their head they can't figure it out ... And the second group is more flexible, more ready to change, and they are doing a bit better.*

His experience of living in Warsaw seems crucial to understanding the complex way in which he used his class background and ambitions to operate in the contemporary market economy:

> *There are different places in Poland, really contrasting places where everything looks different ... I lived in Warsaw and saw that really where you live determines a lot ... You just have a different access to information ... That flexibility is again most important here. Either you try to do something with your life* [or] *... you just do the things the old way.*

Those brought up in the Polish countryside see, then, a choice between a traditional aversion towards risk and a modern willingness to be flexible. As we saw in the case of the 'paradigmatic' seasonal migrant, Adam from Piwniczna, this choice can have very different outcomes—you can either stay in the village or you can have a 'vision' which, in this context, means adaptation and entry into precarious and dangerous but potentially rewarding world of neo-liberal economic order. Rafał contrasts the ways in which he asserts his individuality and develops himself with the traditional life of his parents' generation, which is unwilling or unable to move on. The key phrase which migrants like Rafał use is *wyrwać się* — to 'tear out' or 'break away' from the place you live in. The small world of rural society, supported by traditional values and dominated by the local priest and long-established elites, stifles initiative. Although Rafał acknowledges the influence of family ties and upbringing, he attaches great significance to being a mature, independent, and opportunity-seeking individual exploring the wider world:

> I think that it is the family and culture that determines a lot of who we are ... We are determined by what we take from that Olszanka, the village my parents come from, from their attitude to life ... But, on the other hand, I had a lot of anger in me ... I learn all the time ... and I feel that I want something else, and that I am able to make it ... That's why once I was traveling a lot, hitchhiking around Europe, I didn't have any money and I saw that you can do a lot, that so many things are possible. At the same time I see that so many people are determined by their culture really... It is a closure, an inability to move, and this 'stay where we are' mode of thinking. But ... even when you try to achieve something more ... there are limits there, of course ... When I came here I see that suddenly the world [has] got so much smaller for me, like that [shows his fist] today.

At the same time, educational achievement does not necessarily bring financial reward as Rafal regretfully acknowledges:

> For people of my generation to get education was really very important; it was axiomatic to have a degree, because later you will have a better life. This was the attitude of my generation, but is seems that if they had not gone to the universities and started to do a business straight away to make money — they could have been on a better level financially than they are now. And for me this is a real failure to be honest. Let's assume that I came from that basic class, like maybe some gentry family ... [and] I thought that I will advance by going to university, that I will break away [wyrwać się] so that I will be someone but then it turns out that a cleaner earns the same amount as a psychologist.

Thus, operating in a transnational social field offers Rafal the opportunity to keep a foot in both doors. He owns horses on his grandparents' farm and sends some of his savings to restore a family house. He also recognises that the skills, which he acquired while working on the farm, have helped him find work in London. He supplements his income as a psychologist in a drug charity with occasional carpentry or building jobs:

> Yes, well even before going I tried to look something close to my occupation – I wanted to work according to my qualifications ... So I sent my cv and applications everywhere and all that ... but you needed to live as well. So my neighbour from South Africa was looking for a job as a carpenter and I went with him and got this job as a carpenter for a few weeks. And because I got a driving licence, I got a job as a delivery man in the same firm ....

> When first I got [the building job], I thought: 'Great. I am going to work with the English. I will learn the language'. I came here [the charity] and I have Marian, Wojtek, Paweł – 99% Polish! So this was it. It was manual labour but it was all right, it was cool, I like it ... But with the [charity job] ... I hesitated ... I thought that I should take an even less [well] paid job as a support worker or someone in a centre like [the one in Poland], with the work with addicts ... or do some cool things ... on building sites and have even more money at the start ... I know it's hard work but these people [builders] can surely afford much more, they can buy cars ....

> I thought a lot, talked with my brother, with many people and just told myself: 'What did you study for then? This is a great opportunity to try. I can always work as a builder, no?' And here someone gives you a chance and I can do a lot of interesting things ... I bring to the team a lot since I have a different perspective on some things and I come from a different culture .... This is a great job.

Rafał reflects, then, on his dilemma in London, where he needs to choose between the greater financial rewards as a builder and carpenter and the lower pay as a psychologist in a charity. He consults his brother, his father (who also came to London to work as a builder), and his girlfriend. He cannot consider just his individual aspirations but his financial and emotional ties with his family. His dilemma is familiar to the younger generation entering the world of education and work from the Polish countryside. What is the value of money and work and how do they relate to ones' aspirations, qualifications, and status? Should he settle for more financial rewards in doing something he does very well and which also gives satisfaction, since physical labour is something to be proud of, or choose something that reflects his ambitions and desire to develop as an individual but may be less financially rewarding? Despite temptations, Rafal retains his conviction that life is not all about financial gain and that personal development can be combined with rural family ties. He decides to keep his work in a charity and accepts that he may earn less, but that the rewards for this work go beyond immediate financial gains.

We see here the social and economic function of one of the most interesting cultural characteristics of Polish migrants—their flexibility and ability to fulfil different tasks. Builders who can be plumbers, carpenters who can be good babysitters, car-mechanics who can repair a washing machine, and a psychologist who can be a carpenter are examples of something characteristic about migrants from that part of Europe with a strong legacy of Communism, especially those raised in rural areas where one needed to acquire a considerable amount of practical skills in order to get by. These skills were extremely important in the later stages of Communism when people had to rely on themselves for basic services. At a time when people simply could not buy a washing machine, the ability to repair one was highly prized, and deals could be done with those who possessed other skills. By making self-development and individuality central to his understanding of social class, Rafal provokes a question, which reaches to the heart of transnational class production. Where does self-development take place? In London or Poland? And for what purpose? Again, this is where intentional unpredictability is very important, since Rafal does not know where his quest for development will take him. He is saving in order to make his position 'back home' more secure but other options are also available.

> *I save but also send* [some of these savings] *to Poland. Like now, dad is finishing that house and to help him a bit … I took also a* [loan] *in Poland, since I wanted to buy something in Poland to rent it after, just to invest it.*

Q. Ok, so we are near your plans now, what you want to do next then?

Rafal: I try to save some money. I have some horses for example, I keep them in my grandfather's house in the village ... but I want to sell them, and then keep the capital ... But really if I buy something in Poland, it's not to go there and live there but to earn some money from it, only to rent it or sell it ... to help also my family ... I didn't come here to earn money, save, buy and come back working as a psychologist earning that thousand zlotych [200 pounds] a month or two ... I don't know ... I don't know how it turns up ... Surely I want to invest but ....

Q. So do you want to come back to Poland?

Rafal: Hard to say now ... rather not ... All this is a bit of a surprise for me. I mean I see how the whole world has shrank suddenly ... So staying here does make sense since there are still so many places to see, so many things to do... But ... I don't know. I wanted also to finish my PhD ... I thought also of buying a house here and letting it – this is a good investment ... I could decorate it, repair it ... Also my partner tells me to go the US embassy to go to America ... but I don't know.

The abundance of options may be confusing but it seems that, as in many other interviews, the aim is just to list them but not really take them seriously. Britain is a place where people can enjoy a new sense of freedom rather than make rational plans. The central role of the place 'back there' says it all, since most of migrants, always keep their 'doors open' in their home towns and villages. In times of economic uncertainties, and the post-2008 crisis, this is a tested and well-thought strategy which gives them an edge over competitors. It also provides a psychological advantage when coping with changing conditions of the capitalist labour market. Unlike the British working class, in the case of economic downturn, crisis, or mass unemployment, these migrants have somewhere to go — they can always go back. Operating in transnational social fields is, therefore, not simply a way to have the best of both worlds — it is a strategy aimed at securing oneself from precarious conditions of modern capitalist labour market conditions. Interestingly, the fact noted in Chapter 3 that the economic downturn and recession in Britain has not seen a large outflux of Poles is the evidence that the Poles are quite resilient to the crisis and have weathered in out quite well. By 2015, they still continue to come to

Britain—and leave sometimes to—in search of work in large numbers. For example, Martyna and Maciek from Sokółka came in 2013. In their early 20s, they do not think twice about Britain being in recession or that there is no work.

> *We came and work was there straight away; I took over from Maciek's mum, her cleaning job and network of clients, Maciek started to work in a company run by his brother in law. Crisis? No, nothing like that, we are fine. They should go there and see what crisis really is ....*

The continual working and reworking of this perception of home sustains the transnational field—a field which protects them from the adverse economic effects of the flexible labour market. A potent proof of the popularity of this strategy is a tendency among Polish migrants to buy property in Poland, a continuity of the traditional peasant emphasis on buying land. These days, there are numerous transnational agencies facilitating sale, access to credit, and management. For example, Krystyna, a woman in her early 50s working as a cleaner in London, does not want to return to Poland, but she still decides to buy a flat in her home town by raising a loan from her London bank. An owner of a construction company invests in real estate on the perception that 'one day I may be there again'. Przemek talks fondly of his grandfather's house as a readily available safety net—'you never know with these conditions now; one day I may live there'. People acknowledge that they may never live in these properties; they may remain a leisure or holiday home but their very existence comforts them as they face their daily struggles in London by providing a reminder about the freedom to choose where one wants to live.

On an individual level, perceptions of social class in a transnational field for members of the Polish rural population are the result of several reinforcing cultural norms and practices. A strong ethos of education as the route to mobility is coupled with the reference point of rural class, which is always placed back in their home communities with a powerful emphasis on land tenure and acquisition of estate. This creates a mutually dependent relationship between ones' individual aspirations and construction of the self and the role of the collective social environment, which a migrant has left. Through the constant practice of transnational reflexivity migrants from the Polish countryside reformulate this relationship towards their peers, family, and friends back home. This is where visits to Poland gain such importance, because they help to construct transnationally these perceptions of social class. The home setting then, as well as the perceived British meritocracy with all its negative and positively valued aspects, is a crucial component of class for migrants. These aspects do not operate 'in Poland' or 'in Britain' but are a result of physical movement and reflexivity between the two.

For rural class, as well as those from impoverished regions of de-industrialised Poland, moving out is moving up—social mobility in Poland is restricted and thus one needs to move out. However, for many rural Poles, the fruits of that mobility ought to be consumed back home—this is the main reference point which renders social class meaningful. However, consumption 'back home' is not physically located. It may also mean sustaining and nurturing transnational connections, it can mean simply—for a Pole who is already established and does not think of returning— becoming a crucial part in the migration process through facilitating the migration of *storks*, helping people in finding employment, offering a hand for newcomers—usually family members, close friends. In that sense, as agents, migrants, through their transnational connections, sustain and reproduce their own, deterritorialised notion of class hierarchy, which is suited to their own cultural meanings, life strategies, and transnational ways of being.

The practice of *kombinacje* and the Poles from *blokowiska*

Class is also reproduced and reformulated through different cultural resources and strategies by another group of migrants, who lack the cultural background of Polish rural society and the support provided by relatives and friends 'back home' or the cultural meaning and status attached to land ownership and the relative security of social rural environment. This group's understanding of social class also reveals a deep sense of loss and bitterness towards the socio-economic changes which took place after the collapse of Communism. Even though many of these young people did not actually experience life under Communism, the transformation after 1989 shows how perceptions of class are being transmitted generationally. It also shows how the anti-state and anti-institutional traditions of Polish society are being reinforced and reorientated in new settings.

Individuals who share these attitudes can be found in various settings. During several stages of my fieldwork, I usually encountered them in dozens of night clubs and hip-hop venues, on the street selling goods, or working on building sites. They generally share similar backgrounds, coming from urban working-class families with deep and bitter memories of the post-communist transition. Some, whom I met several times between 2006 and 2009 on a west London main street, were selling cigarettes—one of the most profitable illicit trades quite popular among Polish migrants. British customs officials have taken a keen interest in this multi-million pound industry, and this illicit trade is not new—it clearly predates EU enlargement—and has gained notoriety among many migrants.

For many of my Polish informants, as well as people in leadership positions, people engaged in this illicit trade are the 'bad apples'—the Poles who deserve no mention because they operate at the margins of what is perceived as 'normal' and right. For some community leaders, these people should be condemned as part of the *kombinacje* tradition, with its roots in the *homo sovieticus* syndrome, and therefore not part of the Western, 'civilised' way of life. I will come back to this condemning and stigmatising practice in Chapter 7, but here I wanted to emphasise that, for many Poles, these deviants are seen in social class terms rather than ethnicity.

Before I present more closely at how and why people engage in the trade, the notion of *kombinacje* needs to be brought closer and interpreted. The concept entered the academic literature through the work of Janine R. Wedel and Carole Nagengast, who described the ways in which people survived the everyday grim reality of the command economy. Its inefficiency forced people to adapt numerous informal ways of doing things, having things arranged, and life eased. *Kombinacje* basically is a noun vaguely describing 'doing things' 'arranging', 'getting things done', 'to fix things' with the verb *kombinować* denoting the action of 'arranging'. Ewa Morawska describes the notion as 'informal or shady arrangements as in wheeling and dealing'.

I wish to take this argument further and stress that, despite the normative ambiguity attached to the term, it is a powerful conceptual tool by which people identify their individualistic set of values as well as collective identity. Although the concept of *kombinacje* is seen by scholars, such as Piotr Sztompka, as a part and parcel of the *homo sovieticus* syndrome and an unhealthy and non-modern obstacle to the success of the neo-liberal project,[251] it actually forms an important reference point for migrants, who view their class mobility through the prism of the myth of meritocracy and their ability to overcome obstacles and constraints. 'Doing things' thus loses its aura of informality or shadowy dealings, but retains its validation of creativity, agency, and individual power over hostile structures. The use of the term suggests that it is still value laden—it can still describe undesirable activities, which bring the community into disrespect, but it is also very often used as an assertion of the self as an active, creative, and innovative actor. It is thus an empowering concept. The value is here definitely positive and validates work as well as Eastern identity, which is contrasted to Western identity, seen as spoiled or weak in creativity. The following extract from one of the interviewees working in a construction company captures this attitude well:

---

[251] P. Sztompka. 2000. *Trauma wielkiej zmiany*, p. 55.

When I was a child and wanted to play war-games, I had to find a suitable branch, a hatch, climb the tree, cut the branch and then imagine it being a gun. People with whom I work today were simply buying such a toy in a shop. Nowadays when there is some problem at work – for instance, one needs to get something, then we, the Poles, instinctively kombinujemy [we arrange, we 'do things'] *how to overcome this difficulty and deal with the obstacle despite everything. And they* [the Brits] *just wave their hands and leave for a cup of tea. They think that since they can't find the toy on the shelf, nothing could be done about it ….*

Most often, *kombinacje* asserts the desire to gain control over ones' life. So, it is not surprising that it is something positively valued by those who, objectively, were the victims and losers of the post-1989 economic transformation. *Kombinacje* captures the additional dimension of survival strategy in its distinct anti-institutional and informal connotations. In many instances, it becomes the 'weapon of the weak',[252] the way people contest and make sense of the loss of security due to entry into world of capitalist social relations.

Take Piotr, a 25-year-old man, who came from a run-down suburb of Krakow on the outskirts of Nowa Huta, to London in 2006. He may be regarded as a classic example of the massive social costs the Polish working class had experienced.[253] With a history of time spent in prison for theft and burglary, family breakdown due to unemployment, he saw London as the only option, which could help him to escape the vicious circle of crime and hopelessness 'back home'. Piotr was a typical member of the Polish urban underclass, and his story expresses very clearly how these migrants view their country:

I had all this … you know – a broken family. My sister and me [were] *separated* [and] *this had an influence … While living with my grandma and father I did not complain. I did not miss out on anything* [in a material sense] *… Sometimes I deliberately destroyed my shoes so they could buy me new ones. So there was no problem with money there … but the family was missing … no poverty, no wearing worn trousers … My father worked in PTHW*

[252] J. Scott. 1999. *Domination and the Art of Resistance: Hidden Transcripts*. New Haven: Yale University Press

[253] A. Stenning. 2005. 'Where is the post-socialist working class?': working-class lives in the spaces of (post-)socialism. *Sociology* 39:983–999.

and Iglopool [companies] *as a tile fitter but then lately retired and the last two years was on a pension ... Well, I don't have to hide this ... he died because of alcohol ... He was in a hospital and they told him: 'If you will drink on, you'll die' ... And he got back to* [drinking] *... he did it all his life ... I was in jail when he died; they took me to the funeral.*

Q. And you think that your story tells something about Poland in general?

My story? For sure it does! For sure ...

Q. What?

My story? What do I think ... stories like mine? ... Of the 40 million there are 20 million of these stories in Poland ... There is such poverty ... and, in general, ... if not poverty ... [it is] *being antisocial...*

Q. So for you that's normal?

Yes, it a standard, a norm. ... All the boys I met in jail in Poland, for them this is a rule ... You see here, what criminality is there? They introduced these tags [electronic tagging] *and they manage somehow with this* [criminality] *... but Poland, not ... for a long time and then even will be behind* [laughs]...

Q. So you're pessimistic?

Yeah, if it comes to Poland ... very ... So it means there are inequalities ... because, apart these 20 million, there are another 20 ... who ... stole enough during good times and they live well now ... Apart from these 20 million there are maybe 5 honest ones [laugh]*, but the rest these are all przekręty* [scams, frauds]*. I don't know, man, I never looked at the statistics but this is my view ... Well, ... isn't it this way? You know better, you're older than me; you know how was it, more or less? ... More than me? And you know that these, who stuffed themselves* [stole] *during communist time, now live like kings ... Yeah* [laughs] *so that 5 million of honest ones turn out to be suckers ... and I don't want to be one.*

Piotr's extreme views reflect the sense of loss felt by the Polish underclass—people who, despite their relatively young age, identify all the ills of society with the previous era and see the current inequalities as continuing the divisions of that period. As others such as Buchowski have noted, these beliefs reflect a strong, deeply embedded culture of resistance within the Polish working class—a tradition which is fiercely hostile to state institutions and which is frequently criticised by the supporters of neo-liberal changes as an obstacle towards modernisation. However, Piotr develops his analysis of Poland's class structure through a contrast between two extreme cases which again brings us back to the meanings and values of dichotomisation for individual migrants. His narrative is not much different from that of the highly educated Poles, who are working in the financial sector, and is simply a social critique of state of affairs in Poland:

> *Q. So what do you want to do?*
>
> *What I want? Anything that would let me live. I mean, I would not get into strange things here … I don't know … I don't know how to explain … I just want to live here … I want to work. Even what I have now, I am standing there* [selling cigarettes] *have 30 pounds a day, I get 200 per week … That's fine for me … for food, accommodation … something else* [laughs — he means cannabis], *just my needs.*
>
> *Q. So when you look at Poland and UK what is the difference?*
>
> *Difference? In Poland there is no middle class – there are either these that are very poor or these that are very rich … Here you have a middle class like … all the blacks here are middle class here. They have everything, they are happy … That's the fact that there is no middle class in Poland.*
>
> *Q. So that is how you would like to live?*
>
> *Yes … I mean not like that forever. Obviously, I would like to live from year to year a bit better but not from year to year worse, like in Poland.*
>
> *Q. In Poland there was no way you could work honestly?*
>
> *I did but there was no point, no sense in this.*
>
> *Q. Why?*
>
> *Why? If you would earn for the entire day in the car wash … we were paid a percentage … so I earned 3.40 zloty for a day* [50 p]. *My friend and me we got 3.40 each …* [laughs] *so there was no point.*

Here, the dominant neo-liberal ideology shapes Piotr's understanding of the middle class and the proletarian egalitarianism is replaced by an emphasis on individual effort. People are defined in terms of a middle-class lifestyle, where they can live honestly, can buy some clothes (*ciuchy, dres*) through work, which is fairly rewarded, and entertain themselves like Britain's black population. Becoming middle class entails freedom from subordination, oppression, and disadvantage as people draw on the ideology of *klasa średnia* (the middle class), which has played such a crucial role in the construction of Polish capitalism and the modernisation project.[254] Piotr shares this general quest for middle-class status by reclaiming the notion from the intelligentsia and political and economic elites through a more egalitarian understanding of the 'just', 'fair', and dignified way people ought to live—as Galasińska and Kozłowska notes, a simple craving for social justice of those who are not privileged.[255]

People's interpretations of class are far from constant however, since migrants like Piotr, keep their options as wide open as possible. In some respect, his life strategies were rather basic and constructed with short-term gains in mind, associating class with particular hedonistic lifestyle and consumption patterns—the ability to buy clothes, drink good vodka, or go to a party. At the time of the interviews, he lived in a small room in a house shared by at least six other migrants in Acton and frequently changed jobs besides his £30 a day cigarette-selling activity. His evenings were spent playing Nintendo with his mates and smoking cannabis. Most of his money was spent on clothes, accommodation, occasional partying, and food. Nevertheless, he strongly sees his move and his new life as a breakthrough into normality. Migration is the route to redemption, maturity, and self-respect:

> *I am not going to lie – I fucked up really badly a few times,* [przywaliłem w chuja—meaning got into deep trouble] ... *But here, if you want, if you try, you can make it, you can become someone* [wyjść na ludzi—literally: to become a human being, to take a straight path]. *If you only want you can be normal...*
>
> *Q. So London helped you become normal?*

---

[254] See H. Domanski. 2000. *On the Verge of Convergence: Social Stratification in Eastern Europe.* Budapest: CEU Press.

[255] A. Galasińska, O. Kozłowska, 2009. Discourses of "normal life" among postacceession migrants from Poland to Britain. [in]: K. Burrell (ed.) *Polish Migration to the UK in the 'New' European Union.* Surray: Ashgate, p. 100.

Yes, yes, exactly – you can become normal here ... not over there.

Q. So you're happy you came over?

Kurwa ... [intonation of admiration and satisfaction] *... you know, I can sit here with you, chat about anything. We can hang around, I can help you, we can smoke a lolek,* [cannabis joint] *tomorrow I will go to work, get the money, no stress. This is enough ... I like it, it's the ease ...*

Q. So you don't want to come back?

[shakes his head strongly] *No way ....*

Q. So what would you like to do here?

When it comes to occupation? I can paint. I don't mind, I can be a decorator. I know what I can [do]; *I don't have too much of ambitions, I know what to do best ... so this would be enough for me, really.*

Marcin, Piotr's close friend, had a similar attitude towards Poland, strengthened by the fact that his father had lived in London for four years before he brought his son over. At 21 years of age, he felt strongly that education and work in Poland is something for the privileged few. Born on a tough Nowa Huta estate — called the *blokowiska*, his views about conditions in Poland are delivered though a constant flow of vulgarities:

Poland? Kurwa, fucking drama man ... there is nothing there ... Over there the only things you can get is hospital, jail or grave. Kurwa ... simple ... Kurwa, hard man ... either you steal something, or they will screw you. No future [Marcin says this in English] *... You won't win a fucking lotto, kurwa...*

Q. So any job like ....

What? Job? I go for a job for 600 złotych [100 GBP] *and kurwa, I will buy shoes for four* [hundred] *trousers for two and what I need to get some food, fun some smoke and gone.*

This appreciation of powerful social constraints on mobility experienced among the members of urban working class or their descendants takes various forms. However, the sharp distinction between 'us' and 'them' in terms of social hierarchies transcends generations in Poland. For Piotr and Marcin migration is a form of resistance, even if they bring some of the attitudes and characteristics of the Polish urban underclass, which seems to have been the biggest loser since 1989. The illicit trade in cigarettes, *kombinacje*, petty theft, social benefits scams, everyday lifestyles, and social networks are reproduced in London, as both Marcin and Piotr eagerly exchange news about 'who else made it to London' and frequently invite their friends from the estate to spend time together in London clubs or hip-hop venues. In fact, the extension of the Krakow *blokowiska* into West and North London takes place constantly with some migrants revisiting or coming back, while others engaged in constant contact through modern forms of communication. The beauty of it — as in words of Marcin and Piotr and many others — is that you can actually bring the *blokowiska* social settings to Acton or Wood Green.

Removed from physical space, the endurance of *blokowiska's* social appeal stems from strong personal ties and the generation of migratory capital — so crucial if the whole system is to work. *Bloki* life brings both social support as well as the potential for social breakdown and problems. This influence explains the huge popularity of Polish hip-hop in London where, every week at least, there is a concert by one group or another. The appeal of hip-hop to the urban underclass is, of course, well documented,[256] and numerous studies show that it has had a particular impact on Polish society in transition[257] and packed Polish venues in London are a proof that the hip-hop scene is now a part of the social transnational field between two localities. The anti-state and anti-institutional message flowing from Polish hip-hop song is a powerful one but is not easily translatable, even if it is part of a universal urban culture of resistance, which prizes friendship, masculinity, camaraderie, and trust among peers in opposition to the generalised and hostile 'system'. In fact, in many houses visited during

---

[256] See, for example, M. Foreman, M. Anthony Neal (eds.). 2004. *That's the Joint! The Hip-Hop Studies Reader.* New York: Routledge; or H. Osumare. 2007. *The Africanist Aesthetic in Global Hip-Hop: Power Moves.* New York: Palgrave Macmillan.

[257] R. Pawlak. 2004: *Polska kultura hip-hopowa.* Poznań: Wyd. Kagra; A. Buda. 2012. *Historia kultury hip-hop w Polsce 1977-2013.* Wyd. Niezależne.

fieldwork, the omnipresence of Polish hip-hop was a striking proof that it appeals directly to young peoples' lives and circumstances and forms a sort of background of their daily lives.

The combination of friendship and a cult of independence and individuality present in hip-hop connect perfectly with their emphasis on respect which they deserve as self-made people—individualistic, self-sufficient, and independent actors. This view has clear aspirational, almost victorious qualities and during the numerous hip-hop concerts I attended, the leading hip-hop artists indulged in almost militaristic morale boosting. For instance, during a performance by Kaliber 44 in 2007, one of the main Polish hip-hop groups, the leader stood up straight and screamed violently into the microphone: 'We're conquering London [*Zdobywamy Londyn*]!' The audience burst into wild applause and some screamed: 'Yes, We're at you. Yes, fucking London, we will get you! We're here!'

This reaction, especially the symbolic use of the 'we' in the context of a group engaged in a ritual party, probably tells us far more about the attitudes of Polish working-class migrants than dozens of formal interviews. It captures not only the collective hunger for self-respect, masculine challenge, and a competitive power of self-appropriation but also showed how vital success is to their individual sense of self. The forward-looking and aggressive notion of 'conquering' contrasts starkly with nationalist discourse, which emphasises the costs of leaving Poland behind rather than the benefits of living somewhere else. If we recapitulate the dominant nationalist discourse of emigration as a loss, threat, weakening of the national fabric, the 'body' of the nation—the meanings entailed in Polish hip-hop played during gigs in London forms a powerful counter-narrative a reaction, resistance, and the 'hidden transcript' of Polish migration.

Another interviewee's approach—Marek—illustrates this aspect from a slightly different point of view, with much more self-reflexive depth, drawing on the communist legacy of the *blokowiska*. Marek's story helps us to understand also why hip-hop is so important to Polish working-class migrants. He is a hip-hop artist himself and comes from a working-class family:

> My dad was a carpenter, then he had a heart disease and worked in a swimming pool ... and my mum is a nurse ... [She] worked all her life honestly, didn't do anything to anyone and now lives off a pension of 500 zlotys per month [£80] ... So it seems it didn't pay ... or maybe her clean conscience is the reward ... When my father died, my mum was working, my brother moved out and I was brought up on the streets in my bloki with mates ... I did many stupid things there, some for money ... In this environment no one finished any school, all of my mates from there ended up in jail ... I'm the only one who didn't ... Strange really.

In official communist propaganda, *bloki* or *blokowiska* was the symbol of equality and social mobility for rural society but then became synonymous with decay and disadvantage in the new Polish neo-liberal capitalist environment. Nevertheless, for people living there, it produced new, shared meanings that reformulated rural communities' intimacy in a new space. According to Marek, the intimate proximity between residents was not only a crucial source of support but also created dependency and sometimes stagnation. *Bloki* expresses the contradictions between the legacy of Communism and contemporary capitalism:

> Blokowiska ... I think they create a place where these [human] microcosmoses meet and clash ... People, who are closed and concentrated in a concrete block, meet every day and their problems meet every day and that environment creates additional power. For some this power pushes them to create something to run away from there, for others this is a power that impedes them and stops them from doing anything. As for music I think this bloki, it is a power ... the power of the environment of people, who meet regularly and the more they meet, the bigger the chances that someone will come up with something, make a music group or something ... People [in houses] ... meet only at school, work or restaurant – that's it.

The division between people living in *blokowiska* and houses is a new form of the rural/urban divide mentioned by members of rural class and also expresses the value attached to everyday relationships with relatives and neighbours, the sense of being together in a given space and sharing same social and ecological niche. It also highlights the dilemmas, which people face when manoeuvring between asserting individuality and being part of the group. Hip-hop and the environment producing it helped poor urban working-class Poles to assert their own value. At the same time, Marek reminds us that this may have some drawbacks, since people become entrenched in their class positions and see everything coming from the state as hostile and alien.

Integral to anti-stateism is its implicit egalitarianism. *Blokowiska* share an intriguing atmosphere of equality—one that resonates deeply in Polish minds, reinforced by the communist period, nationalist ideals, and a rural culture of common fate in face of nature.[258] So, it is no coincidence that Marek refers to the ways in which both Polish hip-hop artists and black American musicians fight oppression—'*Yes, yes ... the bloki have leveled* [the class system] ... *It's like in America, where ghettos were made for blacks—they had it also*'. And asked whether, he see himself as middle or working class, he simply answers: '*No, my name is Marek*'. For him, Poles are 'naturally' against the state and class divisions are invented to suppress people and create dominant hierarchies through the creation of titles, economic status, and family connections. 'Real' knowledge and experience is based on working-class life on the streets of the *blokowiska*:

> People look at hip-hop with disdain ... and coming from below ... And they all say that these [people] are smart because they go to the universities and these hip-hop people are bad because they sing HWDP [a Polish hip-hop hit, HWDP is an acronym from chuj w dupe policji which means 'fuck the police'] ... So this is, of course, bullshit ... I don't think that intelligence goes always with knowledge and down there [in the lower social classes] there are a lot people, who are very intelligent, and also I know a lot of professors, who had a huge knowledge, had books in their heads but didn't have any intelligence, didn't know how to use that knowledge ... no life skills.

---

[258] This theme has been extensively looked at in Polish sociology, mainly in relation to youth culture, see: B. Fotyga. 1999. *Dzicy z naszej ulicy: antropologia kultury młodzieżowej*. Warszawa: Ośrodek Badań Młodzieży; I. Borowik. 2003. *Blokowiska. Miejski habitat w oglądzie socjologicznym*. Wrocław: Oficyna Wydawnicza Arboretum.

The claim that working-class people possess 'true' knowledge and an 'authentic' understanding of how the world works is, of course, not new. In Polish culture, it has a strong political flavour. For instance, Polish romantic poets saw the rural culture of peasants as one, which managed to sustain real cultural values and authentic meanings against the corrupt behaviour of the elites and ruling classes, contaminated by the modernistic, often Western ideals. With the introduction of socialist ideas during the communist regime, the proletariat became the repository of true knowledge and robust morality in contrast to the weak-willed intellectuals and stubborn, backward rural society. This is not to say that Marek regards education with contempt. On the contrary, as he admits that he was the only one from his circle of friends who went to university, and he recognises that, in his own words, *'one must leave the past, to have a future'*.

Once again, people's individualistic attitudes and aims conflict with their class backgrounds. They seek to resolve this conflict by arguing that the past need not be discarded but, rather, reformulated and incorporated into a new system of meanings and norms. Just as young migrants from the countryside continue to keep an eye on their family farms, even though they have no immediate intention to live there, so Marek incorporates the cultural values of living in *blokowiska* into his own life and aspirations, as a hip-hop artist living in London. Through his implicit assertion of egalitarianism and anti-institutionalism, he is able to reach out quite successfully across cultural and ethnic boundaries, by making himself known among black hip-hop scene in London, for example.

Freedom and work

Since migrants decided to leave their home environment, moving from what they often call the group of 'passive, rural, backward' Poles to 'active, dynamic' Poles, it is no surprise then that they see Britain as a place where merit and hard work determine opportunities rather than connections. However, this attitude is expressed in very different ways. It can keep migrants in a state of denial, as well as have a real meaning for advancement.

Two cases illustrate this process. Bronek is a van driver from a middle-class background. He came in 2004 and initially was quite excited about his prospects. In Poland, he had tried to study medicine but got frustrated by local nepotism, which helped the offspring of doctors to study medicine, and left for London. During several conversations, he stressed the fact how corrupt things were in Poland and his intention to become a paramedic. However, he continually failed to sit the examinations in London and seemed unwilling to move forward. He was happy to continue moaning about his British employer and his lack of spare time. His criticisms of Poland justify his unwillingness to return, while his plans help him believe that his courier job is only temporary, even though he has been in that position for the last five years. Bronek seemed to be trapped between his negative attitude towards nepotistic Poland and a fear of failure in London.

There may be, however, a different way of understanding this contrast between Poland and Britain. As we have already seen, the references in Polish migration narratives to individualism, freedom, and a sense of independence is a constant feature, whether we talk about a city banker or hip-hop artist, a homeless person or an unemployed carpenter. A good example is the case of Joanna, who comes from a small town in southern Poland where her family was quite 'well off'. She was able to get an office job in a local employment office—a job regarded by her family and friends as a strong status symbol and sign of success. She worked there for a while but got frustrated and decided to go to London. Here she works as a cleaner but insists that she has advanced socially. Her case is a good example of the somewhat casual, accidental way in which migration decisions are made:

> Well, I'm a highly indecisive person really; it takes a long time for me to take up my mind … But in this case it was that in my job it began to be a bit … like boring … and this friend of mine who lives in London came for holiday and she said: 'Look, Wiola, if you want you can come to London, we will find

something … If you want to see how it looks come along.' So, actually, at that time I had small problems at work, had a bad mood and I thought: 'Why not?' … I asked for unpaid leave. My boss also thought for some time and gave me the leave. So as I got it I thought: 'Well, as I have an unpaid leave I will come and see.'

It is her attitude to her current work that speaks volumes about social class in Poland and the ways in which it is contested by individual migrants:

Q. And where would you see yourself?

In Poland here [indicates middle of the graph] *and here… on the very bottom* [laughs].

Q. Why?

Well, maybe not that bad …

Q. Because of the job or the pay? Something wrong with cleaning?

Well I think it's the money … not the job … I mean to the middle class I have a long way [to go] *… 'żadna praca nie hańbi'* [no job is shameful] *really. If I had something against cleaning I would have stayed in the office in Poland. But here it is better appreciated – the job here … Here people are nice and recognise your effort, even if you are a simple sprzątaczka* [a derogatory term for a cleaner] *and doesn't do anything special … So here this job is appreciated … For me it's a big difference.*

Q. Because in Poland sitting in the office is perceived as something more prestigious than cleaning?

Yes, exactly … I heard it from my boss [in Poland] *… That was when I had to decide that I leave … and I haven't heard a single thank you for all this time I worked for him. He just said that: 'I thought that you are changing a job with bigger aspirations' and that I degrade myself to the level of a cleaner …*

Q. And what do you think about it?

For me it's ridiculous … I mean in Poland I worked in office, I had my computer picking up phones … and for me it wasn't at all satisfactory … And what's more important is that there was no possibility there to advance or develop further … It was like I have hit one level and there was no chance of moving forward. And, of course, no thank you, not a nice word. Just these remarks …

Q. And over here?

> *I mean here I think that it depends on your will, on your ability to look for things ... on your stubbornness ... If you want to change a job and look for a new one you will find it. I'm the good example ... because at the beginning I worked for an agency. There are many of them. You work and give a share to them, they give you contacts ... But then I began to find my own contacts and to get my own clients, so I don't have to pay them anything ... So, you see, I can say that from my perspective this is a development; I did something ... In these few months I could do it ... and I think it concerns all jobs.*

Joanna's story is in many ways typical, since she associates freedom from social constraints with individualism, as well as physical mobility with improvement in her social status. Social class is thus associated with rigid, enclosing and limiting ones' own development, it is an obstacle — despite that, in many ways, it secures her position in local setting. As a young woman in rural Poland, her employment opportunities were very limited — 'signing envelopes for the rest of my life wasn't very appealing'. In other words, Joanna's rejects the suggestion that her job as a cleaner in London was retrograde step, since it freed her from Polish restrictions and gave her a base, from which to take several steps forward. She feels free to dismiss her relatives' superficial criticism of physical labour, such as cleaning. Jobs should be assessed in terms of how people perform them regardless of what the job entails. Individualism, then, becomes not a value *per se*, but a self-defence mechanism against the culture of ascribed gendered and economic roles in her village.

School of life and egalitarian Poles

The individualism I refer to is revealed in another interpretation of London that migrants share — the belief that the city and England, generally, is a 'school of life' open to all. Skilled craftsmen and builders often make this claim:

> *Rafal: Well, here I had to make my own decisions. In Warsaw we had a manager who said: 'Do this, do that' ... Here I have the responsibility; it is me who makes decisions ... So it was a school of life ... When I came here first time, I was green. I have learned a lot here ... I had to.*

Kuba: For me it was the first time that I needed to take care of myself ... For the first time in my life I had to think all about myself ... a school of life.

Jan: England? England, it's a school of life ... teaches you everything ... When I didn't have money I needed to survive, how to get tickets [for transport] everything ... slowly but England teaches you.

Marek: As I said there are more possibilities here ... What I said about traveling, schools, so here I am more self-dependent. In Poland I was living with parents, so parents helped there and here ... but here I have to do things on my own ... go to a bank, get an account ... My friends helped me a lot also but I had to mature.

It was not just a matter of learning new things and becoming familiar with a new place. People also learned how to cope with freedom and individual responsibility as they moved away from a familiar, but sometimes socially constrained environment. It is the ultimate freedom associated with growing up, since migration of these young people is coupled with moving of their family homes. Migrants frequently spoke of their need to get away from parents and how hard it was for couples to be still dependent on in-laws and/or parents. Moving out of their parents' home and going to London is intimately bound up, therefore, with self-testing, individual fulfilment, and freedom from social and cultural constraints.

So migration is something that any man or woman can do to prove their abilities regardless of class or connections. Migration thus becomes a way to 'break away' from restrictions of social class in Poland; it is evenly shared by migrants, whether they are builder, a cleaner, or banker — it is an activity with explicit egalitarian and communitarian features. Yet, this egalitarian understanding of migration is not just a contemporary phenomenon. We can see it throughout Polish history, even if it has been overshadowed by the collectivism of the dominant nationalist discourse. What was being challenged by this migrant egalitarianism was the Polish social class system rather than what nationalists focused on — a political system imposed by foreign invaders. In other words, the emphasis on individual achievement was a direct response to the dominant nationalist discourse, which treated migration as a suspicious, selfish act likely to undermine the national community.

What do people mean when they refer to a school of life? School is the new, communitarian and potentially egalitarian context of physical and everyday interaction between people from different social backgrounds. Hence, London is seen as a place where individuals can prepare to return to Poland, stay, or migrate further. It provides a breathing space where people can experience new things, even if they have insecure jobs on building sites, cleaning hotels, or serving beer in pubs, for example. The popular saying mentioned by Joanna '*żadna praca nie hańbi'* [no job brings shame] is very revealing in this context.[259] When asked what people think about the fact that they have studied and now do low-skilled work, people usually draw on the message embodied in this saying. It is an interesting combination of socialist, egalitarian discourse, an emphasis on the value of physical work, and a post-industrial, late-capitalist belief in the meritocratic paradise of a deregulated and flexible transnational labour market.

Some Polish scholars note that this saying has become even more popular after the collapse of Communism, reflecting the individuals' need to be more flexible in their employment choices.[260] Skilled graduates accept work in low-skilled industries because they are based in a city, which provides the opportunity to learn English, social connections, and the thrill of living in one of the biggest and busiest cities of the world. As one of my respondent at some point mentioned, he was not sure how long he was going to live in London but was definitely going to put the fact

---

[259] This is a common feature in other research on Polish migrations, for example, see: I. Grabowska. 2016. *Movers and Stayers: Sociaal Mobility, Migration and Skills*. Frankfurt Am Main: Peter Lang.P. Trevena. 2011. Divided by class, connected by work. Class divisions among the new wave of Polish migrants in the UK. *Przegląd Polonijny* Rok XXXVII z. 1/2011.

[260] W. Kozek. 1995. Tradycje i wartości związane z pracą a przemiany rynkowe w ostatnich latach. [in]: A. Sułek, J. Styk (eds.) *Ludzie i instytucje. Stawanie się ładu społecznego*. Lublin: Wyd. UMCS, pp. 187–200.

that he lived here in his CV. When asked: *'Doing what?'* he replied: *'What? That's irrelevant. The fact that I worked in London is enough'*.

Work, which was traditionally highly valued in rural Polish communities,[261] is thus reinforced and becomes a culturally significant feature in people's perceptions of class. In many migrants' eyes, their class position rests on the pride they take in physical labour. Many — most notably people with university degrees — accept that, at some stage, they may have to do some physical work and that this is nothing to be ashamed about. The British work culture fares much better in comparison to Poland, especially when it comes to everyday, mundane employer–employee relationships. They appreciate British employers, who use phrases like 'thank you' and 'could you?' rather than the authoritarian: 'do it'. Although migrants often recognise that all this politeness may, in fact, be veiled hypocrisy and power-play, the inherent value of physical work and employer appreciation of their effort means a lot, since it resonates with the traditional association of work with self-worth.

For others, especially for those, who come from urban middle class or intelligentsia backgrounds, physical work is approached differently from those who have come from the countryside or the urban working class. The latter are much keener to emphasise how migration was a move upwards, while the intelligentsia wanted to point out the temporary nature of their current jobs and their ability to access other resources. As Maria says:

> People stop because they are happy with what they have, they stopped looking for things ... I just could not live like that ... I had these jobs ... I was cleaning, worked in the shops, and I did it. I was putting my hat, head down and let's get on with it ... but I knew this is just for short period, that this is temporary.

It could be argued that people's widespread respect for physical work was an attempt to justify their position in the labour market. However, the evidence from my interviews point rather to the legacy of the socialist system and its egalitarian discourse which

---

[261]   M. Buchowski. 2001. *Rethinking transformation...*, p. 190.

despite malfunctioning on a macro-level, have appealed, never-theless, to some sense of social justice for the working class. This legacy has been challenged, of course, but survives amid strong class animosities and tensions. Whatever the explanation, the Polish migrants' approach to physical work and their willingness to accept low wages while they save to return to Poland has made them very popular among British employers. Yet, the reasons why they accept it is not that Poles are 'essentially' hard working, it rests on perceptions of their own migration trajectory and also the ways in which people communicate class within their social fields, including to the British audience.

Transnational social mobility

What constitutes social advancement for these migrants is another complex issue. For most of the circular, transient migrants from rural areas, the answer was fairly simple—the dignity of being able to sustain their families, the ability to earn enough to live, buy a plot of land, house or car, or organise a wedding. The free-dom from local constraints on business-making and Polish local nepotism or cronyism was most often equated with notions of self-esteem, individual risk-taking, and seeking opportunities beyond the confines of their locality. At the same time, migrants need to communicate this new-found freedom continually to their peers, family, and friends back home.

Returning to Poland can be one opportunity to improve a person's class position 'back home'. Since people can do this sev-eral times a year to attend family events, for example, where they can bring presents including the almost mandatory British alcohol, transnational movement is intimately bound up with social class. In this way, in a world where social networks are vital to survive in local conditions, migrants are eager to show what connections they have built up while abroad. Migrants from Sokółka, for in-stance, continually remind their peers that they are well estab-lished in London and can arrange work straight away—this is part of the success of the transnational social networks they have built. They show off their enhanced status by giving generous tips to bartenders and putting a lot of money on the collection plate during mass (often in British currency). They also share their migratory social capital by providing addresses and useful information about London to their friends and family. In other words, the shame about not bringing riches back home, which commentators have frequently noted, does not just refer to material goods; migratory social capital has also to be accumulated by developing vital connections and networks abroad.

Migrants are expected not only to send remittances but also to help others to fulfil their migration project. Conversations with families and friends of migrants in Poland reveal that having someone in London is very important when times are hard — a feature of Polish migration for many generations and all classes. What links migrants going to USA at the turn of the century and today's migrants is the transnational social class mobility — the dynamic relation between those who go and those who stay where moving out is associated with moving up 'back home'.

One of the migrants interviewed in London, Wojtek, the builder from Jasło (south-east Poland), was also followed to his home town in 2007 and 2008 and he was eager to show that what he brings back are not only remittances. During meetings, bar-chat, and casual conversations with neighbours, with me present, he was clearly enjoying the status of someone in the know. Over several days of hanging out with him in Jasło, I witnessed lengthy conversations with his friends and family members, which showed how important his position as 'someone from London' was. For instance, at a bar, he was approached by a group of young men, who asked whether he knew of any job offers in London. On another occasion, he told a friend that the person he was going to employ in London was unreliable, while his previous employer asked him whether he had any contacts for building projects in Jasło. With his friend, he came up with the idea of establishing a health-tourism business for wealthy British people in

Jaslo. The idea attracted interest from local power brokers—
people, who would pay little attention to Wojtek if he was just a
local sedentary working-class resident. There is no way of telling
to what extent Wojtek simply took advantage of his status of an
emigrant to make empty promises—last time I talked to him in
2010—he was basically still in the same place—but in a way this is
not that relevant. What is crucial is the potential status-enhancing
features of transnational mobility.

Class can also be manifested within the family, and
Wojtek's status had improved enormously among his relatives. As
during my visit at their home, his sister admitted euphemistically,
Wojtek was not previously known for his entrepreneurial spirit
and work ethic—he was fond of a drink and the companionship of
his friends. Since he began to build a house and decided to look
for work abroad, he had *changed for the better*. Moreover, he had
begun to pay more attention to his own family. He had found
work in London for his brother-in-law and sister-in law and during my stay at his home, he was constantly asked for tips and information by his other sister, who planned to study in London.
Even his teenage nieces were telling him that they also would like
to go to London one day. Clearly, this added to his sense of social
mobility, since he had moved from being an unemployed builder
in Jasło to the facilitator of other people's successful migration,
aspirations, and dreams. Even if his claim to 'have brought over
around 50 guys from the area to London' was exaggerated, it illustrated how being at the controlling end of social networks was the
key to personal gain and social status.

Transnational social mobility, then, does not refer only to
continual comparison between London and Poland but to very
concrete social exchanges, which keep the migration chain moving
and offer certain individuals power and control over who comes
and why, offer them an ability to position themselves in local,
even family power relations. This transnational capital becomes
even more important if a migrant has experienced de-skilling and
a subsequent decline in social status. Paulina, a woman in her late

40s from a family with strong intelligentsia traditions from Kraków, had gone to university and became an urban middle-class
housewife, but now works in London as a cleaner. She sends
money back to her husband and daughter, who have a flat in the
old town—quite a status symbol since property prices have rock-
eted during the last few years. So, in order to maintain certain
status symbols (a flat, car, and holidays), Paulina accepts work
which her family regard as shameful and degrading.

There were also personal reasons for Paulina accepting a
low-status job in London. She had been unhappy about her mar-
riage, hostile to her family's petty bourgeois attitudes, and very
pleased with the freedom she now enjoyed in London. Back in
Kraków, her family and friends would have interfered with her
personal decisions, and she would have been ostracised for taking
a lover—even though her husband was also unfaithful. She had
paid a price though since cleaning flats in London was clearly not
what she wanted to do. She may be bitter sometimes, regretting
that she may have tried to work in other areas, but did not con-
template returning to Kraków. At some point during my fieldwork, she divorced her husband and moved in with a new partner
in North London. In terms of personal trajectory for Paulina, this
was certainly an empowering progress in her opinion, despite still
in 2012 doing the same thing for a living she did when she came
for the first time to London a decade ago.

Urban middle class in the making

The remaking of the middle class in post-Communist Poland
through an endorsement of the capitalist and free-market ideological framework means that individuals who cannot fulfil their
aspirations in Poland often seek them abroad. Yet, it would be
wrong to emphasise the 'push' factor, because many migrants,
especially urban individuals who regard themselves as members
of the middle class, emphasise the 'pull' factor—the very fact that
freedom of movement means freedom to choose how and where

one wants to live. For these people, even the conditions in Poland are not depicted as a black and white affair, and they often admit that Poland is also a place where education and self-determination are becoming increasingly important.

Jola, who moved with her husband and daughter to London in 2002, sees social structure in Poland mainly in terms of the middle class's inability to secure dignified economic standing—a legacy of the communist period where status of certain professions did not carry according to economic profits, but nevertheless was high. She worked in the Polish media, for an estate agent, as a marketing person. Her husband runs a small but successful accountancy and advice firm, catering mostly to Polish migrants. They maintain strong transnational connections—they invest in property in Poland and her husband studies for a PhD in economics in Warsaw—and regard Britain as a meritocracy where hard work and aspirations are rewarded. They see unpredictability and amount of potential opportunities as the main asset in London:

> First of all, everything here is very dynamic. You can change everything in a matter of short time. Within weeks you can change your life totally, in a positive and negative way, of course.

Being middle class, however, mainly means lifestyle for them and is not connected to economic standing. In similar vein, Alek, a young businessman from Warsaw who runs a successful marketing company, decided to come and 'have a go' and almost by accident bought a ticket to London. Despite working in a food factory and disliking the work, he simply regards being in London as a nice experience that expands his horizons. Again, it is individual self-esteem that counts in his perception, and he rejects what others might see as a loss of social status:

> No, I know that I begin from the start, but I don't see it this way – that I've fallen from social ladder... No, it does matter what I think about myself, not what others think about me. So I think that I keep my level really ... Here I think I can say that I'm in the middle, even though I just came here ... Many things adds up to this ... I mean I'm not on the top since I don't work in a bank in the City, but I'm not on the bottom either because, ok, I work in a factory but at the same time I do something else, something mine and I develop

... So I can find myself here because there is that middle class here, unlike in Poland.

For those who were employed in London's financial sector, migration does not depend on the personal networks and connections, which were vital for working class or rural migrants. Almost all those encountered during two focus groups among financial sector employees came to London through more formal avenues; they were recruited through agencies, headhunters, came through internships or their employers in Poland had paved their way into new position. While they often admitted that connections were important in Poland, they believed that they had escaped this system and were totally self-reliant. They believed that other migrants had to use connections, to come over here, because they lacked what they had — high skills. This difference here is vital, and we will encounter it at length in the next chapter; but this difference is not expressed in the language of class — it is through talking about ethnicity and culture that people evoke class.

So, what *is* class in transnational social field? This strong individualistic, almost neo-liberal, appreciation of social mobility and social class, the myth of meritocracy, the ideal of Britain versus the evil of social relations in Poland does look shaky when we look at various data on earnings,[262] exploitation,[263] hours people work, and the general conditions of majority of Polish migrants work in. Overall, we should recognise the cultural value of work for individuals, their constant transnational reflexivity strategy, and notions of 'normality',[264] which render the harsh conditions of British labour market acceptable or the precarious situation of the economy in the times of the downturn bearable.

---

[262] J. Rutter. 2007. *Britain's Immigrants: An Economic Profile.* IPPR. http://www.ippr.org.uk/research/teams/?id=3571&tID=3571

[263] See, for instance, the actions of TUC: http://www.eurofound.europa.eu/eiro/2005/12/inbrief/uk0512103n.htm or http://www.socialistworker.co.uk/art.php?id=9284

[264] A. Galasińska, O. Kozłowska. 2009. Discourses of a 'normal life' among postaccession migrants from Poland to Britain. [in]: K. Burrell (ed.) *Polish Migration in the UK in the 'New' European Union.* Farnham: Ashgate.

Migrants often realise that they form a distinct category on the labour market and they do sometimes refer to themselves as 'cheap labour' but without its negative overtones. They also frequently seem to accept that this is how things are—this is the 'normal' state of affairs. An explanation could be found in terms of resignation, fatalism, a temporary trade-off as in the case of highly skilled working in manual jobs.[265] People may also view it through the prism of 'normality' and the work ethic and believe that future rewards depend on the numerous above-described circumstances. What is crucial, however, is that these views are always constructed transnationally, because social class always *happens* in a transnational social field.

Class, culture, and history

What this chapter shows is, first, that people's perceptions are always embedded in cultural frameworks, which have to be understood in relation to Poland's history and social legacy of last half of century. Classifications and meaning-making stretches back several generations. Furthermore, these perceptions should be viewed not just as symptoms and strategies for dealing with social and cultural change but as known and tested strategies of survival. As Buchowski states in the case of the Polish rural class, *'What appears to scholars as systemic transformation, for rural people it is just a link in the chain of history'*.[266] This means that the practices of anti-institutionalism, anti-stateism, moaning, the division between 'us masses', and 'those elites', individualism, the value of physical work, status as independent from financial gains, perception of London as 'school of life', and transnationally constructed

---

[265] How they cope with that loss, see: P. Trevena. 2011. Divided by class, connected by work. Class divisions among the new wave of Polish migrants in the UK. *Przegląd Polonijny* Rok XXXVII z. 1/2011.

[266] M. Buchowski. 2004. Redefining work in a local community in Poland. Transformation and class, culture and work. [in]: A. Procoli (ed.) *Workers and Narratives of Survival in Europe. The Management of Precariousness at the End of the Twentieth Century*. New York: State University of New York Press, p. 174.

migratory capital have long been familiar to large sections of Polish society. It was not the formal aspect of state formation and its institutions that bound them. Here nationalism clashed with state formation, as the imagined community, not the administration was the aspect unifying Poles. As Chris Hann notes: … *the vast majority of Polish citizens considered their 'pays reel', the source of their most powerful sources of identity, to be not the People's Republic but the Polish nation.*[267]

Secondly, the perception of migration as social mobility needs to be seen as a counter-narrative to the nationalistic dominant discourse of the nation and the state as the 'container' for Polish people and as emigration as a 'moral' issue, which migration is interpreted in terms of individual gain versus collective loss — as depicted in Chapter 2. The ethos of an emigrant as a self-sufficient actor who, in an anti-institutional act, 'tears away' and is independent from state and collective control merges with several other powerful myths that Polish culture has created around migration. One of the most important myth involves the West as the symbol of prosperity, wealth, and a comfortable 'normal' life.[268] Paradoxically, however, this myth carries with itself some peculiar egalitarian undertones where people are viewed as having equal opportunities and it is their individual skills that matter and — in an idealised world of neo-liberal philosophy — will be rewarded.

This myth serves a particular purpose — it seeks to weaken distinctions, barriers, and obstacles that people may experience in Britain. It also serves as a powerful, bottom-up social critique of social relations in Poland. At a deeper level, it also serves to explain contradictions and tensions evident in the Polish road to market economy — the fact that the Solidarność freedom movement brought massive unemployment and misery for many at the heart of that movement, and the fact that the ideology of neo-

---

[267] Ch. Hann. 1998. Postsocialist nationalism: rediscovering the past in southeast Poland. *Slavic Review* 57(4):850.

[268] A. Galasińska, O. Kozłowska. 2009. Discourses of a 'normal life' among postaccession migrants from Poland to Britain. [in]: K. Burrell (ed.) *Polish Migration in the UK in the 'New' European Union*. Farnham: Ashgate. 91.

liberal capitalist transformation have benefited most those who were already holding power during communist times.

The myth of the West is thus the myth of the weak — their 'hidden transcript' of Polish transformation. This hidden transcript has some interesting contradictions — it is egalitarian, but it is also very capitalist-oriented where the ethos of self-sufficiency, social mobility, education, and individualism is very significant. It craves for social justice, but it also has features of unrestricted competition and ruthlessness. It condemns elites but also aspires to become middle class. It condemns the disparity between the ideal and the real, but it allows people to postpone their aspirations and plans for ever or for long period of time, trapping them in the lower levels of the labour market. This hidden transcript offers a justification and framework for peoples' actions but it may also impede their footing in one specific place.

The answer to the question in this subchapter would have to be a nuanced one — class is *made* and *remade* in a transnational social field, since through navigating in two different settings, people try to construct themselves as independent actors, as people who manage to make the best of both worlds. This sometimes ends in failure, delusion, or self-denial; but it may also end in inventing new forms of social class dimensions and status acquisition.

This is where I need to move on to an aspect of class that actually renders class relations in Poland and London much more explicit, potent, and most importantly, meaningful for the everyday use by social actors. Because, new forms of social class articulations in a transnational social field draw heavily on another aspect of social identity — ethnicity.

Chapter 6

Class, ethnicity, and the making of white Poles

As shown in previous chapters, the group we call 'Polish migrants' are a highly diverse and heterogeneous category with differences in education, region, social class background, migration strategies, and time of arrival influencing their ways of meaning-making in the new context they found themselves in. Social settings — a generalised Poland, the 'Polish' state and a mythologised London — act as reference points but for different reasons and for different purposes. Manoeuvring transnationally, both physical and psychologically, between two social stratification systems, Polish migrants are trying to make the best of both worlds by gaining status and prestige in one place and economic resources in another.

It is striking that the majority of Polish migrants I spoke to are keen to emphasise the adequacy and moral superiority of a market economy which places the individual and its capabilities at the centre. They welcome a capitalist culture of individualistic, profit-driven self-development, coupled with a strong belief in an ideal meritocratic system where connections between individuals are sustained through cultural significance of physical labour and deeply ingrained anti-state and anti-institutional attitudes. This is a potent mix, where individualism and anti-stateism both reinforce each other. But these cultural meanings are not borne out of a social void — Polish migrants relate, react, contest, and negotiate hegemonic discourses and narratives constructed within a Polish culture that tried to contain and make sense of constant — 200 years old — outflows of Poles.

These hegemonic discourses frame and sustain individual responses and meaning-making practices. Individual assertiveness, capability, and work ethos, so keenly emphasised by people

215

I interviewed, talked to, and with whom I spent plenty of time discussing various things, is both a reaction to and a consequence of various forms of symbolic dominance—the omnipresent state interventions during communist times, the legacy of rural communities, resistance to the feudal system, *intelligentsia* resistance to political domination, working-class struggle for better conditions during the late 19th century and the first half of the 20th century and, last but not least, as demonstrated in Chapter 2, the powerful nationalist discourse of the Polish nation, whose 'body' is being weakened by constant outflow of its members horizontally connected by metaphoric kinship, hence bound by a specific ethical obligations.

Yet, being individualistic does not mean being anti-social. On the contrary, as we have seen in previous chapters, Polish migration is a deeply social, collective, network-based phenomenon. Polish migrants, reacting to the strong neo-liberal and modernistic discourse of post-Communist Poland, recognise the short comings of that ideal in Poland but seek to fulfil its goals at an individual and family level through their use of personal networks, migratory social capital, value of their labour, and an ethos of hard work. Their individualistic attitudes and strong ethos of self-reliance is not a value *per se* but is constructed relationally in the context of a heavy reliance on social networks, families, and the connections that they so despise but at the same time are so good at exploiting. Nevertheless, the sense of pride of achievement and an attitude that 'I don't need Poland to better myself' must be recognised as one which dominates and has a powerful meanings for migrants' perceptions of social mobility and their understanding and performance of ethnicity.

It is here where class and ethnicity become mutually entangled and interconnected and shapes the way people are able to construct specific classifications and representations and own commentaries on social class and working of society in general. These constructions are borne out of contradictions between two powerful discourses about the self and nation. Bearing in mind the strong, individualistic, aspirational ethos of Polish migrants, whether they are rural, working class, or city workers and trans-nationally or locally oriented, we could expect a strong clash, discontinuity, and dissonance between what the dominant Polish discourse on migration, the nation, the community says and what is being done, told and felt by migrants themselves.

At an ontological level, there is a powerful conflict between the implicit egalitarianism of nationalistic discourse and the particular goals of individuals. Nationalism symbolically constructs a permanent state of *communitas* — a deep horizontal comradeship, a brotherhood of individuals whose backgrounds, differences, and individual characteristics are erased at the expense of communal, collective, and unifying entity[269] — the nation. As the father of Polish nationalism, Roman Dmowski says in a previously mentioned assertion: '*Men are first and foremost members of a nation; only secondly are they divided into social classes within the nation*'.[270] Nina Glick Schiller, Linda Basch, and Cristina Szanton Blanc refer to these modes of perception as hegemonic discourses of ethnicity and nationalism[271] and they show how, due to its dominance in the 20th century, we take for granted a multicultural corporatist model, the dominant tendency which sees ethnic groups as bounded and homogeneous entities where ethnic solidarity and cultural inner cohesiveness is the desirable norm. In a communitarian tradition, ideologies of nationalism[272] link ethnicity and morality, emphasising the normative necessity of communal obligation towards others who are assumed to share the same essential traits, cultural meanings, and symbols. This essentialistic tendency has the effect of overlooking social class and inequality,

---

[269] See, for instance, B. Anderson. 1991. *Imagined Communities: Reflections on the Origin and Spread of Nationalism*. London: Verso, p. 7.

[270] Quoted in F. Millard. 1994. Nationalism in Poland. [in]: P Latawski (ed.) *Contemporary Nationalism in East Central Europe*. London: Palgrave Macmillan, p. 111.

[271] Glick Schiller, et al. (1991).

[272] E. Gellner. 1983. *Nations and Nationalism*. Ithaca: Cornell University Press; B. Anderson. 1991. *Imagined Communities: Reflections on the Origin and Spread of Nationalism*. London: Verso.

especially the role of power relations that influence individuals, groups, and families in their daily lives.

The equation between moral and ethnic community has been singled out as one of most important aspects of Polish national identity,[273] and as I highlighted in Chapter 2, the omnipresent migration experience throughout Polish history has emphasised the moral obligations of those abroad. These moral obligations had strong militaristic meanings and led the 'nationally aware' gentry to see its role as educating the masses in order to rise against foreign oppressors. In reality, this was not always the case, and the subordinate classes remained often indifferent to the elite's fights for political independence. Hence, the question the dominant classes often asked: *'why don't the masses rise up against the occupiers?'* — a question, according to Polish sociologist Jerzy Szacki, which defined the central problem of Polish nationalism torn between elitism and egalitarian consequences.[274] In fact, this question highlights the uneasy relationship between social classes in Poland and shows how the horizontal language of ethnicity and nationalism ('we are all Poles') obscures vertical power struggles between different groups. Freedom in dominant Polish national discourse is constructed as freedom of the whole — the nation — from foreign powers, not the individual from social and economic inequalities. Thus, in many ways, Polish nationalism, by symbolically levelling class distinctions, was actually reproducing existing power relations within Polish society.

Two conflicting discourses — the one emphasising the essential sameness of Poles and the other referring to the individual capabilities that are crucial to a person's life — are the subject of this chapter. However, we need also to recognise that the hegemonic ethnicising discourse, which encourages us to assume that all Poles share similar traits and should engage in collective activities, is reinforced by the practices of modern British multicultural-

---

[273] J. Chałasiński. 1968. *Kultura i naród*. Warszawa: Książka i Wiedza.
[274] J. Szacki. 1987. Naród w socjologii Floriana Znanieckiego. *Przegląd Polonijny* 3:7–28.

ism, too, especially in its corporatist form which sees ethnic groups as bounded entities and political actors. As Gerd Baumann demonstrated, this discourse equates culture, community, and ethnicity and implies that people are passive bearers of their culture and 'have' ethnicity, which is often biologised and naturalised through racial discourse.[275] I will take a closer look at what are the consequences of that combination at the end of this chapter.

Connections in a new setting

Most migrants interviewed in London treat their position on the Polish labour market as determined by negative outcomes of postcommunist transformation where non-transparent rules of promotion and social connections override merit and skills. This is why they are keen to emphasise that migration has been driven by resistance to conditions in Poland and that their migration decisions and life in London were a fulfilment of their individuality and agency, a self-development step where freedom to pursue dreams and aspirations may be accomplished. They attributed their agency to their own capabilities, their own independent choice to be the masters of their life. However, Chapters 3 and 4 have shown us that this overt individualism does not prevent their migration being hugely dependent on social networks and connections. Individual merit aside, Polish migration system is also a quite social and collective endeavour.

Various research conducted by myself and other scholars in the last decade confirm this is the norm. Most of the surveys I carried out and in-depth interviews demonstrate that respondents' migration has been facilitated by pre-existing social connections and through chain migration operating between various

---

[275] Z. Baumann. 1994. After the patronage state: a model in search of class interests. [in]: Christopher G.A. Bryan, Edmund Mokrzycki (eds.) *The New Great Transformation? Change and Continuity in East-Central Europe.* London/New York: Routledge, p. 33.

locations in Poland and London.[276] As an individual act of decision-making and a test of the self and individual skills, migration to London clearly depended on whom someone knew, the amount of migratory social capital one could mobilise, and what social networks in London one could tap into. The role of connections and migratory social capital is not limited to the migration decision-making process. Getting a job, house, or advice from informal sources seems to be the preferred method for Polish migrants who were staying for a long time.[277] In surveys that I conducted in Hammersmith and Fulham, Redbridge, and Lewisham, for example, it was striking that the vast majority of respondents, when asked about how they find employment, stressed the role of friends, family, and informal referrals—around 60% on average. Links with other Poles are crucial, therefore, not only when travelling but also in finding your way round after arrival. Connections with family, friends, friends of friends, and the importance of someone, who could offer support, have been as important as it was in the Polish labour market.

Ethnic ties are not always crucial when migrating. Anna, for example, came after being invited by her English friends whom she met in Wrocław when she worked on a medical journal. Yet, eventually, her social network expanded in London both ways— she began to make friends with other British colleagues when she worked as secretary in the city and, at the same time, began to cooperate with a Polish language website and then moved to journalism working for the media catering to Polish migrants. Some also had jobs arranged through recruitment companies, which operated extensively across Poland. These, however, tend

---

[276] L. Ryan, R. Sales, M. Tilki, B. Siara. 2008. Social networks, social support and social capital: the experiences of recent Polish migrants in London, *Sociology* 42(4):672–690; or M. Garapich's study on A8 migrants in Hammersmith and Fulham Borough. http://www.surrey.ac.uk/Arts/CRONEM/documents/Report_HF_CRONEM.pdf.

[277] See: M. Sumption. 2009. *Social Networks and Polish Immigration to the UK,* Economics of Migration Working Paper 5 Institute_for_Public_Policy_Research. http://www.ippr.org/files/images/media/files/publication/2011/05/social_networks_polish_immigration_1690.pdf?noredirect=1

to concentrate on industries outside London so, generally, having access to someone in the capital was invaluable. After few years, by 2012, she still works in the 'migration industry', this time in promotion of one of the money transfers companies.

The importance of being able to tap into sources of migratory social capital is clear when one visits many 'migratory hubs' of Poland—towns and villages, which specialise in sending their men and women to specific locations in Europe. For decades, this was the case of places like Mońki[278] in north-eastern Poland or Podhale[279] in the south, where links with the USA were forged well before the Second World War. Siemiatycze,[280] with its population shuttling back and forth between Belgium and Poland, is another famous example. In Sokółka, it was clear that migration penetrates all aspects of social and personal life. In these places, migrant visitors enjoyed additional status as those who could provide information, help, or access to jobs in the countries where they currently lived. So, the social and collective dimensions of migration contrast with the individuality of migration experience. This individualistic approach is not only the response to collectivistic and dominant discourses of the nation and obligations towards the whole—as I have shown in previous chapter, but also deals with ethnicisation of these ties and resistance to hegemonic collective discourses. This is where the connection between class and ethnicity becomes apparent.

---

[278] M. Okólski, K. Jaźwińska. 2001. *Ludzie na huśtawce.* Warszawa: Scholar.

[279] R. Kantor. 1990. *Między zaborowem a Chicago; kulturowe konsekwencje isnienia zbiorowości imigrantow z parafii zaborowskiej w Chicago i jej kontaktów z rodzinnymi wsiami.* Warszawa: Zakład Narodowy Imienia Ossolinskich.

[280] E. Kuźma. 2004. Migracje do Belgii : o mozliwosciach i barierach wychodzenia z nielegalnosci. [in]: W. Lukowski, P. Kaczmarczyk (eds.) *Polscy pracownicy na rynku pracy Unii Europejskiej.* Warszawa: Uniwersytet Warszawski, Scholar.

Ethnicity as resource and threat

The strongly moralistic message of Polish nationalism, gaining specific meanings abroad, where Poles are obliged to help each other even more, can be treated as a dominant symbolic structure of Polish emigration culture. However, from a demotic perspective — one that is used and meaningful for migrants themselves — this structure places unrealistic and idealistic obligations on real-life situations and, hence, is constantly questioned, resisted, and placed in context. During hours of conversations, interviews, focus groups, casual talk, and observation, I cannot escape the impression that Polish ethnicity — despite being the source of vital social networks — is at the very same time a subject of unease and tension, a source of constant insecurity and carefulness, rather than enthusiastic endorsement or assumed sense of commonality and solidarity. As other scholars have noted,[281] immediately when the issue of other Poles come up, a sense of ambiguity enters. My fieldwork experience throughout 10 years of talking to Polish migrants confirm this. When Poles talk about it, ethnicity is laden with unease, problematic, and conditionality, it is rarely taken as 'given'.

From the perspective of the development of the migration system — a process taking generations — it becomes clear that, at one level, being Polish is a resource and for thousands their migratory routes were possible because they could tap into specific ethnic networks. Yet migrants never describe these networks or the support they receive as arising from the fact of being Polish, but rather because they were friends, family, or people from the same region. In other words, although their connections and social networks could be classified by the external observer as ethnic, for

---

[281]   M. Svasek. 2009. Shared history? Polish migrant experiences and the politics of display in Northern Ireland. [in]: Kathy Burrell (ed.) *Polish Migration to the UK in the 'New' European Union.* Aldershot: Ashgate p. 129; L. Ryan, R.A. Sales, M. Tilki. 2009. Recent Polish migrants in London: accessing and participating in social networks across borders. [in]: Kathy Burrell (ed.) *Polish Migration to the UK in the 'New' European Union.* Aldershot: Ashgate, p. 161.

migrants 'being Polish' is not equated with being a 'friend' or someone you can trust. How migrants dissolve the connection between ethnic morality and trust will be discussed later when I will analyze the cultural practice of myth-making. Here, I wanted to stress that, almost always when a conversation with Polish migrants gets onto a subject of 'Polish people in London' or 'Poles', the reaction is usually to emphasise internal diversity rather than collective similarity. The immediate reaction is to make a boundary within the dominant ethnic category, and this boundary has a specific social class flavor.

While formal, state-sponsored representations may differ, 'lived' and experienced 'ethnicity' on a day-to-day basis is more a source of warnings and suspicion than a celebration of ethnic solidarity and a cherished cultural heritage. It is important to note that, by 'lived', I do not mean the standard and sometimes oversimplified references to what is 'ethnic' behaviour or 'ethnic traits', when people are asked about what it means to be Polish. Eating Polish food, being a Catholic, participating in Polish social life may satisfy some researchers, but is far too superficial and stereotypical, since these activities are often understood differently by different social actors. People go to Church, eat Polish food, or attend a Polish music concert for diverse reasons, and it would not mean much to describe these as a manifestation of 'ethnic' identity.

As ethnicity is an aspect of social relationship, how it is communicated depends on the context and to whom it is communicated and for what purpose. Hence, a Pole can be eager to boast about the stereotypically hard working ethic of Polish builders to a foreigner since, as we saw in the Svasek article on Poles in Belfast, it asserts a right to 'be here' or as in a fascinating study of Polish builders masculinity by Ayona Datta, it contests structural dominance of their English co-workers.[282] However, to another

---

[282] A. Datta. 2009. 'This is special humour': visual narratives of Polish masculinities on London's building sites. [in:] K. Burrell (ed.) *Polish Migration to the UK in the 'New' European Union.* Aldershot: Ashgate.

Pole, the same person might be very cynical about the Polish working class, their behaviour in public, or clothing. In other words, ethnicity can be communicated and performed in various ways depending on who is the 'receiver' of the message and whether the actor sees any benefits in emphasising a particular trait. Situational and strategic choices, in what Gayatri Spivak calls 'strategic essentialism',[283] determine whether someone would stress that 'Poles are hardworking' or whether the same person would say that 'Poles here are also managers, bankers and doctors.' This is where the intersection between class and ethnicity becomes apparent. It is precisely in the context of relationships between co-ethnics that social class acquires most significant and meaningful semantic power for individuals. It is also where ethnicity acquires specific meaning, since it links horizontally people of different classes and backgrounds. Yet Poles, most commonly in their lived and daily experiences, are deeply uncomfortable with it. It would be wrong to say they reject it—ethnicity is far too resourceful for many to overtly contest and deliberately exclude Poles from their immediate social circle. It is precisely ethnicity's capacity to override class differences, which are taken for granted in Poland, which pushes Poles to express strong divisive, differentiating, and sometimes hostile views against each other. In a way, assumed similarity forces them to emphasise differences—both are relationally dependent and mutually reinforcing. The more tightly the dominant nationalistic discourse of equal brotherhood is tied to the moral ethnic code, the stronger is the reaction to 'other' Poles and the need to stress difference. Hence, individualism and self-reliance, so eagerly stressed by our respondents, is not an independent value but a reaction formed relationally to collectivistic hegemonic discourses.

My interviewees usually suggest that it is only outside Poland where they discovered the variety of Poles and began to be keen observers of their behaviour. When asked about what they

---

[283] G.C. Spivak. 1996 [1985]. Subaltern studies. Deconstructing historiography [in]:
D. Landry, G. MacLean (eds.) *The Spivak Reader*. London: Routledge.

felt about the presence of other Poles, Bronka, a female in her 40s working as a cleaner, responds:

> *Maybe I observe more here. I did not pay any attention to Poles in Poland because … well there were only Poles…but here when you travel by bus and you see someone drunk or … using bad language it is a shame really, a shame. Or a girl, really good-looking, pretty young girl who sits at the back and sips beer from a can. It irritates me. Would she do that in Poland? No, because she would be lynched… and here it is free for all… And these are the things that get on my nerves that Poles show themselves from a bad side … or maybe not all… but it is most obvious in the buses, really because you hear how people address themselves, what they talk about … There are Poles that know how to talk about things and who talk about something else than a boss, and the building site … or girls, boys, parties … I try not to eavesdrop, of course, but traveling on the bus you hear things and specially when someone is drunk then the whole bus hears it … Sometimes I do not admit I understand that because it is really a shame … So here I observe Poles more.*

Others are very keen to point out that the differences between Poles are huge and undermine any ethnic solidarity, as this collection of remarks from different interviews shows:

> *You see, this depends what kind of Poles* [are accepted by the respondent]. *I would prefer if some of them would come back and changed with someone else … because really sometimes what you can observe is scary, is horrible … I mean the way people … I don't mean someone swearing on the street and all that, but overall the whole thing. People not knowing Polish can picture the situation in that country just looking at these people.*

> *What they're like? They are chamstwo* [rabble, rough element, plebeian] *… What I mentioned before all those …and that beer drinking …. There is that Polish guy who is a beggar – he begs for money … and this is worst for me, this is ….*

> *Now I think it changed … I started to see Poland in a more critical way …. I have always been critical but now more than ever … about the system that is out there, where people live and the reality we try to manage to live in … and also on us as a nation … I started to look critically, negatively.*

'Observation' is an accurate term here, as a quite popular cultural practice, a kind of social game among Poles in London is to look out or at least pay attention if someone around in public spaces speaks Polish. Quite frequently, media articles or web forum discussions dwell on the subject on: 'how to recognise a Pole' and a game of 'spot a Pole on the street' is also quite common.[284] The stormy discussions on the web about 'how to recognize a Pole abroad' correspond strongly with discussions held during in-depth interviews, focus groups, or casual conversations.

The emphasis on the presence of 'other' Poles in these discreet games, comments, and observations is usually very strongly connected to class differentiations and focused on identifying a person of working, rural class origin or someone aspiring to a higher status. Thus, a respondent would refer to '*hołota*' in depicting Poles visually displaying unacceptable behaviour (e.g. swearing in public and drinking) or use the notion of 'these are all *chamy*' when talking about Poles he meets in public transport. Maciek, for instance, was careful to emphasise that he chooses his friends he drinks with very carefully and does not include '*różni tacy*' [some others—an euphemism of undesirable element]. Dorota tells in great detail how at her work in a pub she avoids serving Polish costumers, because they are 'primitive'. Dariusz is explicitly hostile but also reflects on how his attitude changed after coming to London:

> Q: *Has living in London changed your attitudes to other Poles?* A: *I avoid Poles .... I avoid them to the extent that I don't want to say that I'm from Poland .... Sometimes observing what happens and listening that here a Poles stole this and over there a Poles did that ... here a band of drunken Poles have beaten up someone ....*
>
> Q: *Like in Warsaw ...*
>
> A: *Well, not really ... Here I think it is because a lot of total scum comes to London to work; all these peasants who work on building sites, typical pros-tak,* [simpleton, rough] *guys who don't know how to say hello or thank you. So that's why I try to avoid them. And also let's be clear—no Pole will help you in London unless someone lives here for a very long time.*

The question about 'Warsaw' is crucial here, in an attempt to contrast the negative attitude of most of our respondents with what

---

[284]   There are numerous examples throughout the years; a simple search on the Internet proves how the topic generates interest. See, for instance: http://forum.interia.pl/jak-poznac-polaka-za-granica-tematy,dId,1101410.

they think of other Poles in Poland. The question brought to the surface the role of the imaginary national boundary and the moral outcomes of crossing it. From the abpve-mentioned quotation, it is striking that Dariusz moves smoothly from distinguishing between the situation in Warsaw and London to evoking the norm of ethnic solidarity and help — something allegedly that has to apply more while abroad. 'Warsaw' is then delegated to the sphere of a different moral order; it is *'London'* where Poles ought to behave differently but also where class markers and boundaries are the source of anxiety and discomfort. Dariusz rejected any sense of solidarity with Poles in general but friendship could be based on ethnicity: *'I thought there is some national solidarity. There is none. Of course, this is a generalisation; we have a friend that is very helpful ...'.* Such statement is very typical — exceptions from the 'generalisations' are framed as 'friends' not 'other Poles' and, thus, are devoid of the ethnic component.

The lack of friends and networks one can rely upon makes people vulnerable and unable to exchange social capital; hence, it is not surprising that those who find themselves destitute are often eager to stress the ideal of ethnic solidarity and cultural norms it evokes. The unemployed Stefan — whose optimism we described in Chapter 4 — is torn between the assumed ideal of ethnic solidarity and the grey reality of struggling in the labour market. He finally, however, makes friends, but this only confirms his belief in luck rather than the view that Poles should help one another. Despite finally finding a friendly soul, he is still bitter about the perceived lack of ethnic solidarity. The exchange below illustrates this tension and has also another connected meaning, since it constructs the notion of *Anglik* [English] as someone who will be friendlier and more rewarding than the Polish employer.

Q: You have not worked in an English company yet ....

A: No, I would like to, I believe that with my skills I would have make it high ....

Q: So you think that in an English company they would recognise your skills much faster than in a Polish one?

A: Yes, I think so.

Q: Why?

A: Because ... er ... I think that Polish nation have always been torn apart ....
They cooperated only in the face of threat, then there was unity ... but now,
for example, seeing all Poles here ... yesterday while going to Acton, from the
'wailing wall' [a window shop opposite POSK] *– this was the second time*
when it happened to me - ... a person stopped and asked me .... 'Are you go-
ing from work?' ... Maybe I looked so ... I was depressed and sad, had little
sleep ... and this lady came up to me and asked .... This was a bit of a shock
... she took my telephone number, talked a bit, said she may help ... We will
see ... I think that not enough Poles are interested in other Poles lives, of their
own kin ....

The contrast between 'English' and 'Polish' employers is thus the contrast between a trusted environment and the one which may end up in disappointment. This tendency is typical and symbolic at the same time. A 'friend', a 'family', or a 'mate' is a category used with positive value, but a 'Pole' or 'Polish' is most often associated with a generalised 'other', who is potentially a source of threat, embarrassment, class transgression, disappointment, or fear of exploitation. A Polish employer may play on a sense of solidarity and could exploit, cheat, and mistreat workers — something that obviously happens but, for reasons described later, is elevated to the level of a dominant myth. On the other hand, this potential, imaginary employer may offer work precisely because someone is Polish. Ethnicity, then, is a double-edged sword. It has Janus-like features: a potential resource and potential threat, an advantage and risk, an opportunity but marred with a possibility of betrayal.

This potential threat is related to the danger of unsettling ones' own class perception and desire to present oneself as 'middle class', that is, as well-mannered and well-behaved 'guest' in a foreign country. These attitudes can be observed in more mundane, subtle, and invisible (to an outsider) manner. Poles, who regard themselves as middle class, for instance, would usually exchange knowing looks when overhearing in public a vulgar

Polish conversation.[285] They would constantly keep an eye on this person on the bus/train/street talking in Polish. This awareness of other Pole out there is a very common feeling among many migrants or established Poles. The appearance of someone 'behaving badly' would provoke a quieter conversation or sometimes even switching to English. '*I speak English when I see these people*' says one and I would argue this is a norm rather than exception, since not just other studies note this tendency as well,[286] but it is an everyday experience of Poles living in London where bumping into a Pole on the street, on the transport system is a very common experience. It is specifically observable and prevalent among those, who see themselves as middle class or members of the intelligentsia.

More crucially, this attitude is also informally legitimised by institutionalised power of the state. It was not surprising for me to hear these comments — more or less veiled — from Polish Embassy officials on various occasions. For instance, during a seminar on Polish migration at one of the major British think-tanks, a Consulate official commented during a casual informal conversation that: '*I don't see why they are so interested* [the think-tank], *they are all, some kind of fizyczni* [manual workers] *lots of hołota*' [scum]. Even one of the Polish diplomats, during an informal chat at one of meetings at the Embassy, expressed to me a form of disdain for working-class Poles, expressing fear that '*they stain our reputation*', where 'they' meant a vague, general but 'different' from participants of elegant cocktail meeting at the Embassy crowd in an untold way. According to gossip from my sources at the Polish Consulate, when I approached the Embassy to organise a one-day symposium in May 2006 on Polish migration to London, there was strong resistance from some senior staffs, who were concerned that the spotlight would focus on the 'wrong kind

---

[285] A similar observation is made by L. Ryan. 2010. Becoming Polish in London: negotiating ethnicity through migration. *Social Identities: Journal for the Study of Race, Nation and Culture* 16(3): 359–376.

[286] L. Ryan. 2010. *Ibidem.*

of Poles'. It was implied that they would welcome a seminar on 'successful, educated' young elites much more than one which referred to people working on building sites.

This attitude is expressed at the highest public levels. In 2006, even the then Polish President voiced his concern about equating ethnicity with class or physical labour. When asked about his view concerning the promotional campaign of the Polish Tourist Office in Paris, which used the stereotype of Polish plumber, Lech Kaczyński replied that:

> Personally, it irritates me very much … our country is perceived as a country of plumbers, while we are also a country of lawyers, who know the languages very well, we are a country of good IT professionals, mathematicians. I would prefer if my country be known also from that side.

In the President's opinion then, as well as the many Poles who see themselves as middle class I spoke to, there is something intriguingly, implicitly, and psychologically wrong about being a plumber and especially about being a plumber abroad, since it projects the generalised image of Poles as working class, as working manually. Their reaction could be read as a strategy of distinction making demonstrating a dislike of being put into the same category as plumbers. This is precisely where the assumed solidarity of ethnicity clashes with social class difference. These attitudes, voiced in public, have many levels of meanings, and I will explore them more deeply in the following sections.

Class markers among Poles

Before I do that, in order to decode the various ways class is constructed, we need to look at what markers are actually used to classify people and how they mark the body, behaviour, attitudes, and norms of interactions between people. The making of class distinctions and boundaries among Poles takes several forms and are usually embodied in specific behaviour, talk, looks, norms, and attitudes people present. As scholars note, these developments are also framed in broader social developments related to economic transition in post-1989 Poland[287] and in this case, additionally bring forward the migratory context of these distinction-making practices.

The influence of hegemonic discourses concerning nationalism and ethnicity creates a situation where migrants are forced to express and highlight class markers in stronger and more meaningful terms in order to disconnect themselves from people who are perceived — by the dominant host society — as their kin or having similar traits. After all, Poles,[288] as many other migrant groups,[289] are confronted with the processes of ascription in a much stronger way than in Poland. Hence, the social class markers centre around terms that refer usually focused on the body, dress, overt use of alcohol, language, *kombinacje*, and general references to a 'rural' and 'working' class mentality.

Dress and looks — the functions of 'how to spot a Pole' game

What people look like is an important marker of social class and in a migratory context, undeniably one that combines both class and ethnicity. The sometimes endless discussions with my interviewees, debates on the web and media, among friends, and casual talk often focused on how to recognise someone who looks distinctively working or rural class.[290] It is usually done in an patronising, if not abusive way by stressing that these Poles are 'bald' with wide

---

[287] See A. Stenning. 2006. *What happened to the working class?*

[288] L. Ryan. 2010. Becoming Polish in London: negotiating ethnicity through migration. *Social Identities: Journal for the Study of Race, Nation and Culture* 16(3): 359–376.

[289] See, for example, how Albanian migrants deal with these processes in: S. Schwander-Sievers (ed.). 2002. *Albanian Identities. Myth, Narratives and Politics.* London: C Hurst & Co Publishers Ltd.

[290] This is actually a constant and passionately popular theme in the Internet discussions and also debated on the media. Enough to type in: 'the look of Poles abroad'.

'necks',[291] with 'stupidity on their faces' with '*morda*' [vulgar for face] showing their assumed lack of intelligence. A moustache is a crucial part of this look, as people often refer to 'that Polish distinct moustache'. Large, worked out hands are also a marker, as well as a scruffy backpack with tools sticking out, or stained clothes which clearly shows that the owner works physically.

Women are described as lacking taste, wearing gold necklaces, dyed hair, and looking like '*ze wsi*,' '*z wiejskiej dyskoteki*' [from a village or village disco]. Now, this discourse of contempt and class stigmatisation operates only one way, since Polish working-class people—apart from also using the same markers to categorise other Poles—do not find similar markers for those, whom they regard as 'higher classes', which mainly means people employed in financial services. People, who regard themselves as middle class, go to great lengths to avoid their dress being associated with working class or alter their image in order to break away with their former image. In a typical case, Wojtek from Jasło decides to change his appearance after a few weeks in London, because he found that his 'Slavic' image was impeding his chances. It was not only his view about how other Poles might see him but rather how the dress and looks related to his chances of interaction with non-Poles in London. He recalls his first trip to London:

> So that was the winter 2003, bit before … I got the invitation from him … January: I am coming to London. And the thing now: they [the Immigration Officer] did not want to let me in. Maybe because I looked like simply like … like a builder, not like an engineer who comes to London to have a visit …. This is my picture, then still with the moustache, typical builder [shows a picture of him with black moustache and a tracksuit. Currently he is clean shaved and has a black leather jacket and blue jeans] ….

He manages to convince the Immigration Officer, but his look haunts him later on:

---

[291]   *Kark*—literally meaning 'neck'—refers to an individual who is bald, with pumped up muscles, and in a tracksuit.

... at the beginning I was a bit pissed of with London; why? At one stage I wanted ... when I was here for three, four months ... to come to a pub. But I was refused entry. I looked as in that picture, moustaches all that ... damn, Australian pub it was ... So right then I came back to my place, cut these moustaches and so, maybe ... Then I kind of ... I started to dress differently, not in these what was fashionable in Poland ... because here it's good to ... you know ... kurwa, not to distinguish yourself, to feel, to feel good ....

'Distinguish' himself actually meant, looking like a working-class Pole, like a 'Slav'. On my visit to his family home Jasło, his relatives enthusiastically confirmed this metamorphosis saying that he looks much better and not like some kind of *Polaczek*.[292] Dress and what people look like is not only a social class marker — it becomes also an ethnic marker but only when it is the lower classes that are marked. One would not find a lawyer or doctor, wearing a suit, being referred to as dressed in a 'typically Polish' way. A 'typical Polish' dress, in the eyes of Polish migrants, is associated with lower social class and it is a marker of hierarchy. It marks people as poor, 'Eastern', ill-fitted to the glamorous world of the global city — as members of the lumpen-proletariat or underclass.

Apart from the dress, Poles often exchange comments that 'someone looks typically Polish' and part of the social game[293] — spot the Pole — focuses on the assumption that a 'Polish' face can be racially identified. It is rather a mystery as to what these features are, but the crucial fact is that it is important for migrants to think that they are able to recognise another Pole — something they frequently emphasise. In this way, class is racialised, and class distinctions cease to be fluid, changeable, and negotiated — as when people are prompted about class in Poland or Britain — and become something biological, natural, given, and objective. 'Knowing how to spot a Pole' is thus a form of racialised social distancing, since the participants of that game/quiz immediately

---

[292] *Polaczek* — a diminutive from *Polak* (a Pole) — is a derogatory term, often implying someone who is cunning, cheating, and not deserving respect.

[293] In one of the many media articles on this subject in the Polish ethnic press, the game is referred to as a 'quiz'. See M. Adamczewska.1898. *Polak — nie da się ukryć!*; www.elondyn.co.uk/newsy,wpis.

put themselves outside the group that is the subject of the game. By contrast, playing the game rises ones' own status and informs others how not to look like a Pole.

Dressing or looking in a way that visually conceals these 'markers' becomes, therefore, a way of disassociation from what are perceived as lower class markers. In other words, to look 'less Polish' means looking more middle class or higher in the hierarchy of power. It is not difficult to find out why this is the case. Totalising and hegemonic discourses concerning ethnicity create a horizontal category, which assumes that every Pole has some specific essential features, and physical appearance confirms this. By associating these features with class markers, those playing the game/quiz immediately remove themselves from that group. Ethnicity potentially entails transgression of class boundaries so people evoke an ethnic hegemonic racialised discourse, precisely to transgress ethnic solidarity and emphasise their social superiority through middle-class markers (suits, Western clothes, and shaved face). It is a complex game of meanings and stigmatising practices where various notions of *Polaczek*, *robol* (working class), *menel* (wino, alcoholic working class), *bilder* (polonised English 'builder'), cham (*brute*) freeze social distinctions but, at the same time, put those creating the meanings beyond the subject of their discursive practices.

Public–private consumption of alcohol

Another important aspect of class boundary making is the set of behaviours associated with consumption of alcohol. An important element of formal and informal social interactions in Poland,[294] alcohol consumption is a paradigmatic example of tensions between the public and private spheres of social life. In general, Poles are well aware of the stereotypes which surround their consumption of alcohol. Their perceptions about how and where one

---

[294] See J. Wedel. 1986. *The Private Poland: An Anthropological Look at Everyday Life.* New York: Columbia University Press.

can drink are strongly affected by these stereotypes, and when they are abroad, a more rigid and reinforced boundary is needed. What would be regarded as acceptable or not worth mentioning or noticing in Poland, such as drinking in parks, on benches, in children's playgrounds, on river banks, or drinking publicly in the early morning, may generate strong emotional reactions in the context of London.

As anthropologists have long argued, alcohol consumption can both create a temporary feeling of *communitas* or brotherhood and yet be destructive and divisive.[295] This feature is quite evident in the context of the relationship between ethnicity and class. Drinking in public spaces is regarded by most Poles in London as something that 'stains' the reputation of Poles in general and, therefore, to be strongly condemned. At the same time, as I have argued elsewhere, collective drinking is a vital mechanism for the homeless Poles to maintain levels of self-autonomy and group ties in a situation of multiple exclusion and class degradation.[296] Among Polish community leaders, one of the most lamented developments has been the erection of Polish language signs in some London parks prohibiting the drinking of alcohol. It is regarded as proof that a minority of *hołota* or *pijacy* [drunks] are destroying the reputation of middle class, aspirational Poles (the 'right' kind of Poles). Again, the ethnic marker of drinking alcohol in this way is constructed mainly as a social class marker, since most Poles would claim that they have a different 'culture of drinking' and that what these people do is maybe 'typically Polish' but associated with the lower classes.

Among certain groups of Polish migrants, whose life oscillates only around work, weekend is the time of heavy consumption. Houses, which are rented mainly by Polish migrants, are

---

[295] See, for example, D. Mandelbaum. 1965. Alcohol and culture. *Current Anthropology* 6(3):281–293; or R. Sulima. 2000. Antropologia libacji alkoholowej. [in] *Antropologia codziennosci*. Warszawa: Wydawnictwo UJ; or A. Zielinski. 1994. Polish culture — wet or dry? *Contemporary Drug Problems* 21:329–340.

[296] M. Garapich. 2013. Homo Sovieticus revisited — anti-institutionalism, alcohol and resistance among polish homeless men in London. *International Migration*.

divided into numerous flats, and most, according to various surveys, live with people to whom they are not related. If we consider also their relative young age and that only a minority has children, then it becomes quite clear that these settings are conducive to heavy drinking. However, this is not an issue which our respondents were particularly concerned about when living in such accommodation, even though they were also substantial consumers and spent their free time drinking and socialising at other people's homes, in numerous Polish bars or at concerts. This kind of drinking is seen as acceptable and normal. What is not acceptable, however, is extending this behaviour into public space. Only *hołota* [scum] drink on the streets and parks, and this *hołota* is constructed as typically Polish.

Related to this is another set of markers focusing on the use of the Polish language, especially loud vulgarities. This can be seen as the discursive equivalent of public drinking, since swearing in private is acceptable but doing so loudly in public is strictly associated with the lower classes—it 'pollutes' public space. Many of our respondents claim that this is precisely what Poles do and how they are—they simply swear a lot in the presence of others. Hence, many public leaders and people in positions of power and even priests during their sermons remind Poles to be aware of this and not to swear in public. Language also is a marker within different groups of Poles, as I will describe it in Chapter 7.

Shame, reputation, and class

The aforementioned markers are negatively constructed, since as Jenkins notes: 'the categorization of 'them' is too useful a foil in the identification of 'us' for this not to be the case, and the definition of 'us' too much the product of a history of relationships with a range of significant others' (Jenkins 1997: 53). While referring to ethnicity, Poles very often create images, practices that present a negative reference point and through these they create a moral ordering of classes and a normative hierarchy of what should be regarded as the image of the 'right' Pole—essentially someone who does not commit above-decribed offences. These distinctions do not mention anything about earnings, status, or social standings of people identified as *hołota* or those, who are being called 'typically Polish' in their behaviour as drunks, thieves, or *kombinator* (someone who does *kombinacje*). People use these distinctions in their everyday lives, since they must confront hegemonic discourses at an individual level and make them meaningful. The strategies they employ and feelings they experience are vital to understand what is at stake.

In the interviews carried out as part of the ESRC project at the end of conversation, I inserted a question entailing a hypothetical situation: *'You travel on the underground and there are some drunken Poles talking loudly and swearing. What do you feel?'* What was fascinating was that, in the majority of cases, people reacted in a way that suggested that this was not a hypothetical situation—that they had indeed experienced it.

The overall response was encapsulated in one word: shame. This was combined with many instances of social mimesis (*I pretend I'm English*) or sometimes active involvement (*I would stand and tell them not to behave like idiots*) or indifference (*What can you do? But it's a shame because it is true, I've seen* it). Overall, however, shame is vital in deciphering why class distinctions become such a crucial issue for Poles in London when it relates to other Poles. It can be called an individual sense of shame, which arises from both the hegemonic discourses of the nation and the belief that Poles are somewhat all the same and that the outsiders—the imaginary 'English'—also think and view groups in totalising and essentialist terms. People generally say that it bothers them more than in Poland, because a reputation is being cemented and that reputation is worryingly dependent on the lower classes, on the *hołota*, *chamstwo*.

> Very much indeed, it bothers me … because I am in a different country and people look at our nation, at the Polish, and they just think: 'My God what kind of nation it is'.

It seems, then, that Poles are trapped by their own acceptance of nationalistic and essentialising understandings of ethnicity. Shame — the emotion of committing a social gaffe — is the result of their belief that nations, groups, people like the 'Poles', 'French', and 'English' share specific substantial and essential characteristics and if someone behaves 'badly', this will be extrapolated to all Poles. In straight and simple words, Wojtek describes this as simply taking care of one's own reputation:

> Well, there could be two answers ... First of all it is normal stuff. A group of English can drink and be loud as well. Second, it is a shame a bit... we are guests after all ... I do not speak Polish then [in this situation] I hide even ... not only because I am ashamed but to avoid a situation where they would start to be friendly with me and raise the fact that we are co-ethnics ....

Others share the feeling and try to understand it:

> I mean ... I don't talk to them for sure .... There are some situations where I do interfere but in this case I would just feel sorry ... I would be sorry that I also come from that country, I would not think of them in good terms .... They are in an alien country, they make noise, they make a mess ... so I think people are wondering about what English think of them. But they are working on that at the same time .... You hear stories that English are sometimes bad towards foreigners ... and you kind of understand it.

> I feel ashamed. Because really do you see any other nationalities that are sitting on the benches in parks and drinking? I didn't see other nationalities ... really ... maybe some homeless English yes ... but here you see Poles like in towns in Poland sitting on the benches in parks and drinking. National sport or what? Maybe some group of young English would walk with a Smirnoff or something but it usually covered .... These Polish ... it just reminds me Poland and that's sad.

> I feel a bit ashamed ... on the one hand because they swear and are drunk and just get on my nerves and also because they are Polish so they bring shame to the ethnic group I belong to.

> Not on these Poles specifically but generally about Poles no? And that's why I was ashamed. That these people [the British audience] think now that everybody is like that in Poland. Because they don't understand that only a certain type of Poles come here; that there is this kind and other kind of Pole; and that there are divisions [among Poles] ... educational, social and all that ... They form their opinion on the basis of these guys.

Shame is a complex notion, and there has been an extensive anthropological literature on its function in diverse societies.[297] As a tool of social control, it acts as a reminder of cultural norms and practices. Yet, several crucial components stand out, which inform us how difficult it is to assert ones' individuality and at the same time recognise the existence of collective notions of the nation and ethnic groups. Shame is an individual experience—one that prompts people to refer to his reputation and background. To fully decipher it, we must look more closely at what people mean by these strongly emotionally charged comments.

First of all, it was a familiar real-life situation, one that people remember, mainly since it is qualitatively differently experienced when occurring in Poland and when happening on the London Underground. Secondly, shame is a direct result of the strong individualistic attitudes people endorse, something I discussed at length in the previous chapter. They regard themselves—or would like to regard themselves—as masters of their own destiny, but suddenly they are confronted with the fact that their reputation may depend of someone else's actions. At the very same time, they assume that the observers—the imaginary English—will stereotype Poles and so they take for granted that all people think in totalising, homogenising ethnic terms. Shame, then, is the result of a very strongly felt unease about the fact that, despite their optimistic outlook concerning individualism, meritocracy, and social advancement, their success can be affected by stereotypes, the overgeneralised reputation of a group, and so on.

In this sense, shame, is a personalised experience of social class markers that become ethnic ones. It is the individually experienced interface of both class and ethnic dimensions of social identity, hence the strong emotive reactions to its—sometimes negative outcomes. But through shame, people also experience the limit of their individualistic attitude since it has also the effect of

---

[297] See, for example, D. Gilmore (ed.). 1987. *Honor and Shame and the Unity of the Mediterranean. American Anthropological Association Special Publication 22.* Washington: American Anthropological Association.

reactivating and renovating the collectivity. Shame reminds people that they are categorised as Poles, and this ascribed identity equates them horizontally with people, whom they avoid having contact with and would not even notice while in Poland.

> *I put up the volume in my walkman and read the book. That's what I do and I had several times such a situation. And I just don't show that I anything in common with them lot.*

> *I hide the book in Polish I read and take out an English one … [laughs] … I mean I feel stupid … but really, I don't care why I should be responsible for these guys? And what I've got in common? No … this issue of nations … no ….*

The words: '*No … this issue of nations … no ….*' is a realisation of the paradoxes implicit in putting people into 'ethnic' categories, in the eyes of this respondent it is full of unjust assumptions because at the end: 'why I should be responsible?' Shame has also a strong gendered association, as this woman reflects on the Polish lower class behaving 'badly' having actually males only in mind:

> *A: I actually avoid Poles … as for guys* [Polish men] *I avoid them …*

> *Q: Why?*

> *A: I'm ashamed of them really … If I am on the bus and I hear kurwa, chuj, all the time … you know … I swear also sometimes but I control myself. These guys think that no one understands them but I am there and I do … They haven't got a clue how to behave. When I argue with my boyfriend I tell him to shut up and that we will talk at home … because I feel that people can hear me ….*

Shame is, therefore, a powerful emotional reaction to the deeply ingrained cultural categorisation of people into ethnic groups and the belief that people in these groups share similar features and that others—especially the positive reference group, the 'English'—share the same opinion. Shame brings to the surface the integral contradiction borne out of both the belief in the self and the power of own aspirations and the belief in the social world divided into ethnic/national groups where class difference is levelled. This confronts individuals with forces seemingly beyond their control. Suddenly, it is not the merit, hard work, and aspirations which can be sufficient qualities to 'make it' in the new social world. Behaviour of other Poles, negative stereotypes, and the reputation of a drunk member of an 'uncivilised' lower class can also have an influence. So again, the collective identification process clashes with the individual. How people deal with that contradiction?

The myth of the Polish conman

People, as producers of culture, are not defenceless against these contradictions. I argue that confronted with dominant hegemonic ideological traits, they do try to dissolve the crucial, in nationalistic ideologies, link between morality and ethnicity. The tool to achieve this is an old human invention — by telling a story, a myth.

As is quite obvious by now, a constant feature in my interviews was the story of a Polish employer who is cheating others, Poles that behave badly and 'stain' the reputation of the entire group and the need to insist that there are 'different kinds of Poles' with difference going along the class lines. While talking about other Poles, my respondents chose the discourse of vertical class difference, rather than horizontal ethnic solidarity.

That feature of distance-making and alleged distrust within Polish migrant's social world in London also struck other researchers and various explanations were offered. Franck Duvell and Bill Jordan faced with sometimes seemingly Darwinian behaviour of Polish migrants state that: *'by their economic behavior, they pose the question of how much mobility is consistent with a well-functioning democracy, with loyalty and solidarity, and even with the accumulation of social capital (norms of reciprocity and trust) that is required for the efficient working of a market economy'*.[298] Drawing on his research experience, Jordan was asking: how these people who

---

[298]   B. Jordan. 2002. Migrant Polish workers in London. Mobility, labour market and the prospects for democratic development. Paper given at the conference: *Beyond Transition. Development Perspectives and Dilemmas*. Warsaw, 12–13 April 2002, p. 3.

in their ethnic group cheat, exploit, and report each other to Immigration Service (these were still the old days of visas) how can they create a functional, prosperous, democratic society? Poles:

> 'engage in unrestrained competition, including informing to the authorities on each other, in order to get other's jobs. Every service, ever amenity has a price. They exploit each other mercilessly; they cannot be relied on to keep promises. Is this the shape of social relations beyond transition? Is this what happens when hypermobility under global capitalism replaces the rigidities and stagnations of socialism?'[299]

This sense of mistrust, described in other studies,[300] is common, and some scholars cite this as a proof of the 'dark' side of Polish migration. Other scholars also comment on the issue, however, in much less objectifying way and offering less analysis, rather elaborating on what interviewees have said and offering a short explanation. For example, Svasek notes that 'Polish migrants tend to have ambiguous feelings about other Polish migrants' as on the one hand they offer support and network, but from the other they are a potential threat to their public reputation.[301] Ryan, Sales, Tilki, and Siara highlight that 'the idea that Poles do not help each other was a recurring theme in many interviews and that there is a binary opposition between particular Polish networks and more general population of Polish migrants who were constructed as unhelpful and even dangerous'.[302] They explain this opposition as a consequence of internal

---

[299] B. Jordan. 2002. Ibidem, p. 4.

[300] Apart from Jordan's approach, see, for instance, the account of Polish migrants in Belgium by Grzymała-Kazłowska: A. Grzymala-Kazlowska. 2005. From ethnic cooperation to in-group competition: undocumented Polish workers in Brussels. Journal of Ethnic and Migration Studies 31(4):675–697; or already quoted L. Ryan's article on the issue: L. Ryan. 2010. Becoming Polish in London: negotiating ethnicity through migration. Social Identities: Journal for the Study of Race, Nation and Culture 16(3): 359–376.

[301] M. Svasek. 2009. Shared history? Polish migrant experiences and the politics of display in Northern Ireland. [in]: K. Burrell (ed.) Polish Migration to the UK in the 'New' European Union. Surrey: Ashgate, p. 129.

[302] L. Ryan, R.A. Sales, M. Tilki. 2009. Recent Polish migrants in London: accessing and participating in social networks across borders. [in]: Kathy Burrell (ed.) Polish Migration to the UK in the 'New' European Union. Aldershot: Ashgate, p. 161.

economic competition within a group sharing similar range of networks which leads to ghettoisation due to the 'weakness of strong ties'. The theme of ambiguous perception of co-ethnics and even hostility is a feature of numerous publications[303] also in the USA,[304] and it is clear that researchers in the field encounter this attitude fairly frequently. An in-depth analysis of the phenomena has been presented by Małgorzata Irek[305] who argues that, contrary to the standard account, Polish migrants demonstrate features of trust and cooperation and that the perceived anomie and internal conflict has been overstated. She demonstrates also that the perception of Polish migrants as divided into neat categories and groups is misleading and that there is lots of evidence pointing to mutual cooperation and networks between groups described in the literature as separate and isolated. What's maybe even more revealing is the level of interest about the issue from the traditional and social media. It is enough to search in one of numerous Polish migrants' Internet discussion forums for themes that circle around 'trust', 'cooperation between Poles', 'solidarity among Poles' to be met with a deluge of comments, debates, and feature-long essays. As an occasional commentator to the Polish press in Poland and UK, I lost count on how many times journalists asked me to comment on the issue on whether the old saying that 'Poles to a Pole is like a wolf' reflects the true nature of intra-group relations. The very fact that this discussion is kept alive not just in the academia but within the public domain as well as private conversations is a testimony of the crucial cultural significance of the question about trust between Poles, whether they do cooperate and form a cohesive group or is it just a pure fantasy. This fact has not been noted by researchers, but I argue here that it is this eagerness and willingness to debate the issue which holds the key to the question why migrants, as well as people researching them

---

[303] //Garapich (2007, 2008, 2012); Eade et al. (2006); Ryan et al. (2008); Pietka (2011); Lassalle et al. (2011); Andrejuk (2011).

[304] Erdmans (1998); Schneider (1995); Bukowczyk (1996); Rabikowska (2015).

[305] Irek (2011).

pick upon the subject of trust—both as a subject for an academic article as well as an online discussion.

Such similarity between researchers' findings and eagerness of the public debate on the issue is worth closer attention. This theme is also, as we have seen, very present in the conversations with Polish migrants where often they maintained that Poles should be avoided and that their behaviour 'stains' the reputation of the majority. For example, such comments are quite common-place:

> *Because from the part of Poles you can expect only a scam and you can be cheated.*

> *Because what you see is that Poles are exploited all the time, but by whom? By other Poles! So this is really horrible for me.*

> *What does it tell about Poles? Kurwa ... where should I start?! [laughs] there is a lot I could tell you about ... First of all ... they are mean, bad, envious ... rarely it is otherwise.*

Anecdote, gossip, or personal experience frequently refers to Polish employers breaking their promises or being cheated. Someone stresses the fact that he/she was not paid the proper wages, another recalls that his employees stole from him, or someone else says that he/she was stopped by security in a shop, because the shop had bad experiences with Poles shoplifting. These stories are very common not only in the interviews but also in the media, web forums, and even national debates. A popular saying—'a Pole to a Pole is like a wolf' made its way to the popular parlance, but also academic studies, as an account on Poles in Holland demonstrates,[306] as well as an article by Rabikowska using that popular saying[307] where she also highlights the importance of class discourses among Polish migrants. From one perspective, it

---

[306] S. Toruńczyk-Ruiz. 2008. Being together or apart? Social networks and notions of belonging among recent Polish migrants in the Netherlands. CMR Working Papers. No 40/98.

[307] M. Rabikowska. 2016. 'A Pole Like a Wolf to Another Pole': Class (Im)mobility and Group Resentment among Polish Immigrants in London. *International Journal of Politics, Culture and Society.*

gives support for the interpretation by Jordan and others about the moral vacuum created by increased mobility and the assumed breakdown in mutual trust among migrants.

However, it is often missed that, all the respondents quoted earlier (as well as Jordan's), mix mostly within a Polish environment. They live with Poles, work with them, go out with them, and engage in relationships with them. As we have shown, their social network is Polish. They go to Polish churches and read Polish papers. Moreover, as we seen, they very often come through migration chain networks established by other Poles — pointing to a considerable amount of migratory social capital being in use. This clear contradiction between rhetoric and the actual use of networks has not escaped other scholars. As Louise Ryan notes: *'this suggests a binary opposition between particular Polish networks and a more general population of Polish migrants, who were constructed as unhelpful and even dangerous'*.[308] This combination of hostility towards co-ethnics and an acceptance of Polish friends and the use of Polish networks as a source of capital is very significant, and scholars, who have noticed this rhetoric of mistrust, have failed to grasp fully the significance of this cultural agency and failed to explain why people seem to fully engage in social networks composed of co-ethnics while at the same time maintaining a strong hostility towards more generalised 'Poles'. The emphasis on 'friendship' rather than 'Poles', means that people are saying: 'watch the other Poles — my mates are ok'. So where does the problem lie then? Why is it such an emotional issue for respondents?

From my perspective, a lot of previous research has assumed that peoples' discourse is based on facts rather than as something sociologically constructed. In that sense, explanation of researchers take what people say at face value and lack interpreta-

---

[308] L. Ryan, R.A. Sales, M. Tilki. 2009. Recent Polish migrants in London: accessing and participating in social networks across borders. [in]: Kathy Burrell (ed.) *Polish Migration to the UK in the 'New' European Union*. Aldershot: Ashgate, p. 161.

tive analysis taking this story, not as an account of facts but as an expression of cultural significance. There is something beyond the story itself, such as its commonality and repetitive omnipresence. Anthropologically, every story as such, has a layer of meanings beyond the narrative — norms, values, and complex meaning-making practices, is expressed through stories to make sense of the tensions and contradictions between, the world of norms they were socialised in and between the harsh realities of everyday life. So, why have researchers taken what they hear for granted? It is impossible to escape a conclusion that scholars have been implicitly reproducing a romanticised version of the dominant discourse, which sees migration as a threat to the moral fabric of the community. The view that social relations between migrants collapse in London, Belgium, or Berlin rests on the assumption that they were better back home. This assumption not only is hard to prove but also assumes that a sedentary and stable home community creates trust and moral order. The assumption romanticises and reifies the notion of a cozy 'home' community where everyone trusts another. It rests on the belief in an ideal 'ethnic community' where ethnic ties create mutual trust, social capital, and solidarity. It perpetuates the belief in the world of horizontal brotherhood replacing the brutal reality of vertical class differences. All in all, it is a kind of continual revitalisation of *communitas*.[309]

What is striking about that repetitive negativity towards co-ethnics is that people's accounts stand in stark contradiction to the character of the social network they are embedded into. In other words, by engaging in the simple story of a Polish dishonest employer/employee or a Pole committing a crime, people are commenting on the social world around them by using cultural resources they know — the notions of morality of ethnic ties, the symbolic value of ethnic solidarity, and the egalitarian notion of the collective. They are sending a particular message, rich in cul-

---

[309] V. Turner. 1995. *The Ritual Process: Structure and Anti-structure.* New York: Hawthorne.

tural and social meanings, which relates to the dominant hegemonic nationalistic discourses described above.

Anthropologists have a soft spot for looking at disparities between what people say and what they do and they seek to understand how concepts and ideas are applied, used, manipulated in everyday life and interactions. So if people are eager to present negative attitudes towards other 'Poles' but, nevertheless, do other things (engage with them, live with them, use their ethnic ties as sources of social capital, etc.), they are not necessarily lying. Rather, they are trying to problematise and contextualise the very notion of 'Polishness,' which—as the grand narrative would have it—should bound them together in a set of mutual moral obligations that exclude non-ethnics.

In describing that discursive agency, I call it the *myth of Polish conman* using the understanding of myth in a way Anthony P. Cohen or Levi-Strauss did. As explained in Chapter 2, this approach sees myth as a particular set of discursive performative actions, a narrative that tries to ease and diffuse the cognitive contradictions stemming from the tension between the ideal and the real, between the dominant ethos imposed from above and the grey reality of everyday. The myth of the Polish conman contrasts two identities in order to create a sense of unease—national identity, with all its symbolic power, implicit morality, and notion of romantic sentiment, is combined with the *conman*, who violates the rules and social norms. In contrasting these two identities, people try to show that they belong to two different social orders and the social praxis should not mix them together. The myth contests, therefore, the notion that ethnic ties translate into moral obligations. By telling a story of a Polish migrant cheating, or breaking social norms, people send a message that in a labour market, in real life, ethnicity is not an *a priori* source of mutual trust or expanding networks or getting along.

Although not quantifiable, while conducting fieldwork in various places in London, I have an impression that the hostility towards co-ethnics is particularly significant when performed by

Polish construction workers. It seems, this is not just about competition and should not be surprising. The construction industry labour market, with its all casual, flexible, informal structure, and recruitment practices, is an area where social capital and mutual trust are highly valued assets, and the price of a broken promise or dishonesty is high. Polish builders, then, constantly remind each other that just being a Pole is not enough to make conclusions about their ability to keep a promise. In fact, a naïve faith in the link between ethnic ties and morality may be a source of deep disappointment. The *myth* is a daily, constant, casual way of reminding people about this fact.

Another group, which eagerly engages in the reproduction of this myth, are the Polish homeless who were interviewed on several occasions and who were the focus of the study funded by the Southland Methodist Trust in 2010. In their narratives, the presence of dishonest, rich, and ruthless Polish employers achieves almost Dickensian proportions, as this homeless man: '*Never work for fucking Polish … they will rip you off, they will use your last breath and let you go with nothing*'. At the same time, ethnic bonds and ethnic solidarity among the homeless is clearly very strong, and mutual support is very strong and is often a matter of life and death on the streets of London. As one homeless person notes:

> *You have to be in the group … You have these guys letting dogs on to you, our friends almost died because some fuckers had a game with their pit bulls – setting dogs on us … but also you need to defend yourself from others … Russians are bad … Albanians … You know life is a jungle on the streets here.*

So, what is the purpose of the myth about the cheating Polish employer, Polish conman? I can identify two specific social functions. First of all, it is a kind of moral preaching. By stigmatising and condemning the behaviour of Poles who are cheating, people are projecting an ideal mode of ethnic ties where ethnic affinity involves a set of moral obligations. Consequently, instances of Poles cheating each other are perceived as morally far worse than cheating outsiders. So, by showing what is wrong, individuals establish what the desirable state is. However, this is a function that stays in the domain of the ideal—it is an ideal to which the group should aspire, but at the same time, it falls short of being the *real* state of affairs.

The second function is more pragmatic and has an everyday value. By its immediate, and 'reality checking' character, it can be considered much more important than the 'idealistic' one. It is a case of what may be called—reversing Michael Billing's famous term[310]—strategic banal 'anti-nationalism', that is, through individual activities, day-to-day actions, and agency-dominant discourses concerning nationalism, ethnicity and morality are challenged, and their pragmatic usefulness questioned. It says: 'ok, this is the ideal but this is the reality'. It is a decoding message to make people aware of the perils of dogmatic thinking.

The message rationalises an emotional sentiment or as Max Weber saw it the 'affective criteria' about not treating other Poles as a source of social/human capital and trust *only* because they are co-ethnics; 'Don't trust someone just because he is a Pole'—says someone who tells a story about exploitative Poles. Among people looking for work, this information forms a piece of crucial knowledge—the same as that concerning employee insurance on building sites—about how to find accommodation and so on. It is a reminder that sentiments do not count very much on the labour market, or rather that the idea that they count is a form of wishful thinking. In Poland, people do not trust other co-ethnics *a priori*, of course, but somehow, through the search for information, networks, and capital, ethnic ties seem more valuable when abroad. This is true to some extent. As we have seen, the circles of Polish friends, the migration chain networks, the booming migration industry, and ethnic economic niche are proof that ethnic ties do, indeed, translate into business, cooperation, economic interest, and, in certain circumstances, are an important asset. Migration does not lead to the collapse of social ties. However, as with all

---

[310] M. Billig. 1995. *Banal Nationalism*. London.

sentiments and ties based on an ideology and an imagined vision of 'sameness', this assumption is vulnerable to abuse. The Polish conman myth is a reminder to all that it is nice to talk in Polish with a stranger but being Polish is not enough to trust him. Ethnicity is a double-edged sword. It may be useful as a potential platform where people can share resources, but due to its emotional character, it can easily be abused. Knowledge of this ambiguity is transferred via the urban myth of a 'Polish conman'.

Another aspect that needs to be raised here relates to the constant reminder of internal class differentiation. As described earlier, the narratives by Polish migrants about their co-ethnics are full of complex ways by which class differences are established — through education, behaviour, geographical location (rural–urban), language, dress, or appearance. So, the playing down of ethnic affinity is a necessary outcome of raising class barriers. These barriers are set to prevent people being associated with the 'wrong crowd'. From my experience, both middle class and working class Polish migrants are sensitive to this particular issue — that misbehaving, lower class, and generally not 'presentable' Poles 'stain' the reputation of the entire group. Now this is something, which can also happen in Poland, but what migration does, is to highlight ethnic horizontal bonds, mainly through the fact of external ascription by the host society. This, in turn, requires a stronger and more powerful counter-response in the form of the constant storytelling about Poles being *wolves* to each other.

The above-mentioned argument puts into perspective the argument held by some social scientists that Polish society suffers from a moral vacuum and lacks the crucial components of a healthy and prosperous society — social capital, trust, and norms of reciprocity.[311] Just because people express their reservations

---

[311] Trust and social capital in Poland has been the subject of considerable and ongoing debate: See, for instance, P. Sztompka. 1999. *Trust: A Sociological Theory*. Cambridge: Cambridge University Press; or B. Wciórka. 2008. *Społeczeństwo obywatelskie 1998-2008 (Civil society 1988-2008)*. 'Opinie i diagnozy' ('Opinions and diagnoses') no 8. Warszawa; J. Dzialek. 2009. *Social Capital and Economic*

about ethnic ties, does not mean that they do not engage in mutual cooperation, trust building, civil society construction, and so on. It is the very *categories* that are used that are questioned, not the notion of trust. It would be overwhelmingly wrong to assume that Polish migrants, due to their migration, *really* become more cunning, mean, untrustworthy, and lacking in basic social norms. On the contrary, the very existence of a vast and strong transnational social field and multiple ways of belonging and being shows that Poles strongly rely on and value their family and friendship connections. Their criticism, disdain, and contempt relate more to the ideologies of the nation and the dominant cultural norms, which derive from the history of Polish nationalism, than to direct reality. This is not to say that there are no instances of migrants cheating each other or committing acts of crime but these do not differ in scale or form from what is happening in Poland. The transnational field perspective helps us to understand that we should avoid seeing social relations as *qualitatively* different in one state and different in another.

Poles in multicultural London and whiteness as resource

The British context involves, of course, other opportunities for ethnic and class differentiation. While keen to show the 'best' side of Polish ethnicity by stressing the work ethic, ambitions, and individualism, Poles are also well aware that, in the complex British hierarchy of ethnic groups, certain traits need to be emphasised and strategically used. So, if 'Polishness' is seen as too inclusive and regarded with strong ambiguity, there is something that potentially has the opposite effect of unwanted class transgression, something that makes them align with a group, which is perceived as dominant — the white English middle class.

Growth in Polish Regions MPRA Paper 18287. Germany: University Library of Munich.

The new social environment Polish migrants find themselves in is marked both by the presence of co-ethnics engaged in similar economic activities and by huge cultural diversity, which they encounter on the streets, on public transport, in shops, and at work. In interviews with Polish migrants, the London urban jungle is described often as a culture shock—a place which is 'not England', since the latter is associated more with whiteness and middle-class status. Unsurprisingly, when Poles are asked what social divisions they see in London, they emphasise cultural differences, and by 'cultural',- they mean mainly racial differences between 'black' and 'white' people. This attitude has many nuances and shades, but again, we must stress the relational way in which differences are perceived and how those differences are produced and revitalised though people's cultural assumptions and the local context of London's urban environment.

By emphasising the black and white division, Polish migrants very often use a very simplistic division of the social world they encounter on an everyday basis. 'Diversity' or 'multiculturalism' does not mean for them the presence of French, Americans, or Spaniards, but those who are phenotypically 'black' and hence automatically neither British nor English. It should be noted that Poles rarely use the notion of 'Britishness' and *Anglik* (English) is understood in purely ethnic terms. With exceptions, Poles would never regard as *Anglik* a Gujarati who was born in London and speaks impeccable English.

The racial marking of people from the Indian sub-continent as *ciapaty* also refers to skin colour and is seen as essentially non-British. This phenotypical marking is often totally monochromatic, since many Poles interviewed on various occasions, would not distinguish between a black person from Africa and third-generation descendants of an African-Caribbean migrant. For some respondents, being alien is unchangeable—aliens are not from *here* and *here* refers to a generalised European space or European culture. For example, Maciej, who has lived in London for almost 10 years, has strong views on this and is not bothered by factual inaccuracies:

> A: … we need to see that 68% of population in London are people of colour, and the majority of them are black living in council flats [and] are making that model [multiculturalism] look differently despite that there are people who work and earn …
>
> Q: […] So you think that multiculturalism is working? …
>
> A: The British government has enough of it …they tell it officially … because, as I said, 68% are people of colour ….
>
> Q: … .eh … is it not just some boroughs?
>
> A: No, well maybe, you have some statistics but… you know whatever paper like Metro I find I read so I see … but because lot of people are leaving [Britain], the arrow is up …
>
> Q: Even though some of these people are here for three or more generations?
>
> A: Listen, this is a global problem, and if they are here three or five generations it does not matter because, despite all, a black is a black and for me he will always be black and … they are able to use the fact that they are black … Always when something economically will not work this problem will come out … It is an aggression in the waiting … Like in Yugoslavia, nothing happens for some time and then … if there would be a problem with fuel or money … So this [multiculturalism] functions on a bit of superficial level … At the end I do not know really what these English are thinking but I think they have a problem with that … that there are too many coloured people.

Damian, the builder from Sokółka, arrived in 2004 and also sees the divisions along racial lines:

> when the influx of immigrants would be on that scale, people would get used to it. Like here it was slowly here, but if it was to happen suddenly it would be different … this happens … I think that's why this is a divided society we have the English, Asians, blacks and the rest.

Implicit in these and many other remarks is also the fact that despite all meritocratic dream of having finally ones' skills and aspirations recognised, there are strong divisions and inequalities in Britain; that despite the cherished story that 'you can make it here', there are some who clearly do not, or who are perceived as not being able to pick up the opportunities London offers. If they cannot, this means that there is something wrong with them, rather than social divisions and — well known from Poland — informal and class-based ceilings, which separate people between the elite and the poor. Being 'black', then, is not only about racialised positioning but a stigmatising specific position in social hierarchy. A well established and often repeated in Polish literature, press reports, web forums, and everyday discourse notion of describing Poles as *biały Murzyn* — 'white blacks' — is strongly indicative. Being 'white blacks' means predominantly doing a heavy, degrading, and low-paid job. It means not sharing the privileges of the white dominant group. This expression is not a Polish invention since it was also used against the Irish in the USA during the 19th century, but it reveals how social class is racialised in everyday discourse.

It is sometimes explained — by both Poles and British — that the racial lenses through which people view social divisions in London come from a dominant construction of Polish society as a relatively homogenous ethnically.[312] Although this is surely part of the explanation, it does not reflect the fact that many Polish migrants interviewed in London are in a place which has a particular history of immigration and ethnic diversity, and this affects peoples' perception of whiteness and race. In order to understand what people mean by stressing some attitudes towards diversity and multiculturalism, we need to weigh both the Polish and British contexts and interpret how individuals position themselves in a complex hierarchy of groups.

When confronted directly and asked what they thought about London's diversity, over a half of my respondents from the ESRC study expressed positive views, aligning describing London as the 'school of life'. For many, especially young students and those from urban areas, London's character as a 'world in a city' added to their everyday education of survival in London. Many spoke with pleasure about the people they had met from all the

---

[312]   L. Ryan, D'Angelo A. 2011. Sites of socialisation — Polish parents and children in London schools. *Przegląd Polonijny*. Rok XXXVII z. 1/2011.

continents, their experience of difference, and the thrill of the ethnic and cultural cosmopolitan bazaar in certain London areas marked by restaurants, festivals, music, and shops. This everyday enthusiastic approach to diversity is, of course, much more nuanced than the black/white division described earlier and arises from both everyday encounters and the realisation that diversity is more complex than this simplistic division.

So, the views of Poles could be seen as ranging from strongly cosmopolitan, enthusiastic, and carefully nuanced to covertly or explicitly racist. The former stressed more the numerous and complex mosaic of cultures, lifestyles, and ethnic groups, the latter would focus on a totalising dichotomous picture of 'us' whites, Europeans and 'them' *kolorowi, czarni* [blacks] non-Europeans. It is difficult to state the percentage in each group, since people's views on diversity are not so clear cut and people do contradict themselves. However, in general, younger people with education and English skills were far more cosmopolitan than those who were less educated and came from more rural backgrounds. Even so, one can also find some middle-class, aspiring, and educated person from an urban area who will elaborately explain that England is 'going to the dogs' due to accepting so many *kolorowi* and that Poland's main asset is its whiteness. I also encountered people from rural Poland, who demonstrated high levels of tolerance and curiosity towards other cultures.

The issue of racialisation and hostility towards people of different skin colour came out also very strongly in our local surveys for the London boroughs of Redbridge and Lewisham. Here Polish respondents made explicit, negative remarks about racial diversity, particularly about the presence of black people. Some were expressed in clearly derogatory terms, while others were thinly disguised, such as references to the area being 'too diverse' or that there are 'too many cultures'. What is important is that these responses were given to an open-ended question about likes and dislikes in the local area. Around 16% of Polish respondents in Lewisham and 15% in Redbridge expressed such views as '*too*

*many of them here; really it's like Africa; what the fuck they're here ...
too many of them blacks here; yes, blacks this is a problem'* (notes from
fieldwork in Lewisham).

Any sweeping generalisation about the causes of such attitudes (whether identified *there* in Poland or *here* in UK) often
masks the fact that some respondents during an interview were
making racist comments and at the same time felt comfortable
with dealing with diversity on an everyday basis. This practical
orientation and treatment of a multicultural environment as lived
practice, acquired in a global city, is expressed in the frequently
heard phrase: 'one can get used to it'. This pragmatic approach
contrasts strongly with sometimes overtly racist remarks. Maciej,
for example, confirmed that he has plenty of Hindu and black
customers, whom he respects. Asked also whether he would ob-
ject if his child would go out with someone of different colour, he
said no, although added that 'races should be kept separate'.
Hence, it is perfectly conceivable for people to discursively delineate clear boundaries and at the same communicate across them.
As Frederic Barth would argue, this is *precisely* what makes cultures, ethnic groups, and identities happen in everyday interaction; the boundaries, which people make, are meaningful only
when there is someone else on the other side.

The examples of everyday multiculturalism as practice are
numerous. The behaviour of those belonging to the network of
cigarettes sellers described in Chapter 5 are good examples of the
apparent contradictions between what is accepted within their
peer group with regard to others and actual behaviour. Hanging
around with them was quite monotonous, since they were making
racist comments almost non-stop. Yet, this did not stop them from
discussing at length the price of cannabis with their black neigh-
bour or exchanging hip-hop style comments with a group of black
teenagers on the same street. Furthermore, their business relied
heavily on support from newsagents, who were almost exclusive-
ly South Asian. Mutual cooperation in an illicit activity between
these Polish migrants and South Asian shopkeepers required con-

siderable mutual trust and an acceptance of the rules of interaction. Shopkeepers needed to learn a few words in Polish, and Poles were often referring to them as '*ciapaty*, but all right really'. In these interactions, race, colour, ethnicity, and religion does not play any part. The behaviour and sometimes aggressive comments from this group of young, working-class Poles, loaded with masculine uncertainty and an ambition to mark their immediate space around them, was actually directed towards Polish elites rather than the racialised other, who happened to be a companion in illicit business transaction or simply was sharing a joint of cannabis.

Moreover, contrary to the aforementioned stereotypes and the generalisations, the 'one can get used' to approach was very often encountered among people with secondary or vocational education, from small rural areas. Adam, the *stork*, has these words to describe his attitudes towards multicultural diversity, when asked whether he liked it:

> A: *Neither … I don't feel neither sympathy neither dislike … it's ok … I can live with that … These are people, humans, so they can be here … so what?*
>
> Q: *So that diversity is working well here?*
>
> A: *Oh yes, I think it works … Everybody has its religion, Hindus or others … they have their things and nobody sticks their noses in their affairs … It's very good that.*

This mundane, down-to-earth, demotic multiculturalism is a pragmatic one dwelling on personal, intimate experience, as the last few words from the above-mentioned comment show. Adam, as we recall, is a migrant who understands well the restrictive and unjust system of immigration control and barriers migrants had before the EU enlargement and he knows what it means not to be allowed to *be here*. He links his views to *being* here and to have the right to do so. It means that others — whoever they may be — may have a legitimate moral reason as well to be here, not because they have specific traits, come from a specific country, or have a particular cultural background but because they are human beings who, like Adam, seek to better themselves and their families.

This attitude towards what we call 'diversity' varies, since people's experiences were extremely diverse. Women generally commented more positively on this diversity than men, but often complained about attitudes of Asian or Turkish men towards them and sexist remarks from Asian employers. Lucyna, a young aspiring woman in her early 30s, who came from Warsaw, comments that she had been anti-racist in Poland but began to have doubts once in London and now understands that the issue is very complex. Julia, in her 20s, says that she dislikes the attitude of black teenagers and is afraid to go at dark. Another person complains about the Roma, while yet another thinks that he likes the cosmopolitan atmosphere, except the presence of Muslims. While simplistic, these comments are often combined with an overall acceptance of diversity and the realisation that they are also a part of it. After all, the presence of people from all over the world, for a migrant, is often seen as validating their cherished meritocratic myth and living proof that 'anyone can make it here, if they could, they I can'.

This proof is also a double-edged sword since, if for some reason, someone does not 'make it', then it is easy to find who to blame. Some of the most overtly racist comments come from people who have not fulfilled their dreams and are full of regret, resentment, and looking for a scapegoat. It is not surprising that among the homeless, gangs are formed along strict national code and conversations with homeless or unemployed Poles, conducted for various projects, are littered with arguments along the line: *'They [the English, government, establishment] all help black; fucking English, they won't help us'*. A typical reaction/comment is usually made with reference to the fact that the Polish Centre employs security guards, who happen to be black.[313] Here the animosity and criticism of the established Poles (see next chapter), combine

---

[313] Informally, some officials of the Centre admitted to me once that this is an informal policy that seeks to prevent the security guards from becoming too friendly with 'some undesirable element', that is, Poles who would take advantage of their connections with the guards at this important centre for Polish community life.

with racist views, to give an explosive reaction, such as the following quotation from an unemployed man in his 40s: *'Yes, they fucking employ these czarnuchy* [blacks], *instead of us. What kind of solidarity this is? We are unemployed and they take some of that scum'*.

As we have argued, this black versus white perception of diversity reflects something deeper, something directly connected to social class and hierarchy in the British context. During interviews, we were careful not to impose any views but it became clear that referring to 'blackness' equated with diversity for some respondents, usually those not keen on enthusiastically endorsing London's cosmopolitanism. In other words, by talking of 'blacks' in broad terms, they identify themselves as whites and, thereby, closer to the dominant English group.

The following exchange with Arek, an engineer and long-term migrant, who came during the mid-1990s and now runs a construction company, shows how this is done.

> Q: So you think Poles are treated better than immigrants from other parts of the world?
>
> A: Yes, because we assimilate very quickly. Because we are white migrants and people come here to achieve something…
>
> Q: You mean that skin colour helps?
>
> A: Oh yes definitely yes …Between Poland and UK there never was a conflict …there is always a positive story … because there are so many times when Poles did something good for the English… It is rather the British who have a problem with us, with who killed Sikorski[314], with the absence of Polish troops on Victory Parade in 1946[315] … They have moral problems with us, not the other way round … At one party I met Prince Philip and told him: 'I am from Poland' and he said straight away: 'Oh, how great!' And he said that he was there and there … very nice.

---

[314] An ongoing issue related to the circumstances of the death of Gen. Wladyskaw Sikorski, who was killed in a plane crash in Gibraltar in 1943. One version (largely dismissed by historians, but popular nevertheless) blames the involvement of the British in the crash, possibly with the help the Soviet KGB.

[315] A reference to the absence of Polish Armed Forces during the victory parade in 1946. In fact, many Poles in Britain did not participate, because they did not see the end of the Second World War as a victory at all.

From race, assimilation concept, and the notion of the history debt, which Britain owes Poland, Arek moves straight on talk about class and Prince Philip as a stereotypical Englishman (not many Poles actually know, that he is of German descent and born in Greece) in order to show that the relations between the English and Poles is of qualitatively different character than the one between Britain and those with whom there was a conflict, or lack of 'positive story'.

This physical affinity between a Polish owner of a construction company (a migrant, who is proud of 'making it' by grasping the opportunities Britain offers) and a member of the British monarchy involves, then, both class transgression and the symbolically laden association of whiteness as a binding principle. In another exchange, it becomes clearer that what Prince Philip cannot overtly express, many English families do towards their Polish employees, and it is precisely this support for their prejudices, which renders being 'white' or 'European' meaningful and, more importantly, resourceful. A young female, who works as domestic help, comments:

> A: Here, what I observed is that [surprise in her voice] *they talk about Poles in good terms.*
>
> Q: And you were surprised by that?
>
> A: Yes, because there are so many nationalities here but it is about the Poles that they [the British] say good things about…
>
> Q: And about other nationalities what do they say?
>
> A: About other nationalities … hmmm … where I work, in that English family, these people do not tolerate the Hindus. They say that there are far too many of them … and that they own this country, that England belongs to them and they are pissed off that there are so many of them.
>
> Q: And what do you think about this?
>
> A: I think partly this is true because wherever you look around you see the Hindus … I didn't expect that there are so many of them here … because there are too many of them ….

Her friend, working also as domestic help, supports this view:

Q: And knowing some English, what do you think they think about it [multiculturalism]*?*

A: They hate them, they just hate them. Where I work there aren't many Hindus so they are very happy ...

Q: Where?

A: Kingston, Richmond ... it is very rare to meet a Hindu, and they [the English] *are very happy that there are no Hindus there ... in offices or anywhere ... They tolerate the blacks, but not Hindus.*

Q: So it is an advantage for Poles that they are white?

A: Yes it is ... to be a white person is a plus here.

A young, educated journalist, who previously expressed a very positive attitude towards ethnic diversity, reflects at the same time:

Q: You mentioned something interesting that it's an advantage for Poles of being white ...

A: Yes because that's how it's here ...

Q: ...how do you know this? You experienced it from the English?

A: No, not that it comes from the English ... you just know it ... you don't talk about it but you know it ... Of course, the English law is that in every place there should be that amount of blacks and others but it's always harder for blacks ....

Anna, whose migration was facilitated by an English couple whom she met in her hometown, also reflects on this, was sad that this view entrenches racial divisions which she despises:

Q: You told me about divisions in Poland. And in London?

A: Yes, London ... racial divisions ... yes ... two months living with [names of the English couple]*... they are very tolerant people and they accept a lot ... but in some way they do not accept the influx of other races ... Or I mean — maybe I put it another way — they have this feeling ... both* [are] *over 60 ... they do remember London when it was ... white ... clean ... peaceful ... Now London isn't like that any more. Neither white or clean ... due to the influx of others ... It's not that they are racists but ... they are more hostile towards a black villain than a white one ... you know? ... It is, I think, very common ... better ours than theirs ... better our own drunkard than someone else's ... Yes, I think it does matter* [being white] *... We are made from the* *same ... white flour ... It isn't only in UK like that ... it's all over the world ... that a white feels himself more secure with a white and a black with a black ... It's a pity really ... Depends which group* [of British society] *also... ... I try to generalise, of course, that's what you ask no?*

Another example comes from a typical member of *intelligentsia* who, after studying history in Kraków, works as a forklift driver in Heathrow. As it happens, during his employment period, a strike broke out involving mainly Indian staff from one of the catering companies. The respondent made clearly racist comments and then notes that he simply learned from talking to English colleagues that ethnic diversity is something socially negative and that one of Poland's main assets is its homogeneity and 'whiteness':

A: I think that Poland has better prospects than the UK.

Q: Why?

A: We don't have to make the same mistakes that UK did in regards to ... how I should put it ... I am talking ethnic policy here ... It is already a huge problem for the UK and probably there will be situations like that one in Paris now [interview taken during the Paris riots in November 2006] *... This is where it is leading to ...*

These English I work for are aware of this, but they are 'grounded' [as immobile, cannot do anything about it] *because of all that political correctness and they talk about on the level of a joke, but on one stage I can feel a pressure to be silent on that issue ... for them it is unacceptable that their streets where they were brought up are now literary black — because that is how it should be called. They are pissed off that every shops belongs to some... that in a bank and everywhere they need to meet ... because, let's not fool ourselves, these are not English higher spheres, they earn not much more than me, they use the same services but they are in their own country. So for them these things may be irritating... like the accent, for example ... These may sound nationalistic but I agree with all that ... Generally, I think that because the society starts to radicalise itself and going towards these movements like in Netherlands ... I think this is only a matter of time when these national movements will appear in the UK.*

Q:... well they are not here ...

We can speak about a conspiracy here ... but if the media didn't so viciously attack these movements, they would appear very quickly. But the question is that will some services [he means secret services] *allow that. I think that mentally the English would like that to happen, they do not like it* [the diversity]. *I mean the white English … And it is not only the question of the elites that work here, but finally they are starting to understand that they are being fooled, that these immigrants are coming here get the money and do not work … I encounter that in my work … They tell me that I am not a problem for them, I pay taxes.*

Although clearly politically charged and to some observers, strange (this particular interviewee has some specific conspiracy theories, referring to the role of the secret services), these views are not rare among a segment of young, educated Poles. Yet, these similar stories and reflections point to something more — to the fact, that whiteness is constructed in a mutual interplay between what Poles think of themselves and what the British dominant group would like to think of them.

We need to be careful not to overgeneralise, since the 'dominant group' is, by definition, a fuzzy set. However, we need to bear in mind what sometimes hides beneath the often heard enthusiasm towards Polish migrants expressed publicly, especially in some media leaning towards the political right. For instance, Anthony Browne writes in *The Spectator*: 'The New Europeans are hard-working, <u>presentable</u>, well educated, and integrate so <u>perfectly</u> that they will <u>disappear</u> within a generation'[316] (emphasis added). Clearly, 'disappearing' means not only integrating but also becoming less visible, having a less observable, and 'sticking out' appearance. Similarly, one of the most vocal opponents of immigration, who strongly opposed the opening of the labour market for Poles and other Accession States, Sir Andrew Green, after a while changed his mind and pointed his finger elsewhere: '*We have no problem with immigration from Poland, which is valuable to all sides …. The government must make a reduction in numbers from elsewhere. What they could do is reduce the number of work permits for*

---

[316] A. Browne. 2006. *The Spectator 2006.* http://www.spectator.co.uk/2006/01/invasion-of-the-new-europeans/

264 London's Polish Borders

the rest of the world' (Sir Andrew Green, Migrationwatch; BBC Today).[317]

This exclusionist and sometimes covertly racist view, which
often saw Poles as having a 'similar culture' to the British, is difficult to detect in public debate, given people's anxiety about the
implications and effects of political correctness. Furthermore, not
all the views, which prize Poles *en masse*, have this meaning. Yet,
the possibility that Polish workers may be welcomed encourages
not only the migrants to see this as a resource. During talks and
casual conversations with people in positions of power, such as
Embassy officials, ethnic leaders, journalists, and politicians, the
theme of Poles being 'naturally' better workers and exemplary
migrants than (non-defined) others is fairly common. It also affects the vocabulary. One prominent member of a Polish community organisation, a second-generation Pole, advised young journalists at the Polish Daily not to refer to Poles as an 'ethnic community', because it puts us on the same level as 'Hindus' and
'blacks'.[318] A young Polish activist, who champions the case of
underprivileged and homeless migrants, and who strongly criticises Poles for their racism, reflects:

> *Sorry, this will be terrible ... I heard once how someone very well educated,*
> *someone important ... an English* [person] *... said that the English are more*
> *keen to accept Polish than blacks coming here ... so we are a step above ...*
> *Maybe I shouldn't say this ... but this is important* [being white].

Being 'a step above' speaks volumes, and in this context, our argument is clear. Racist as some of these comments and perceptions may be, they do not emerge from a social void, the assumed
homogeneity of Polish society or the taken for granted assumption
that Poles are intolerant due to their history and struggle for na-

---

[317] Sir Andrew Green, Migrationwatch; BBC Today. See: http://www.theguardia
n.com/uk/2005/nov/04/immigration.immigrationandpublicservices

[318] Quoted also in: M. Garapich. 2008. Odyssean refugees, migrants and power:
construction of the 'other' within the Polish community in the UK. [in]: D.
Reed-Danahay, C. Brettell (red.) *Citizenship, Political Engagement and Belonging.*
Immigrants in Europe and the United States. New Brunswick/New Jer-
sey/London: Rutgers University Press, pp. 124–144.

tional identity, that they are nationalist 'by nature'. Racism, through the emergence of whiteness as a social class marker, is constructed relationally in response to what the dominant group, or people in positions of power say — British, second-generation Polish Brits — about the newcomers in the continually made and remade hierarchy of ethnic groups and their political representatives. Being white equates in many Polish eyes with what Poles are aspiring for — middle-class life styles, being independent, self-reliant, and individualistic — and these social and cultural features are dominated by the white English. In a recent study, undertaken before the London mayoral elections, similar attitude was also quite significant. During focus groups among Poles based in London, the issue of race was clearly conflated with masculinity, youth, and welfare dependency.[319] Whiteness and Englishness was seen by most participants as markers of middle class, achievement, and power — hence the most popular candidate among this small sample of Polish Londoners was Boris Johnson.

It should be noted here that one group of migrants from Poland stands rather differently on this issue — that is, the Polish Roma, their different trajectory described in Chapter 4. In several interviews with the Roma, the fascinating insight was that their perception of London diversity stems from their experience of racism in Poland, and there was no doubt where they feel better.

> *This is how things should be, this tolerance and friendliness ... London is just paradise, I mean no one points fingers at me ....*

This Polish Roma person has a particular telling comment, which in a way shows also how racial hierarchies in the UK are perceived:

> *In Poland I was black ... here I am white ...*

---

[319] S. Driver, M. Garapich. 2012. 'Everyone for themselves'? Non-national EU citizens from eastern and central Europe and the 2012 London elections. http://www.sociology.ox.ac.uk/documents/epop/papers/EPOP_article_garapichdriver_SEPTEMBER_07_mg.pdf

Polish Roma, with their distinct migration networks, social capital,[320] and institutional setting, with a highly effective and well-established centre in Newham (Roma Support Group), are probably the ones benefiting most from diverse cultural and ethnic environment of London. They face other important barriers, due to discrimination on labour market but, overall, are a group of migrants from Poland that demonstrate how difficult it is to generalise. Their new relationships with ethnic Polish migrants show, however, that they are able to change the unequal power dynamics.

To recapitulate the argument: Since ethnicity is a set of relational features rather than 'natural' objective characteristic,[321] its dynamics change when the environment changes. That relational individualised ethnicity directed more towards inwards and co-ethnics than outwards acquires different meanings and value when confronted with different 'others'. In the multicultural London environment, Polish migrants reconstruct their ethnic identity on the backdrop of a plethora of never seen before ethnicities, cultures, and lifestyles at the same time being strongly immersed within Polish ethnic networks. With two effects: one is related to their contestation of ethnicity as horizontal bond which carries with itself a set of specific moral obligations; this contestation takes form of a myth, a specific narrative so distinct that it has been noted by numerous studies, but so far, no one has showed its cultural significance and explained, why it is so important for Polish migrants to express distrust towards their co-ethnics. The second is a realisation of whiteness as a class marker. As in the case of the Irish and other migrants groups in the USA,[322] Poles 'become' whites in their own eyes as they move to a more diverse environment since, in their perception, it moves them closer in the hierarchy of groups towards the top—which are the white Eng-

---

[320]   T. Staniewicz. 2011. Negotiating space and contesting boundaries. The case of Polish Roma and Polish migrants. *Przegląd Polonijny* Rok XXXVII z. 1/2011.

[321]   F. Barth. 1969. *Ethnic Groups and Boundaries*. Oslo; R. Jenkins. 1997. *Rethinking Ethnicity*. London: George Allen and Unwin.

[322]   A. Hartman. 2004. The rise and fall of whiteness studies. *Race Class* 46(2):22–38.

lish, middle and upper classes. As I showed earlier, Polish migrants do get a positive feedback legitimising their prejudices. They also realise that whiteness has become a key feature in the racialisation of ethnic difference. Poles can 'become' white' and move up the racialised ethnic hierarchy towards the white English, middle class. According to these Polish migrants, this is a move which many white English people are happy to endorse together with their hostility towards black and Asian citizens, however ambiguously expressed.

Chapter 7

Making *Polonia*. Power, elites, and the hierarchy of belonging

In April 2014, a Polish organisation called Polish Professionals in London, organised a meeting with several key figures in London's Polish diaspora, along with some British politicians with Polish roots or connections — Daniel Kawczyński, MP, Stefan Kasprzyk, a Lib Dem councillor in North London, and many others. The meeting in the Atthlee Suite next to Westminster was entitled 'UK, EU and the Polish Question', and the room was packed with young people. The local elections were just around the corner; so, clearly the occasion was to raise the often discussed issue whether Poles — so numerous now in the capital — can make any political impact. Speeches were made, questions asked, and every speaker was eager to emphasise how Poles 'are well integrated' into British society, how much they contribute, and, essentially, how welcomed they should be. It was striking that every speech began with reference to the post-1945 generation of emigrants, and everyone was eager to infuse a sense of continuity rather than rapture between war veterans who spent their last 60 years in the UK and young Poles, IT, bankers, professionals who were glad to hang around the Westminster. At one stage, a young Polish activist thanked publicly one of the present war veterans, a participant in the Warsaw Uprising, by stressing that Europe and free world would not exist without her, and that all subsequent emigrants owe her and people like her the fact that they can move around Europe freely. So if there were strong emphasis on 'togetherness' and ethnic unity across generations, this 'oneness' was vertical, not horizontal. It was almost as a group have suddenly bowed to a symbolic figure that defines their identity. And although the meeting was about Polish migrants and coming European elections, one could sense that this embodied symbol — a frail old lady — is being put to the front as a unifier, one of very few symbols that links very different groups of Poles.

As Mary Erdmans notes: '*we perceive the distance between groups as being greater than the distance within groups and 'this epistemological tendency, causes us to overlook heterogeneity within groups and dismiss internal borders*'.[323] It is crucial to overcome this tendency, the 'ethnic lens' as Glick Schiller calls it and see through the codes of difference and commonality that are being produced by those, who control the sources of symbolic capital within a particular group. Groups are made through discursive reification of its boundaries, and, as Gerd Baumann notes, part of that discourse has been the feature of contemporary 'formal' British multiculturalism that sustain and perpetuate difference and boundaries[324] 'between groups' not within. But what if these 'within' are in fact fundamental to group identity?

Recent migration from Poland provides us with the opportunity to observe the 'in-house' dynamic relationships between the groups of Polish emigrants, produced by different periods of settlement, generation, social class, lifestyle, and culture. In this chapter, we look beneath the surface of group representation in public discourse and explore what and why certain things are being done, said, and emphasised. In this way, we can see how power relations shape the politics of ethnic representation and how those relations relate to the wider socio-cultural context of London during the first decade of the 21st century. In particular, I will examine the impact which recent migrant flows have made on the established structure of British Polish institutions and what is involved in the interaction between people, who share some traits, symbols, concepts but not others, what aspects of ethnic identity are performed, and to what audience. The case of Polish London shows complex constant adjustments of various groups

---

[323] M.P. Erdmans. 1998. *Opposite Poles. Immigrants and Ethnics in Polish Chicago, 1976-1990.* Philadelphia: The Pennsylvania State University Press, p 7.

[324] See G. Baumann. 1996. *Contesting Culture. Discourses of Identity in Multi-Ethnic London.* Cambridge: Cambridge University Press

and institutional structures struggling for power to speak on behalf of the wider whole. Sometimes this struggle turns ugly, sometimes public, and these moments are particularly interesting from ethnographic perspective as they remind us how ethnicity is relationally constructed not in isolation but with reference to class and gender.

The history of Polish migration to Britain is very often interpreted by a simplistic schema of consecutive waves: the postwar *emigracja*, the Solidarity dissidents of the 1980s, and the post-1989 'economic migrants'.[325] As I have shown in previous chapters, on closer inspection, all these groups are closely interconnected, merge into one another, and often occupy a similar social niche. Most crucially, they also symbolically and politically relate to one another for their own purposes using tested tools.

This is not a new observation but I would like to develop this alternative view further. Both Sheila Patterson and Kathy Burrell note,[326] for instance, that, although the Second World War refugees and their leaders rejected the Warsaw regime and were hostile to anything that originated from Communist Poland, they still maintained close contact with their kin through frequent visits, sending parcels, and inviting them to come and stay in Britain. Furthermore, a strong gender imbalance in the early years of Polish settlement in Britain meant that there was a constant flow of women to Britain from Poland and elsewhere. As Keith Sword shows, in the 1991 census, a third of people born in Poland came from waves of migration after the 1950s.[327] Furthermore, many of my interviewees from post-Accession waves had built migratory

---

[325] This division is explicitly held by K. Sword and P. Stachura and is accepted as a valid one in academic literature.

[326] K. Burrell. 2003. Small-scale transnationalism: homeland connections and the Polish 'community' in Leicester'. *International Journal of Population Geography* 9(4):323–335; S. Patterson. 1964. Polish London. [in]: Ruth Glass (ed.) *London: Aspects of Change*. London: University College, p. 338. Also, C. Bogdan, B. Sulik. 1961. *Polacy w Wielkiej Brytanii*. Paryż: Instytut Literacki, recorded the numbers of Poles visiting Poland when the social ban on doing so was strongest.

[327] K. Sword. 1996. *Identity in flux. Polish community in Great Britain*. London: SSEES UCL, p. 81–82.

networks using their kin, friends, or family from previous waves, including the Second World War refugees. The famous town of Sokółka, which I described in earlier chapters, has proved to be so rich in migratory social capital precisely because migrants from there were able to use their connections with families staying on in Britain after the end of the Second World War and also later migrants, who came during the early 1980s.

So, what are popularly, politically, and academically[328] seen as three separate and detached groups — as the young activist mentioned earlier was eager to stress — are, in fact, specific localised social constructions that obscure the dense mutual transnational networks, which members of these groups maintained from the 1950s onwards. So, it is crucial to examine that insistence on the separateness of these groups since it is clear that members of the first cohort *see* themselves as totally different from other migrants, and this perception rests on important cultural meanings woven through Polish culture establishing and legitimising important relationships of power between the state and its citizens. I would like to explain why this is so, especially why these distinctions are maintained with such vigour despite the declining numbers of first-generation *émigrés,* or in fact their actual absence, as most of them are by now deceased. I argue that the discourse of detached groups will survive its original producers, because it supports a specific power relations structure shaping relations between the established and newcomers, supporting a specific nationalist and exclusionist discourse of 'right Poles' who retain 'true' and 'patriotic values'.[329] As Gupta and Ferguson note:

> The presumption that spaces are autonomous has enabled the power of topography to conceal the topography of power. ... For if one begins with the premise that spaces have always been hierarchically interconnected, instead of naturally disconnected, then cultural and social change becomes not a matter of

---

328   From English literature see, for instance, Stachura (2000) and Sword (1991); from Polish: Habielski (1999); Friszke (1999); Topolska (1999); Radzik (2001); etc.

329   See, for instance, N. Elias, J.L. Scotson. 1994. *The Established and the Outsiders — A Sociological Enquiry into Community Problems.* London: Sage.

cultural contact and articulation but one of rethinking difference through connection.[330]

Hence, the concepts of *emigracja, Polonia,* and *zarobkowi* (another description of an economic migrant) are social constructions used relationally to present *political* and *economic* migrants as opposing one another and by attaching an implicit moral value to each in order to construct a specific hierarchy of power and legitimise ones' claims to leadership positions. These binary oppositions define an individual's relation to the collective and the state. It justifies a specific field of power and does not necessarily accord with the reality of people's individual motivations for migrating. As we know, these motivations are a complex set of factors and the degree of autonomy, which individuals have over their decision to migrate, settle, return, migrate further, or move back and forth is a frequent theme in the literature on migration, illustrating the much deeper dilemma of agency and structure. As I have shown, the existence of diverse and distinct groups of identities within the Polish ethnic group—especially in recent years—is not principally the result of objective processes and migratory histories but rather the outcome of local struggles for power, specifically through claims to represent the entire group and maintaining hierarchy at the same time. In other words, *political* emigrants are not political because they pursue a specific political objective but because, in Polish traditional dominant discourse on emigration— as we described in Chapter 2—being *political* guarantees a higher social position within the local hierarchy of an ethnic community and in relation to the state.

This is not to deny that differences exist between, for example, a Second World War refugee whose almost entire adult life was spent in Britain, whose children are British citizens, and whose political loyalty is much more firmly attached to the British than the Polish state, and a working-class builder from an impoverished town in eastern Poland whose entire life was spent under

---

[330] A. Gupta, J. Ferguson. 1992. Beyond culture: space, identity and politics of difference. Cultural Anthropology 7(1):35.

Communism and then in the tough and difficult years of economic transformation. The focus will be rather on how these differences within the Polish ethnic group in Britain are maintained,
reproduced, and legitimised by individuals in London and how
recent migration flows have affected these infra-political[331] and
backstage power relations between people from different cohorts,
generations, and backgrounds. In other words, why and for what
purpose differences and similarities are emphasised in one context
or brushed aside in another.

This approach helps us understand how 'groups are being
made and constructed' especially in post-'7/7' Britain and how
multicultural dominant discourses continually reinvents itself.
Through the exploration of different ways in which Polish nationals relate to each other, negotiate their power positions, and use
specific symbols, myths, and rituals to maintain commonality and
difference, we learn a great deal about what processes are involved in the construction of ethnicity in everyday life in London
more generally. Ethnic 'communities' are not isolated from what is
going on around them and the public discourses that shapes their
understanding of social structure, hierarchy, and access to power.

As Eriksen observes, ethnicity is an 'aspect of the social relationship between agents who consider themselves as culturally
distinctive from members of other groups',[332] so it is something
people *do*, rather than something people *have*. He further states
that this social relationship entails 'both aspects of gain and loss in
interaction, and to aspects of meaning in the creation of identity'.[333] The relationship has, therefore, symbolic and political consequences, by shaping ways people organise themselves and
achieve collective agreement or agency in a given context. In the
particular circumstances of a multicultural urban context of London, which is caught between the liberal notion of civic integra-

---

[331] J. Scott. 1990. *Domination and the Art of Resistance: Hidden Transcripts*. New
       Haven: Yale University Press.
[332] T.H. Eriksen. 1993. *Ethnicity and Nationalism: Anthropological Perspectives*. Lon-
       don: Pluto Press, p. 12.
[333] T.H. Eriksen. 1993. *Ibidem*, p 12.

tion and the recognition of difference,[334] ethnicity becomes a political resource and is interlocked with issues of power struggle between specific individuals over the control of group representation and the group's agenda. In particular, legitimacy of that power becomes a locus of increasing importance. This in turn, results in cultural meanings being reinvented and redefined in order to suit immediate political purposes. In these meaning constructions, in our Polish case, class in never far away, in fact as I will demonstrate, various cultural performances of class identity is the implicit element in Polish debates over migration and diaspora.

A key, *emic*,[335] notion of *Polonia* is crucial here. In everyday speech, political statements, and academic discourse, it denotes broadly Polish communities living abroad. Despite its popularity its meanings and assumptions are rarely looked at closely and unpacked. This notion defines spatial and temporal dimensions of migration in Polish culture through its symbolic power and associated meanings. The existence of a specific term describing co-nationals living abroad is a common theme among cultures with strong migration traditions—the Jewish Diaspora, the 10th Department of Haitians,[336] and many others. What makes the concept of *Polonia* particular is not only its state-centric and nationalistic assumptions but also its strong temporal and spatial meanings. Historically, this notion was formed during the settlement of Polish emigrants in the USA at the turn of the 19th century and described communities of rural and working-class folk.[337] It gained popularity after Poland became independent in 1918 when the new state increasingly recognised the potential value of its co-ethnics abroad for its foreign policy. In an extreme case, members

---

[334] C. Joppke. 2004. The retreat of multiculturalism in the liberal state: theory and policy. *The British Journal of Sociology* 55(2):237–258.

[335] By *emic*, we refer to the 'native' point of view, a term laden with specific meanings but with little analytical value.

[336] L. Basch, N. Glick Schiller, C.S. Blanc. 1994. *Nations Unbound: Transnational Projects, Postcolonial Predicaments, and Deterritorialized Nation-States*. Langhorne: Gordon and Breach.

[337] M. Cygan. 1998. Inventing Polonia: notions of Polish American identity, 1870-1990'. *Prospects* 23:209–246; K. Paluch Andrzej. 1976. Inkluzywne i ekskluzywne rozumienie terminu 'Polonia'. *Przegląd Polonijny* 2: 37–48.

of the *Polonia* in South America were regarded as potential colonisers, who could help Poland to gain its own territories abroad.[338] The notion has undergone considerable evolution in its meanings,[339] and although used in descriptive ways, it is in fact a complex symbolic term where self-identity and ascription are negotiated in the face of changing social and economic changes. Its multiple meanings and strong symbolic resonance, as well as the ways by which social actors contain mobility, migration, and settlement, turns it into valuable source of symbolic capital.

I use here Pierre Bourdieu's concept of symbolic capital, since it emphasises the ways in which meanings and distinctions are shaped and maintained by conflicts and power. His approach shows how social positions and the division of economic, cultural, and social resources (capitals), in general, are legitimised with the help of symbolic capital. Social capital, for example, acquires its *symbolic character* and is transformed into symbolic capital through mutual cognition and recognition.[340] In other words, symbolic capital exists only in the 'eyes of others' as its renders specific distinctions and social differences inevitable. In his words:

> *Symbolic capital ... is nothing other than capital, in whatever form, when perceived by an agent endowed with categories of perception arising from the internalization (embodiment) of the structure of its distribution, i.e. when it is known and recognized as self-evident.[341]*

As symbolic capital, distinctions are 'the product of the internalization of the structures to which they are applied'.[342] In this way, the distinctions defining different migratory experiences are a form of symbolic capital.

The notion of *Polonia* draws its symbolic power from the past—from the specific traditions constructed around the sacral-

---

[338] M. Kicinger. 2005. *Polityka emigracyjna II Rzeczypospolitej;* CEFMR Working Paper, 4/2005. http://www.cefmr.pan.pl/docs/cefmr_wp_2005-04.pdf

[339] M.M. Drozdowski. 1974. Ewolucja pojęcia 'Polonia' w XIX-XX wieku. [in]: M.M. Drozdowski (red.) *Dzieje Polonii w XIX i XX wieku.* Toruń, p. 5.

[340] P. Bourdieu. 1985b. The social space and the genesis of groups. *Social Science Information* 24(2):204.

[341] P. Bourdieu. 1985b. *Ibidem,* p. 204.

[342] P. Bourdieu. 1985b. *Ibidem* p. 204.

ised story of the nation and the act of leaving the sacred territory. This story presents the emergence of an independent Polish state in terms of an inevitable, linear progression; a *natural* state of affairs is for Poland to be an independent state and the nation living under Polish state administration. Due to historical events, Poles were scattered outside its sacred territory (which empirically was not of course solely Polish but also Jewish, Ukrainian, Lithuanian, and so on) and in need of symbolic reintegration with the source of its culture — the land. Polish culture constructs migration as a 'moral issue' and *Polonia* is a symbol, which reintegrates those scattered abroad and assumed to be lost without the safety of the national community under — Polish of course — state control. If emigration, therefore, due to the 19th-century partitions and unsuccessful uprisings is a story of loss, deportation, suffering, and passivity, the notion of *Polonia* is a reintegrating symbol of return under the safe umbrella of common tradition and language. This return does not mean returning in physical sense — it is a symbolic return to the community, to the collective, to the group to the sacred imagined source of moral national spine — Poland. *Polonia* is thus Poland recreated abroad; it is a way with which the nation can form a collective outside the borders of Poland.

In the dominant constructions of Polish history, the objective forces of foreign occupation, hunger, economic decline, and war act as the principal push factors for most migrations. It sidelines issues of individual agency, people's autonomous decisions to leave, and the *forward* and *going to* aspect of all migrations. Through a feudal-like, intense symbolic attachment to the land using specific sedentary and biological metaphors,[343] this official nationalistic and state-centric discourse presents mobility as unnatural, even pathological, something that people *ought not* to do since it exposes the land to foreign powers, settlers, and aliens — for example, 19th-century moral panics around emigration were about emigration of ethnic Poles, not Jews or Ukrainians. Yet, the reality of massive population movements presented that national

---

[343] *Korzenie* (roots), the notion of *Macierz* (mother), *ojczyzna* (fatherland), etc.

discourse with a problem—was it really unnatural to leave? So, these feudal, land-oriented symbols and meanings needed to be reformulated in order to accommodate and socially control the growth of diverse Polish communities from Poland from Berlin to Detroit. The concept of *Polonia* was developed to not only help people find their natural home and sense of belonging abroad but also maintain a culturally meaningful grip on social identities. Since this nationalistic-communitarian approach sees all migrations as individual acts against the collective and threatening the moral order of the group and its traditions, the only way to restore the moral order is to create *Polonia*, a sort of second Poland, a recreation of home. *Polonia* enables migrants to return spiritually to the body of the nation without physically moving.

Polonia as timeless settlers

In everyday speech by both migrants and political actors, *Polonia* may be used in two different ways. One way is to refer very broadly to all Polish nationals or people of Polish origin living outside the borders of the nation. This mode is often used in official discourse where the size of the *Polonia* is also evoked.[344] The second and more interesting way the notion is evoked is to associate *Polonia* with the more formal, established ethnic organisations, which are found throughout the world. If *Polonia* is generally seen as the nation reproduced abroad, then its formal representations — in the eyes of its representatives or the Polish state — are or should be the reproduction of the nation's state institutions.[345] Hence, the

---

[344] References are usually made to 20,000,000 people but it is not clear how this figure is arrived at. It is, however, much more clear that this figure is politically manipulated.

[345] G. Babiński. 1992. Uwarunkowania przemian organizacji polonijnych w Europie i Ameryce. [in]: B. Szydłowska-Cegłowa (eds.) *Polonia w Europie*. Polska Akademia Nauk, pp. 77–90; M.M. Drozdowski. 1974. Ewolucja pojęcia 'Polonia' w XIX-XX wieku. [in]: M.M. Drozdowski (red.) *Dzieje Polonii w XIX i XX wieku*. Toruń, p. 5.

power of the state is outsourced to the formal voluntary institutions abroad.

Who ultimately remains in control is a problem, of course. The history of the Polish diaspora or emigration has been marked by the struggle to both accept that the ultimate source of its existence is the spiritual relationship with the territory and maintain some degree of independence from state decision makers, but also remain loyal to their new homelands. Right up to the Second World War Polish state policy was to view *Polonia* as an extension of its interests. Government funding of *Polonia* organisations was made on the assumption that Poles abroad constituted a kind of informal ministry of foreign affairs.[346] We cannot overestimate the importance of this emergence of the 'deterritorialised nation-state'[347] and the subsequent growth of nationalism in Poland, these two are closely linked as demonstrated in Chapter 1. What is crucial is that the notion of *Polonia* also acted a nationalist filter because not all migration flows from Poland have the potential to turn into the *Polonia*. Polish Jews, Roma, Ukrainians, or Silesians are not included in literary and official discourse. So, if *Polonia* is a reintegration symbol it also acts as an 'ethnic purifier'. In addition, it has also a strong class dimension, since the adjective *Polonian* is always used with reference to responsible and respectful roles and class-related notions, such as *Polonian* writer, activist, organisation, newspaper, artist, or journalist. One would never hear of a *Polonian* gangster, cleaner, plumber, or mafia. It is an oxymoron; it would sound odd and disrespectful to use these terms in that context.

For the de-territorialised state, *Polonia* has obvious policy benefits. One of the legacies of this history is that, although Poland

---

[346] An example is the Polish state relations with its American *Polonia*—the call to arms in 1914 resulted in massive response and thousands of Polish Americans traveled to Poland in order to fight for independence. The same call, however, in 1939, received a much more modest response.

[347] L. Basch, N. Glick Schiller, C.S. Blanc. 1994. *Nations Unbound: Transnational Projects, Postcolonial Predicaments, and Deterritorialized Nation-States.* Langhorne: Gordon and Breach.

has still to work out its immigration policy,[348] post-1989 Polish politicians agree that the state must support the *Polonia*. This—as Joppke calls it—re-ethnicisation of state policies[349] not only consists of specific laws relating to immigration and naturalisation for potential returnees but also a policy of funding and sponsoring civil society organisations abroad—those, of course, which are 'sufficiently' *Polonian*. As with all diaspora engagement policies, where funding is concerned, the inevitable issue is the criteria under which some receive it while others do not.

Starting with how the members of state institutions define *Polonia*, we can see how spatial and temporal symbolic categories reveal the metaphysics of the sedentary, bounded nation, reproduced in the *Polonia* concept.[350] Various state documents, especially those produced by the Polish Senate, which officially 'takes care' of issues related to Poles living abroad, define the *Polonia* as 'People of Polish nationality or origin permanently living abroad.'[351] The Polish Ministry of Foreign Affairs defines it in similar way as a relatively integrated population of people of Polish origin—*'emigrants from Poland, their descendants and other people admitting Polish origin, with a permanent residence outside of Poland'*.[352]

These definitions evoke notions of permanence, settlement, and establishment. As one of the leaders of the pan-European network of *Polonia* organisations, who is also a prominent sociologist, said in a press article: *'I think that the term Polonia should be used to describe Poles living permanently and in an organized fashion abroad, not the entire mass migration movement, which is today rather a*

---

[348]   A. Kicinger, A. Weinar. 2007. *State of the art of the migration research in Poland.* CMR Working papers.

[349]   Ch. Joppke. 2003. Citizenship between de- and re-ethnicization. *European Journal of Sociology* 44:429–458.

[350]   L.H. Malkki. 1997. National Geographic: the rooting of peoples and the territorialization of national identity among scholars and refugees. [in]: A. Gupta, J. Ferguson (eds.) *Culture, Power, Place: Explorations in Critical Anthropology.* Durham/London: Duke University Press.

[351]   https://www.msz.gov.pl/pl/polityka_zagraniczna/polonia/definicje_pojecia/

[352]   http://www.stat.gov.pl/gus/definicje_ENG_HTML.htm?id=ANG-82.htm

seasonal movement, transient and basically economic'.[353] Various other documents point to an understanding of *Polonia* as a rooted, stable group of ethnic Poles living in abroad, ideally with a formal representation of an organisation calling itself *Polonian*. This stability and timelessness symbolically separates a group from its migratory past, the 'permanently' refers to how a group communicates its sense of sedentary stability — everything that renders its past mobility void. So the term denotes specific relations of power through exclusion and ascription of symbolic capital to certain individuals.[354]

The movement in space is, then, forgotten and changed into timelessness; the migratory past is transformed into spatial sedentarism. By making itself, *Polonian,* the liminal status, associated with migrants, guests, or people without a home, is replaced by those who belong, are rooted, stable, and can legitimise their presence with a considerable amount of time. There also clear political meanings as, in turn, this assumes that *Polonia* is straightforwardly integrated into a 'host society', where its members are respected, settled, and well-accommodated citizens — natives almost.

This implicit understanding of time is important, since, through this understanding, a group defines itself not as temporary guests but as settlers. This sense of permanency has been one of the main reasons why some groups of Polish émigrés, which created a government-in-exile in Britain after the Second World War, strongly rejected the *Polonia* label. Their political mission and ideological commitment has been to return to a free Poland and to reject putting down roots in Britain, such as adopting British citizenship, taking an interest in British political affairs, or joining the

---

[353] *Polonia w nowej Europie. Z prof. dr. hab. Grzegorzem Kaczyńskim z Zakładu Integracji Europejskiej im. Jeana Monneta Uniwersytetu Szczecińskiego, wiceprezesem Związku Polaków we Włoszech rozmawia Leszek Wątróbski.* London: Cooltura, nr 3/2006, pp. 40–42.

[354] In 2014, the Polish government attempted to make the term 'diaspora' a more inclusive way to include other minorites that emigrated from Poland (Jewish, Armenian, and Lithuanian) as part of its engamement policy; this was, however, attacked by the right-wing opposition.

post-war race to social mobility.[355] They have much preferred the notion of *emigracja,* and in many official documents today, one can find references to both *Polonia* and *emigracja.*[356]

Crucially, the notion of *Polonia* for the old generation of Poles in Britain had also a distinct class flavour, as one of the émigrés explained to me once: '*Polonia* is all these *chłopi* [farmers] in Chicago.' This struggle over the meaning of *Polonia* involved a fight against the tide of assimilation and eventually a redefinition of the role of Poles in Britain, whose political leaders believed and hoped for a third World War right until the mid-1950s. So, it is not surprising that, throughout the 50 years of Polish settlement in Britain, one of the most common themes in public debates in the Polish ethnic press (notably the *Polish Daily* and *Soldiers Daily)* has been the fear of 'becoming' part of the *Polonia.* This process would entail accepting that a belief in temporary fate and quick return had to be replaced by acknowledging that they were becoming permanent settlers in Britain. Nowadays, the notion of *Polonia* is not contested so strongly and second-generation Poles in Britain accept this as the description of their status. Nevertheless, as a reporter on the Polish Daily back in 2003, I was often, however, reminded not to use the term *Polonia,* but *emigracja.*

The point is that the notion of *Polonia* is much more than a description. It is a normative prescription of a formal, bounded, and highly organised unit also with clear generational and gender roles.[357] It also strongly related to the formal and institutionalised

---

[355] In the early 1950s, one of the émigré authors in *Kultura* spoke of his moral outrage at seeing 600 private cars at a beauty contest at a Polish community event. This was treated as proof that Poles enrich themselves, work, and look at their own material well-being, which may undermine the success of the mission of *emigracja,* which is essentially political comeback to Poland and overthrow of the communist system. This suggests that, by definition, a political refugee needs to be poor and not looking for financial gain. In fact, those, who were rich, were very often criticised for taking individual advantage of being a political *émigré.*

[356] See a historical monograph on Polish émigrés in UK by A. Friszke. 1999. *Życie polityczne emigracji,* Warszawa: Więź, p. 424.

[357] This was noted by B. Temple. 1994. *Polish Identity and Community.* University of Manchester Occasional Papers in Sociology no 38.

side of the community, something that is captured by the notions of *organizacje polonijne* the *Polonian* associations, which are *a priori* seen as legitimately representing the voice of the entire group. It has the temporal dimension of a settled, permanent group, which also denotes an intimate knowledge of the 'host society' which, in turn, translates into dominant power position.

Polonia and the Other

We touch here upon something that is intriguingly common in the literature on Polish migrants or communities abroad. In a monograph which explores this issue most in depth, Mary Erdmans describes how 'ethnics' and 'immigrants' of Polish origin interacted throughout the 1970s to the early 1990s in Chicago[358] and how different orientations towards the USA or Poland shaped their patterns of cooperation or animosity. She also shows how formal *Polonian* institutions insulated themselves against newcomers and how politics back in Poland affected Polish society in Chicago. In similar vein, Jo Schneider depicts how a Polish American parade was marked by discrete boundary-making between Poles from USA and (often undocumented) Polish immigrants, who were often excluded from the 'Polish' parade.[359]

These boundary-making mechanisms extend further into the past. Erdmans notes that, in the USA, tensions also manifested themselves in the aftermath of the Second World War when Polish war refugees, soldiers, and political emigres were confronted with the institutions and culture of those descended from rural Polish migrants, who had arrived half a century before.[360] Ethnic self-ascription may not be the result of a particular group migrating at

---

[358] M. Erdmans. 1998. *Opposite Poles. Immigrants and Ethnics in Polish Chicago, 1976-1990*. Philadelphia: Pennsylvania State University Press.

[359] J.A. Schneider. 1990. Defining boundaries, creating contacts: Puerto Rican and Polish presentations of group identity through ethnic parades. *Journal of Ethnic Studies* 18(1):33–57.

[360] See also: S. Blejwas. 1981. Old and new Polonias: tension within an ethnic community. *Polish American Studies* 38(2):55–83.

particular times, therefore, but the product of competing discourses within a group. How a group presents itself is the result of power struggles and competition for leadership positions within formal organisations, where newcomers may seek inclusion and, ultimately, power on the basis of a shared culture.

Keith Sword also observed that *emigracja* had strong reservations towards their co-ethnics, who came to Britain for work during the early 1990s.[361] Yet, Sword missed the cultural role that post-1989 migrants have played in reinforcing the *emigracja*'s sense of being an established group and representing Polish identity in Britain.[362] Their presence acted as a negative reference group against which the Polish British (but also the émigrés from the Solidarity period) could define themselves. A perfect example of this construction comes from a review of the book by the historian, Peter Stachura, mentioned earlier. Here a US-based Polish historian describes the topic of Stachura's book:

> British Poles are traditional, Catholic, conservative, nationalist, patriotic, proud of their Polishness. They do not accept Yalta with all its consequences, including the national borders imposed by Stalin. In one word they are an in-version of the omnipresent type of today's post-socialist Pole.[363]

It may be striking that historians use these stereotypical clichés and demonstrate a degree of ideological nationalistic rhetoric but bearing in mind the importance of these contrasting symbols — the binary oppositions of political/economic; elite/working class; settler/migrant — for mapping out the relations of power, that is

---

[361] K. Sword. 1996. *Identity in Flux. Polish community in Great Britain.* London: SSEES UCL, p. 204.

[362] The fact that there were still some members of the old institutions, who were reluctant to use the notion of *Polonia,* is irrelevant here — the crucial thing was that old organisations were suddenly confronted with a growing mass of other Polish nationals, who could claim the right to participate in their institutions on the basis of shared language, culture, and traditions.

[363] [My emphasis, the 'post-socialist Pole' in Polish, model post PRL-owca has a strong derogatory tone, which is difficult to reflect in English] M.J. Chodakiewicz. 2004. 'Brytyjska Polonia' — a review of the book by Peter Stachura. *The Poles in Britain, 1940-2000: From Betrayal to Assimilation.* London/Portland: Frank Cass. [in]: *Glaukopis,* 2–3 2005, p. 413.

who *ought* to be the leader of such and such organisation, trust, fund, and institution, then all becomes rather clear. Obviously, this historian also has a well defined idea who is a 'better Pole' and who requires to be further 'educated' to become one — quite similar to Jerzy Zubrzycki's ideas of 'soldiers' being the kind of morally superior to 'peasants' in his quite nationalistic rethoric.

By taking a relational perspective to group identity formation, we can see that it was the growth of newcomers from Poland that continued to reinvent and strengthen the response from the Polish émigré elites to the question: 'Who are we?' 'Are we Polish enough? 'Is it the newcomers who are insufficiently Polish?' They answered these questions by asserting even more loudly and vigorously their claims to be the authentic voice of Poles in Britain, the 'true' Poles, the ones fulfilling all the nationalistic criteria dreamt up by Roman Dmowski, the father of Polish version of pre-war fascism (whose ideas still are alive both in Poland and among Polish emigres and migrants in the UK, for example, in the radical right groups called collectively Ruch Narodowy). This development should not surprise us. After all 50 years of life in Britain a respected and prominent group of relatively wealthy, politically conservative Poles had emerged, who were integrated into mainstream British culture, economy, and political system. They continued the tradition of the Anglo-Polish Societies of the mid-19th century, went regularly to church, mostly voted Conservative, and carefully maintained their military traditions and rituals which were praised, understood, and endorsed by — at least some sections — of the British public. These rituals also discretely marked them out from other ethnic groups, further maintaining their privileged position of power. This applies mainly to formal Polish institutions as these days, one may find Brits of Polish origin in all walks of life, but the distinct conservative and nationalistic aura of Polish associations is still being preserved. This time, it was the newcomers who gave the impetus for maintaining that identity.

These military and political traditions were their great symbolic assets and guaranteed them a prominent place in the hierarchy of ethnic groups, which have rapidly multiplied over the last 20 years. During this post-1989 period, Britain also saw the increasing presence of a number of relatively young, often working-class people who were seeking work, accommodation, luck, opportunities — migrants with different set of values, perceptions and capitals, who happened to be Polish too. They came from various regions in Poland and came from the second or third generation, which had been born under communist rule. Although they participated in the same social networks, religious, and cultural rituals or sometimes were even close relatives of the British Poles, the two groups were separated by a symbolic boundary between insiders and outsiders, *us* and *them*, the *emigracja* and *zarobkowi* [a term basically meaning 'economic'], *ci z Polski* [those from Poland].

This boundary enabled the *emigracja* to protect its identity from the new Poles. It also prevented their sense of permanence and acceptance by the British mainstream from being undermined by newcomers, who were seen as lacking any sense of attachment to Britain. Indeed, the arrival of the migrant workers helped to define the *emigracja* even more strongly as a group with symbolic power, elitist, well integrated, and higher class. The newcomers were not only the *Other*, but the *Other* who was too close, since they were often cousins, distant relatives, friends, etc. Consequently, more powerful symbolic tools were needed to maintain the distinction between natives and newcomers, settlers and migrants, those marked by liminality and those embodying settlement and establishment. In practical terms, this boundary needed to be maintained in order to retain control over the vast economic and social capital that *emigracja* had built up — institutions, museums, buildings, charities, trusts, estates, etc. In 2003 and 2002, while working as a reporter at the *Polish Daily*, I was reminded of that boundary on the everyday basis, that there were constant reminders from senior management of the paper to address to the 'old' *emigracja*, that they are different, distinct, and, crucially, that due to their political opposition to Communism, far superior. While trying to stick to the line, at times, as a reporter, I wrote things that drew critical responses from the old guard. Some of them, blamed my misunderstanding of some issue on my 'soviet' upbringing and being, basically 'from Poland' which essentially meant someone stained mentally and morally by being born and brought up in Polish Peoples' Republic.

This symbolic boundary is usually maintained through the media, public speeches, and rituals, and the symbols had not changed much over the years. A similar set of stereotypes about Poles from Poland were promoted by the press during the 1950s[364] and 1980s, as well as more recently. The best example comes from a sermon by one of the leaders of the Polish Catholic Church in England in September 2005. It illustrates well the discursive maintenance of this boundary:

> We wish in this pilgrimage to offer to God by intercession of Immaculate Mary those who 60 years ago in defense of freedom and sovereignty of our Fatherland, have paid the tribute of their blood. We offer in this Mass also you, dear combatants, and the generation who found itself abroad. The Sanctuary of Our Lady of Mt. Carmel in Aylesford was and still is the Polish Częstochowa. Here after difficult war experience you rebuild your faith in God and the faith in humans and faith in human dignity. We bow our heads to you. We would like to offer also through intercession of Our Lady of Częstochowa, these that call themselves Solidarity Emigration. It was you who took into hearts the words of the Slavic Pope: do not be afraid. You came here expelled from your Fatherland and for long years you experienced the bitterness of emigration lives and then you found your dignity. And you, who call them-

---

[364] In the 1950s—which is understood given the political climate—all Poles from Poland, all newcomers were suspected of being communist spies. These were not just conspiracy theories. In fact, one of the Prime Ministers in exile turned out to be one. Later, a typical example of such stigmatization would be the numerous articles in the press about young Polish females from Poland, who were looking to meet Poles in Britain only for their passports, not true love — see Sword (1994). Another version of this tension is evident in frequent conflicts between the Polish émigrés and the Polish Catholic Church, which parachuted into local parishes priests who were sometimes seen as 'communist spies' or 'Soviet-minded' — see A. Romejko. 2000. *Duszpasterstwo polonijne w Wielkiej Brytanii*. Wy. Marszałek, p. 255.

selves, the John Paul II generation, you have a special task in the new Europe to carry a real Christian culture in your country of settlement. You have to defend strongly against a consumerist way of life, which always brings moral and spiritual emptiness. Your input in the life abroad should be a positive, Christian model of the family, shaping the life of the emigracja. I address these words also to these who came to Great Britain for economic reasons, for bread [idiom]. I welcome you from all my heart. Let yourself be known at Holy Masses, involve yourself in the liturgical life of your parish. The Church is your second home, where you often seek support and consolation. Youth is a great gift but a duty also. Don't be tempted by what is easy and pleasant. Take care of your spirit your 'be first and have next'. Your conversations should be an example of the culture of language and customs. Take care of the good name of Poland, your Mother. (Fr Tadeusz Kukla sermon, Sep 2005)

First of all, we see how by grouping Poles in different categories, the sermon establishes a strict hierarchy and relation of power through the emphasis on which group is more 'political' or more 'economic.' The almost platonic dualism (between the soul and body, idea, and the material) is deeply rooted in traditional notions of the *emigracja* or *Polonia*. Since exile is so powerfully linked with Polish political struggle, those involved in it have a strong claim to control the community's agenda and public image. The newcomers are literally 'new' and need to be treated as not quite adults, as not fully participants. They need yet to prove their faith and identity (their Polishness) by participation in rituals, which accepts established power relations.

This speech identifies several groups of people and sends a different message to everyone that the old, established diaspora is to be cherished and acclaimed for its strength and resistance. The newcomers are invited to engage with the life of the British Polish community but are reminded that anyone entering the *community* has certain obligations. There is a moral 'examination' to pass in order to be accepted into the club. The newcomers are reminded to behave properly so as not to undermine the reputation of established British Poles. The reminder about 'language' in the last sentences is a direct reference to the class markers of foul language in public, which will 'pollute' Polishness.

This group hierarchy is performatively reinforced and re-produced on most occasions during holy mass. On Sundays or special occasions, churches like St Mary's in Ealing or St Andrzej Bobola in Acton are now packed. However, these congregations' seating patterns demonstrate that they are far from a random grouping of individuals. The way in which people occupy seats and rows in relation to the altar reflects their position within the Polish community. The oldest members of the Second World War generation, trustees of all organisations and presidents of associa-tions occupy the front rows, middle-aged individuals, and the second generation sit further back, while the recent migrants sit at the back near the entrance or in the foyer, or even stand outside. This reflection of community hierarchy embodies not only the spiritual journey of a Catholic, who gets closer to God with age, but also the structure of who are the most important and promi-nent people in the group and who has been around for the longest period of time.

In other words, the distinction between *Polonia* or *emigracja*, on the one hand, and migrants or *zarobkowi* (economic migrants) as symbolic capital accepted by all parties, supports the power structure and subordinates the new participants to a specific cul-ture of place making. The distinction also helps to resolve the problems raised by assumptions about ethnic solidarity — how to accommodate the horizontal and cultural bonds among people, who are believed to have something in common, with class differ-ences, hierarchy, domination, and subordination. As bearers and producers of the dominant discourse of Polish emigration laden with symbolic capital obtained through the connection with myth-ical past and military achievements, leaders of Polish formal insti-tutions position themselves as controllers of public opinion. This claim to possess the knowledge, respect, and symbolic power of the community meant that fellowship with Polish newcomers was acceptable only if it entailed the latter's acceptance of hierarchy and a subordinate position. At this point, it is worthwhile to re-mind the reader the opening scene of this chapter. The ambitious newcomers, in order to enter the circle of diasporic social circles, need to accept the rules of the game—and the game is a strongly nationalistic one.

This hierarchical system was influenced, of course, by the wider British society. Members of the pre-war Poland elites encountered structural constraints, anti-Polish sentiment, and language barriers in the post-war labour market. Their loss of class status encouraged the emergence of a parallel system of hierarchy and prestige, which could compensate for a sometimes dramatic fall in status.[365] Nevertheless, the persistence of the distinction between *emigracja* and *zarabkowi*, despite the personal interconnectedness, family links, and interdependence, suggests that the figure of economic migrant (*zarobkowi)* has developed into one of the main '*Others'* against which the established group could define itself. This division between insiders and outsiders incorporated a number of binary distinctions: political versus economic, idealistic versus materialistic, charitable versus consumerist, collectivist versus individualistic.

These distinctions directly play on the Polish dominant discourse described in Chapter 2, one, which juxtaposes soldiers against peasants and constructs a normative hierarchy of personal identity. *Zarabkowi* are presented as ignorant and those in power are there to teach them and equip with specific traditions and understandings of not only how British society works but what it means to be Polish. Recent migrants are at the beginning of their journey and should learn what it means to be 'Polish' abroad, to respect Polish traditions in a new, stronger way and to submit to a specific national ideology binding *Polonia* together. In November 2005, the Polish Prime Minister at the time, Kazimierz Marcinkiewicz, paid a visit to the Polish Embassy and in his speech clearly described who was who:

---

[365] It is very common to refer to the so-called 'silver brigades'—high-ranking Polish officers working as servants polishing silver cutlery in London hotels and restaurants in the late 1940s and the 1950s.

'When I see you [the emigracja] I feel that I do not have to worry about all those Poles who come here... I can see that you will take them under your wing and teach them the best values of Polishness, what it actually means to be Polish'.

In the same way, the meeting described at the beginning of the chapter used the figure of the old veteran to create an aura of respectability, settlement, integration, and close links between the military history and migration history. The figure of the soldier is a powerful one, and it is not surprising that it is and will be used by new migrants in order to gain recognition in public. In 2012, a strong legal conflict related to right to property (and a lot of it) torn apart one of the most respected and wealthy Polish diasporic organisation, the Association of Polish ex-Combatants (SPK — Stowarzyszenie Polskich Kombatantów), with court battles, flurry of press accusations from both sides, and so on. A young organisation linked to Ruch Narodowy — the far right groups in Poland — composed of recent migrants, took active interest staging demonstrations and voicing strong political support for one side. One of the members of the 'old guard' remarked then to me: *'Who the hell are these people? Why do they stick their noses into affairs that are not theirs? They should go back home, to Poland, not stir up trouble here'.*

But symbols do not have owners, so the military symbolic aura of the Association was simply used by these new migrants to laid claim for some space in the diasporic community. Keith Sword notes that the Polish associations were notorious for closed, clique-like structures and the second generation was most often kept at arms distance. So the shock of my informant above is understandable. But so is the seizure of opportunity to gain power of representation by new comers. Not accidentally, the new organisation that took part has strong nationalistic ideology and sees its aims at improving Poles stance in British life through historical references — to the Second World War, Polish pilots, anti-Communism, and so on. Involvement in the legal chaos within the SPK was part of that battle. In a way, one of the only ways to participate in that field of power was to use the same discourse as the *emigracja*, or even surpass it with a new convert's fervour.

Formal representation and its contestants

The leaders of the diasporic Polish organisations, which were created after the Second World War, often claim to be the official
representatives of the Polish community in Britain. They are led
by the Federation of Poles in Great Britain—an umbrella organisation based at the Polish Centre in Hammersmith. Their leadership
is often chosen from a small pool of first- or second-generation
Poles, and its president in 2005, Dr Jan Mokrzycki, acknowledged
to me that the Federation is very under-funded and can only afford one full-time staff member with the remainder working on
voluntary basis. Not surprisingly, many of my interviewees and
those catering for migrants through social service organisations
criticised the Federation's inability to support its claim to be the
official representative of British Poles with adequate resources but
not really living up to its expectations. The heaviest pressure on
welfare resources came in the aftermath of EU enlargement. Despite a massive effort by the few volunteers at the Federation, its
reach seems quite limited. My respondents, and it can be said
Poles in general, know little about the Federation or the complex
web of Polish organisations. If they do, they often contest their
status as representants—from interviews I conducted as part of a
study on political participation of Poles in 2013[366]—it was evident
that power is being strongly decentralised and the role of Federation increasingly contested. Many, who did know something,
dismissed the idea of seeking contact or help from a Polish organisation which, they assumed, would be highly traditional. Anna,
who worked in the electronic media, made a typical comment:

> *I heard* [that] *Polonia is a closed circle … When I enter POSK I have a feeling
> that time* [has] *stopped, that they live in their world that they have created …
> They don't want to accept that there is a young Polonia that young people
> came here … You know they think that: 'Who are they? They may be illegals.
> What* [do] *they want? and 'They will bring some trouble upon us'. But it's
> hardly surprising really, they are over 80 years old.*

---

[366] J. Kucharczyk (red.). 2013. *Nic o nas bez nas. Partycypacja obywatelska Polaków w
Wielkiej Brytanii.* Warzawa: Instytut Spraw Publicznych.

In one respect, her comment is not typical, however, because she distinguished between a young and an old *Polonia*. Konrad reflected a much more common view:

> This is Polonia – not the Polish [people] – this is important. All the time I regard myself neither as an emigrant nor a member of Polonia … I have a Polish passport and I am the citizen of the world … There are Polish in London, who are not Polonia, it's as simple as that … Polonia is a closed unit – that's it … They live in the UK where they try to invent Poland abroad and that's how Polonia is being made … Because they are not in their own country, this sort of a mutant is being born… This is Polonia, which is a closed world that does not want to open

Konrad sees *Polonia* as a fixed entity, then. It is opposed to cosmopolitanism and, as a closed cultural unit; it seeks to preserve the values of the past, which are alien to a young Pole. Furthermore, although Konrad was negative about the diasporic leaders, he somehow accepts that membership of the *Polonia* is an individual choice and if people choose not to, then they are not obliged to belong to the group. From opposing sides, Konrad and those articulating the hegemonic discourse about the role of the *Polonia* in nation building accept that the *Polonia* is sustained voluntarily. Membership, then, is an ideological and political statement. This is not a group into which people are born but, rather, one which they choose to join, drawing on the specific symbolic and economic resources which formal organisations can offer. This is why these institutions have a reputation of being very conservative and traditional. One needs to really take its ethnic identity seriously to participate. Membership becomes an individual statement, just as religious conversion for an adult is something far more serious and meaningful than baptism at birth. As one ethnic leader said: '*These people are, well, migrants – they are not yet a community, a Polonia, yet'*.

New participants in the game

To understand how power relations develop in practice and how differences are maintained in this context, we will consider a notable example, which took place in 2006—the emergence and development of a new organisation called the Poland Street Association, which sought to organise recently arrived Polish nationals in Britain. The following account is based not only on interviews with several of its acting members but also on participation in several closed meetings during late 2006 and 2007 where decisions about strategy were formulated.

Poland Street was set up after a spontaneous and highly successful vigil after the death of Pope John Paul II. In April 2005, around 20,000 Poles marched from Trafalgar Square to Westminster Cathedral, and the event was organised by a group of young migrants, who managed to spread the word across the capital mainly using social media. Similar marches had been organised in Poland during this time of national mourning. The group began to meet informally in pubs and cafes around central London and, in October 2006, formalised its existence by calling itself the Poland Street Association.

In this context, the most interesting feature was how different emerging leaders regarded relations with the Federation. The main point of controversy was whether they should join straight away—and hence accept the leadership position of the Federation—or start a specific activity and accumulate enough social and political capital so that they could operate as equals with the Federation leaders. There were some heated discussions over what course the organisation should take. Some members of the initial founding group stressed the need to establish links with British organisations, which welcomed young representatives of Polish migrants. Others claimed that it was much better to build contacts and good relations with the Federation and that this would enable Poland Street to gain wider recognition.

Eventually, the elected president chose a compromise. Bridges would be built with the older generation but a high-profile event or action would also be launched, which would make the organisation known well enough so that it would not be forced to seek the Federation's recognition. Zenon, the leader, had a rather negative view about of the prospect of joining the Federation which he regarded as 'backward and useless'. Even so, he still came up with an idea, which aimed at gaining favour among the members of the older generation. The first occasion was the highly symbolic but also political act of organising the cleaning of graves at the Gunnersbury cemetery where a lot of Polish soldiers and members of the establishment are buried.[367] The cleaning was scheduled for November 1 (All Saint's Day, a 'day of holy obligation' when all Catholics are supposed to attend mass). In a remark heavily laden with social class references, the president declared: *'We need to do it, to show them* [the older generation] *that we care about these values, that we are not some bunch of dresiarze* [men in tracksuits] *but you know, some intelligentsia as well'.* When asked whether that was what they did in Poland on that day most activists, including the president, responded that this would be the first time they would engage in such ritual.

Clearly, the cleaning of graves has a deep symbolic meaning. It is an act of respect, an acknowledgement of one's moral value in life, and also an act of submission and subordination—a cleaner is usually situated lower on the social ladder than the one who is being cleaned or whose material possessions are being cleaned. Moreover, class distance needs to be communicated by overcoming physical proximity, since washing one's house, body, or grave is a physical job, which requires close bodily contact with domains that are seen as private and intimate. Cleaning as work and duty simultaneously, then, presupposes proximity and distance. Although the person comes closer, what they are doing reinforces hierarchy at the same time. Cleaning graves as a mark of respect for the dead also purifies the memory of that person. The cleaners, therefore, bowed to certain military and cultural traditions but at the same time appointed themselves as guardians of these traditions, which preserved the memory and mythical

---

[367] An important aspect of that activity was that funds for grave cleaning were obtained from the Polish Consulate, showing how state's policy in fact encourages such activities.

legacy of the Second World War Polish émigrés for subsequent generations. Interestingly, this combination of death, memory, and intergenerational tensions was reflected in an interview with Bartek, a seasonal migrant from Kraków, who had contacts with some members of the older generation:

> Still there are not enough of relations between [different groups of] the emigrants — horizontal contacts between different generations of migrants are absent … These people are not integrated. It's always the older generation that sets the tone and the level of cooperation … they set up the relations … In some way they may be right, but this is a road to nowhere because [the] next generations if they won't stick together then … I allow myself this joke sometimes that then, [if there is no integration] on the last journey [funeral] of the oldest, it will be the Rastafarians who will accompany those oldest Polish … but no Polish.

Like the grave cleaning ritual, this comment sends a signal to the older generation that it is the younger ones, who can preserve the memory and traditions of the group, otherwise 'aliens' (Rastafarians act here as culturally distant group) will do it and the memory will be lost. In a way it is a sort of a gentle blackmail — we are here and want to continue your work, that is, cultural traditions, but also, crucially, the maintenance of the institutions, estates, charities, and so on. The blackmail operates through the disturbing vision of fervent Catholics and Polish patriots being accompanied on their last journey by 'exotic' Others. The suggestion that this simply amount to blasphemy and insult to the pathos of death is obvious.

The grave cleaning ritual shows how a formal association of newcomers attempted to gain some recognition from an established institution. The strength of this symbolic action is demonstrated by the fact that few years later, in 2013, another new organisation set up by the young generation of recent Polish migrants initiated exactly the same ritual in recognition of the role of pre-war migrants. *Patriae Fidelis* Polish Youth Association, an organisation with distinct nationalist emphasis, has begun to establish links with older generation through events immersed in historical-political discourse of anti-Communism, heroic war time martyrdom of Polish soldiers (the same organisation that got involved in conflict within the SPK). One of explicit aims of that organisation was to 'unite' various groups of Polish migrants and to create 'one voice' but crucially, with the old diaspora and their symbols as its leadership.

The problem is when an organisation attempts to address a wider range of Poles. At the time when they were most active, Poland Street took an opportunity to address a different group of people—the post-Accession migrants. The issue concerned double taxation, which was introduced during the 1970s but not repealed after accession. It penalised Polish migrants, who are still connected to Poland through work, property, or family, since it made a charge on money already taxed by Britain's Inland Revenue. In 2005 and 2006, the issue slowly gathered a massive grass-roots response and protest. Online petitions to various ministers, officials, and ombudsman were sent, the media in Poland got involved, and the issue gained considerable attention. At Poland Street meetings, members were strongly in favour of some kind of high-profile action, which would legitimise their existence and help them gain popularity among Polish migrants. The decision was made to organise a street rally, and on 17 March 2006, around 1,000 people turned up with flags, posters, and flyers. The event gathered huge coverage in the Polish media.

Characteristically, the Federation of Poles and many members close to the established institutions opposed the rally. Dr Jan Mokrzycki declared in public that it was a wrong idea because 'we should wash our laundry at home'. This reaction was highly indicative of the relationship between established groups and the new migrants, since it shows that entering a public space in Britain was seen as a transgression if it was not agreed with the establishment. The Federation supported the idea of abolishing double taxation but, at the same time, it wanted to retain its dominant role as the public face of the debate. Privately, a lot of members of the elite and the second generation feared that the rally could turn nasty as some participants might be drunk or aggressive. There was a clear sense of fear that a protesting crowd, composed of Polish migrants near Oxford Street in London, might have unpredictable consequences and perhaps 'stain' the reputation of Poles, in general.

The other reason behind opposition to the rally was, of course, the anxiety that the Federation was losing its position as the official representatives of the group. This was a reasonable fear because, according to what leaders of the Poland Street said at the time, it was precisely their intention to—as one said—'break the monopoly of representation the granddads have'. This sense of competition led to very critical voices being raised in private from both sides and considerable hostility.

In the end, it turned out that long-term survival triumphed. The group most opposed to closer links with the Federation has dissolved—the president has simply gone back to Poland to take up a civil service job in local government, while others lost interest or became caught up in their professional life. The Association elected a new leadership whose strategy was to strengthen relations with the Federation, and this eventually resulted in Poland Street joining the Federation and *de facto* accepting its presidents as the leaders of the umbrella organisation and its representatives. In doing this, they accepted the hierarchy embedded in the decision-making process which marks the structure of the Federation, whose aim—as Sword noted a decade ago—was to 'insulate the Federation and its leadership from the potential shocks that direct democracy might involve'.[368] This development has clearly been a success for the Federation and shows that old established institutions can be adaptable, can evolve, and open their doors to newcomers. However, it could be argued that they are, indeed, open but on their terms only.

The rifts within 'Polish London' emerged out in the open during another dispute, this time without Poland Street which was clearly less active. The rift cut through many groups of active Poles through political rather than generational lines. It concerned

---

[368] K. Sword. 1994. *Community in Flux*. London: SSEES UCL, p. 90.

the sale of one of the establishments associated with post-war emigres, the *Ognisko Polskie* in the heart of Kensington. The board of directors decided at some point that it was financially not viable and needed to be sold. The decision mobilised a campaign led by some newspapers and newly formed organisations, such as Patriae Fidelis, along with a very heterogeneous collection of recent migrants, Solidarity era political refugees, second-generation Poles, or even Brits with no Polish family connection whatsoever. As in 2015, the threat of sale of the building has been removed, the *Ognisko* gained few new hundred members and has clearly reinvented itself; however, the financial position still remains unclear. The story of *Ognisko*, however, shows another dimension of the processes of construction of ethnicity in diasporic context — its closely implicit relationship with social class distinction constructions, an issue I will describe in later sections further.

Establishment as buffer zone

It would be wrong, therefore, to argue that the first or second generation of the *Polonia* has turned their backs on recent migrants. As we have seen, the presence of newcomers is crucial, symbolically and practically for the process of reinforcing the establishment's own political dominance in the local context, but crucially also to prove their own superiority described in social class-related terms (educated, professional, respectful, and cosmopolitan).

The Federation has actually a quite good legacy and track record of publicly standing in favour of migrants from Poland. In 1993, it successfully lobbied the John Major government to lift visa restrictions for Polish nationals and in early 2004, when the Conservatives attacked the government's decision to open the labour market, the Federation issued a public letter to the Prime Minister urging him to resist political and media pressure. By encouraging migration, they ran the risk of being toppled by a young generation of leaders, who emerged from the very process they had supported. These younger activists had different problems and pursued different agendas but, as we have seen, the Federation's leaders have so far been able to resist this challenge.

The ethnic leaders also take on a role, which the British state would be reluctant to adopt—acting as a buffer zone where certain things can be done and said that would be incorrect on the part of British institutions. One example is the information office run by the Federation of Poles, which as I have been repeatedly told, often advised many people to simply return to Poland. Set up during the busiest period right after Accession, it dealt not only with straightforward matters, such as guiding people to the nearest job centre or translating a document, but also helped people who had been robbed of their money, cheated by employers, had become homeless or alcoholic, or experienced serious problems adapting to life in London. The frequent advice, which the office gave to many people, according to both my interviewees and employees at the Federation, was to go back to Poland. Now, it would be very difficult for any British service provider, such as the Citizens Advice Bureau or a borough council office, to give this advice. For example, saying to someone: 'Go back to Poland if you cannot speak English and cannot adapt or cannot behave' may sound rather xenophobic but is seen as perfectly acceptable when delivered by a second-generation Pole during a meeting with fellow Poles at the Polish Centre.

Polish ethnicity and making the political transnational social field through exclusion

The success of the grave cleaning ritual and subsequent engagement of Poland Street in various activities, and the emergence of new associations such as Patriae Fidelis which reproduced the nationalist discourse and militaristic traditions of the Polish *emigracja,* showed how formal ethnic organisations can easily gain a specific, traditionalist, patriotic flavour. Poland Street, in its statement of goals, declared its desire to 'promote Poland as a modern and European country with a rich and beautiful history'.[369] One of its activities, which the Federation strongly supported, was linked to the issue which questioned the 'beauty' of that history, mainly the uneasy Polish–Jewish relations. In response to an article in *The Times* which referred to the participation of Poles in the Holocaust, Poland Street and the Federation orchestrated a vigorous campaign of protest. Poland Street's involvement in many commemorative events, which were the main rituals of the *emigracja*, enabled it to align itself with a group which possessed resources. It also strengthened class barriers and distanced it from Poles, who do not want to reproduce the historical narrative of Poland as the 'Christ of Nations' and or who regard other issues as more important for Polish migrants. A similar series of actions against the portrayal of Poles as endemically anti-semitic were also carried out by a nationalist youth organisation Patriae Fildelis as well as an organisation tellingly called Polish Professionals in London.

It is significant that Poland Street, as well as Polish Professionals, is composed mainly of people with a middle-class background or who work in highly skilled professions. From interactions and conversations with that group in 2006 and 2007 and my conversations with Polish Professional members in 2012 and 2011 it was clear that these people fund it difficult to engage with the working conditions of migrants, exploitation and the capitalist labour market, the London Living Wage campaign, agency workers, and so on. In 2008, one of my projects involved working closely with London Citizens – a large London-based coalition of civil society organisations, which campaigned for workers' rights, a living wage, and the rights of undocumented migrants. London Citizens wanted to involve Polish migrants in their campaigns and through my connections approached Poland Street to see whether it would join the coalition. However, from conversations with the leader of Poland Street, it became clear that he was not interested in campaigning on behalf of Polish migrants, who were poor, des-

---

[369] http://www.polandstreet.org.uk/index.php?page=sekcja_ogolna&dzial=5&kat=2

titute, and exploited. After a presentation of London Citizens' aims and goals, he commented: '*It is all very nice, but it all looks very left wing ... you know, it is not our kind of thing ... it's very leftie*'. Being a 'leftie' among many of Polish established institutions was a stigma, and although two of the old guard leaders of the Federation belonged to the Labour and Liberal parties, this did not prevent them from framing their understanding of Polish history and ethnicity in very traditionalist terms, reproducing the grand narrative of Polish romantic nationalism, which often excluded any interest in class dimension of identity which in turns functioned as a way to prevent any internationalization of ethnic institutions engagement— for example, in joining the trade unions or multicultural coalitions, like London Citizens (now called Citizens UK).

This clash between ethnicity and class is obvious in another campaign Poland Street and Federation joined forces in, notably the reaction to a fictional representation of Poles in London. This time, however, it did not involve the British media but Polish state TV, which in 2008 and 2009 issued a soap TV programme depicting the life of emigrants called *Londyńczycy* (The Londoners). The programme was immediately attacked for 'falsely' depicting Poles as racists and the women as promiscuous. The underlying issue was that the fiction depicted Poles who were 'losers' and as one of Poland Street leader said: '*They also have success, have good jobs and are respected*'.[370] The controversy provoked some Polish MPs to protest against use of public money to 'tarnish' Poles abroad and the Federation formally complained to the Polish TV that the programme: '*spits into ones' nest*'. The dispute revolved not only about community reputation but the questioning of the myth of the successful, self-made Pole, which as we saw in Chapter 5 is an important part of Polish migrants' class identity.

The fear of blurring of class and ethnic markers leads the Polish organisations, created among newly arrived migrants, to acquire a specific class character, based around education, work-

---

[370] http://www.mojawyspa.co.uk/artykuly/22839/Polacy-na-Wyspach-bojkotuja-Londynczykow

ing in a particular field (not below one's qualifications), behaviour, and appearance. Besides Poland Street, an active organisation I became familiar with is Polish Professionals. Apart from the name, tellingly they are explicitly exclusionist on class basis, as according to their membership status it accepts only people with higher education degrees or those, who have worked at least two years in an 'appropriate' position.[371] Most of its members come, not surprisingly, from the financial and managerial sector and as one member commented: *'We want to be elite, we want to create elites. As you know, there are many kinds of Poles around there ... you know ... others'.* The Polish Professionals website is designed to appeal to energetic, young, aspiring, urban, cosmopolitan Poles — the pictures construct a message of clear aspiration but also class distinction. Like Poland Street, the organisation also participates in events orchestrated by the Federation of Poles, in commemorative events, or the 'struggle for historical truth.' The Polish City Club is the third active organisation and describes itself as linking businessmen and businesswomen and City workers. The interesting question is that, at the very same time, these institutions have relatively modest membership — given the overall Polish population in the UK. When asked why they do not recruit more widely, one of the leaders said: *'You know, we are focusing on the quality of people and ideas that we generate, not how many members we have'.* Quality in this context means simply — not people with lower class markers.

Here, we can see that ethnicity acts as a form of umbrella concept that assists people with substantial economic, social, and cultural capital in their activities. They seek explicitly to connect 'certain' kind of people and 'certain' kind of Poles, and this strategy provides a firm basis for identity politics among Poles abroad. 'Certain' here usually implicitly refers not to those involved in *kombinacje,* who may be working class but those who are cosmopolitan, open and last but not least, financially successful. This reference can lead to misunderstanding, because people use an

---

[371] https://www.polishprofessionals.org.uk/dolacz-do-nas.html

inclusive notion of ethnicity to pursue their exclusive goals. The function of the nationalist discourse concerning migration resolves this tension. By symbolically legitimising community leaders, it reasserts the relationship between classes, between the elites and the subordinates. For this reason Poland Street, Polish Professionals, and others participate in rituals and meaning-making practices, such as grave cleaning or protests against 'staining' of reputation of Poles or in numerous historical patriotic events—all practices in which these people are unlikely to participate in Poland—since this is the source of their power and legitimacy in the eyes of the elders.

It is then not surprising that, despite being part of Polish society, for centuries, Polish Roma are radically excluded from these diasporic networks. Through not only class-based exclusion but also clearly racialised forms of stigmatisation, Polish Roma in London were not welcomed, from the late 1980s right to late 2000s. Through family connections and the role of Roma Support Group, one of most active Roma organisations in the UK, set up by Polish Roma, these things began to change and there seems to be a greater acceptance of the Polish Roma, but I still remember the advertisements at the shop window near the Polish Social Cultural Centre (POSK) in early 2000s reading: 'room for rent. Not for *Cyganie* [Roma] ' or 'Looking for a room, but not with *Cyganie*'. It is also telling that the Polish state, the consular office, has until recently been not engaging at all with that group of migrants from Poland. Again, there are signs of change here as the Embassy is starting to foster some relationship with the Polish Roma. Interestingly, these relations on a grass-roots level are quite common, for instance, some Polish Roma are active at Polish Saturday School, or a large part of Polish-speaking Jehova Witnesses, are Polish Roma.

As shown in above- described many examples, the Polish state is an active stake holder in this process. Following a long tradition of actively engaging its compatriots abroad, the Polish state uses economic and symbolic resources to legitimise, support, and to some extent identify who ought to represent the *Polonia*. It is not a unified policy, as various factions, political sides and parts of administration compete for influence and funds. The main axis of conflict runs between the Polish Senate and the Polish Ministry of Foreign Affairs. The outcome of this conflict is that the state actively promotes those formal institutions that reproduce the story of the *emigracja* as 'successful' and the authentic representatives of the *Polonia* and, as result, supporting class boundaries between Poles in London. The political transnational social field offers then direct benefits for middle-class migrants.[372]

Hence, the elites and formal associations work with Polish state institutions to project a specific image of a 'Pole' by dismissing some issues, problems, and aspects of migration from Poland as controversial or unhelpful or carefully avoided any discussion of them. I have already mentioned the initial unease, with which the Polish Embassy officials reacted to my idea of organising a one-day conference on migration in May 2006, and in similar attitude, their reluctance to engage with the Roma arises from deep-seated racial prejudices, that Roma struggle in Poland. However, it is the issue of homelessness among Polish migrants in London that poses a particular challenge. *'hey are all criminals really, they probably escaped the law in Poland'* was a comment heard in casual conversation with a Consular official during a meeting in 2008 at the Polish Centre, and this attitude does not seem unique to this individual. In 2010, a British service provider, working with homeless Polish migrants, noted during an interview that Polish consular officials are particularly unsympathetic to the plight of the homeless. For them, the typical response is to send people back to Poland, most preferably to prison. The attitude of the Federation of Poles was much more positive and as we have seen, despite their limited resources, they have acted as an information point for newcomers and a link between various groups of Poles

---

[372] This is a process summarized well by L. Basch, N. Glick Schiller, C.S. Blanc. 1994. *Nations Unbound: Transnational Projects, Postcolonial Predicaments, and Deterritorialized Nation-States*. Langhorne: Gordon and Breach, p. 280.

as well as sections of British society. Yet, the Federation still sees the problem of poverty, homelessness, and unemployment as one, which *'gives us a bad name'* rather than issue of social justice. One ethnic leader remarked: *'Well, these people cannot expect us to help them all the way. They came here on their own, they made a decision and expect us to help them. We build all these institutions and all they want is to use them .... I think ... they should have some respect'*. The standard advice then given to Polish migrants in difficulty is to go home, go back to Poland. In informal conversations with leaders, they do not hide the fact that the main reason to act so, is to preserve 'our reputation'. An unemployed, homeless migrant is thus a threat to one's own class position.

Despite plenty of goodwill, it is clear that the Federation — trapped between their own class producing status and an implicit ethnic egalitarianism — has limited ability to engage in social work aimed at those who need help. They seek to preserve a particular power balance and helping the destitute is not on their agenda. It would undermine their power base, would mean unnecessary class transgression, and could threaten the carefully crafted picture of the 'Polish community' as respectful, ambitious, middle-class, and a model ethnic group.

Post-7/7 London and history recreated

The crucial effect of these cultural and social processes is the fusing together of two powerful discourses concerning Polish migration — one discourse interpreted the implications of emigration for the nation and upheld the power of those who 'fought' for Poland, while the other celebrated a mythologised West where an aspiring Pole goes, becomes successful, and is recognised by strangers as an individual struggling in a highly competitive labour market. The fusion of these two creates a cultural norm, which explains why members of the Polish Professionals or the Polish City Club are so eagerly accepted by the leaders of the *Polonia*. It also explains why these newcomers accept the dominant narrative of

Polish romantic nationalism as the main point of ideological reference when it comes to various activities. Their organisations made their mark (except for the action on double taxation) by supporting what the Federation was already doing. They accepted that these are the symbols and discourses to be used in order to be approved by established groups as well as the Polish state.

However, focusing only on internal power relations would be incomplete. These people do not operate in a social void but in early 21st-century London with its contemporary debates over multiculturalism and the effects of the economic crisis. So, in order to position themselves in a particular hierarchy, those who are involved in formal organisations and in shaping the public sphere have to consider carefully what the dominant group thinks and says.

It is in this context that several threads of dominant discourses in Polish culture, individual agency, and social and cultural conditions in London meet and reinforce one another. The notion of the Polish 'soldier' the defender, the active freedom fighter against foreign oppression and demonised 'other' meets the idea of the economic, neo-liberal actor who in pursuit of his/her dreams works hard, pays taxes, climbs the social ladder, gets a good education, and accepts middle-class values. Both discourses seek acceptance from the dominant British society and are received favourably, since they offset negative stereotyping of an 'immigrant' as a 'benefits cheat', 'asylum seeker', 'burden on the tax payer', which impacts so much on other migrant groups. This fusion of two notions seems inevitable, since they form a coherent narrative which justifies the newcomer's presence by legitimising one's place in the modern mosaic of ethnic groups.

Bleeding for Britain during the Second World War and sweating through hard work to support, its economy on a minimal wage merges into one, single narrative. It should be no surprise, then, that numerous speeches by British politicians move smoothly from talking about post-Accession immigrants to 'Battle

of Britain' Polish pilots.[373] It may be read as good manners towards constituents, but symbolically, it is powerfully charged and
encourages Poles to see themselves as somewhat better than other
minorities. The messages mix diverse experiences and groups in
order to send one particular message. For example, during a rally
to commemorate the 90th anniversary of Polish independence in
November 2008, the MP for Hammersmith and Fulham addressed
the 3,000-strong crowd of Poles gathered at Trafalgar Square with
the words: *'You are Britain's most popular migrants'*. This followed a
speech by the Labour MP Denis MacShane, who drew on a range
of historical references to Poland and its fight for freedom.

This fusion of the two discourses has practical outcomes,
which are crucial for new organisations. It shows who has political
connections, particularly with the elite, and the symbolic capital to
'enter' British society. One of the leaders of Poland Street tellingly
commented: *'These* [the established British Poles] *have good connections. They know the establishment, they know people in politics and it is
obvious that we need to use these connections for our own advantage'*.

The belief that the *Polonia* has retained its integrity while
fully accepting the values of British society is particularly popular
among members of the second generation. They witnessed the
growth of multicultural policies in Britain from the 1970s and re-
sented their leaders' failure to take advantage of those policies.
We have mentioned one leader saying that the term 'ethnic group'
should not be used because it *'puts us on the same level as Hindus
and blacks'* and they should be treated as a role model for other
ethnic groups. During a meeting with the Mayor of London, Ken
Livingstone who invited members of the Polish associations in
2006, one of the Federation of Poles representatives put this claim

---

[373]   For example, during the Polish President's Lech Kaczyński's visit in November
2006, Tony Blair says: *'And there is a very close bond between Poland and Britain as
a result of the heroism and bravery particularly of Polish pilots but also of many other
Polish people during the course of the Second World War. And today, of course, we
have many Polish people who are here in our country working and living – a very
strong community here. And the outlook, both in terms of Europe and in terms of
NATO, of Poland and of Britain is, I think, very similar'*.

in these words: *'The Polish community offers an ideal of integration for British numerous ethnic communities; they show how others should integrate'*.

The political courtesy behind all these speeches masks something more. By identifying a group with particular features — the 'fighter' spirit, self-reliance, individualism, freedom — the authors are constructing a hierarchy where some groups are closer to the 'dominant' majority. By claiming that Poles are the 'most popular migrants', the Hammersmith and Fulham MP is understood by many Poles to be saying that there are 'other' migrants, who are far less popular and their closeness to the British much less clear.

Another proces, which reinforces such attitudes, is the racialisation of social divisions so omnipresent among Poles, as we have seen in Chapter 5. The perception of London in terms of ethnic, cultural (understood as racial) boundaries rather than class or power juxtaposes Poles against others seen in racialized tems as 'Indian' or 'black', *ciapaty* or a generalised Muslim. Like the 'soldier' and economic actor narratives, this perception sends a message to the generalised 'English' in order to come closer to the sources of power and prestige. Exceptional circumstances provide an opportunity to send these messages with a stronger, clearer, and more explicit symbolic content. The London bombings in July 2005 illustrated well the role played by the symbols and meanings described in this chapter. Just after the bombings, the Polish National Tourist Office in London, staffed mainly by Poles who had arrived in the 1980s and 1990s, but also with some post-Accession migrants, issued the following poster on their website:

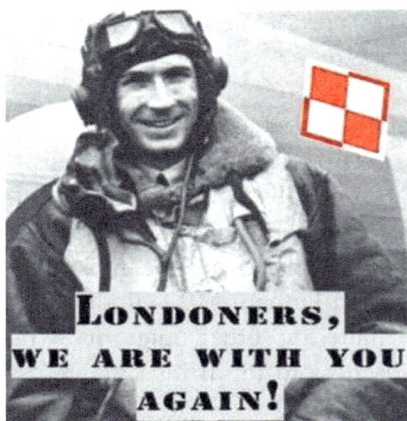

LONDONERS, WE ARE WITH YOU AGAIN!

The poster visually used an image of the Polish pilot[374] to create a link between the Second World War effort of Poles and current presence of Poles in London. The image of war tuned well with the war on terrorism propaganda and the idea that London is again under deadly threat from people who are bend on ending the dominance of the West. But, its meanings also carries a message that, since 'Poles' are here again, again they may be able to offer some helping hand in defeating that mortal enemy, that Poles are 'with you' unlike, those British who for some reason may not be 'with you'. The silent reference to Islam and its place in Britain is clear—Poles are here again and again it is a time of war and again they will defend you. Obviously, I am not arguing that these lines of thought are consciously woven among Poles. However, as described, three sets of meanings and discourses combined result in many Poles constructing a similar narrative— as shown in Chapter 5. These narrative are channelled through the formal world of ethnic associations and results in Poles eager to stress particular issues over the others: The fusion of the narrative presenting the 'Poles' as defenders of Europe, soldiers, émigrés

---

[374] This campaign was short lived, however, and the poster removed from the Office website a month later. That was not due to any controversy (however, some officials admitted that the message was not sensitive) but because someone pointed out in local Polish media that the pilot in the picture is actually Czech, not Polish.

who serve the values of freedom and the narrative of self-sufficient, anti-institutional, individualistic, and socially mobile economic actor form a powerful claim on British establishment that Poles are somewhat different and more valuable as citizens. The proximity is constructed through implicit reference to gener-alised other — the Muslim most commonly, but usually described in broad strokes — non-European, alien, culturally distant, or more mundanely and in street terms: *blaksy, czarny, ciapaty, Araby.*

So, the established institutions, now populated by second-generation Poles or newcomers, are involved in both control and supervision — a role which is made possible by the way British multiculturalism works. The recognition of the established com-munity and its dominant place in hierarchy is not only based on the possession of particular symbolic capital implicit in the notion of *Polonia* or *emigracja* – it is also created through the way in which the British state expects hierarchy and class distinctions to operate and reproduce themselves at the ethnic community level. Polish migrations have, however, a particular role in these debates and in the post-7/7 world, the place of the Polish ethnic group within the British hierarchy is evolving.

Is there a counter-narrative?

In this chapter, I showed how through the concept of *Polonia* a group constructs its sense of permanent settlement in relation to the newcomers who may be from the same ethnic group. Ethnicity turns to be an ambiguous relationship being exclusive from out-side but clearly too inclusive from the inside. In order to offset this, a group that can operate and reproduce the symbolic capital that makes meanings and assumptions about migrating in Polish culture indisputable maintains a distinction from the newcomers. These meaning includes sedentary metaphysics and hierarchic order of migrants whose individualism threatens the health of the community hence the need of a reintegrating symbol of *Polonia* along with the nationalistic discourse of the historical role Poles have in the grand scheme of European politics. At the same time, nationalistic narrative has an implicit class exclusion discourse interwoven into it, as it creates a particular hierarchy of those who leave and those who reconstruct communities of Poles abroad. These processes are influenced by both de-territorialised politics of the nation-states as well as the context of multiculturalism in London. The result is a fusion of two discourses that proves beneficial for the formal representatives of the group. This in turn preserves and reproduces power relations in a way that maintains symbolic capital even if one generation takes the place of another. In fact, the relationship between different groups in Britain can be seen as a version, a modality of natives' versus newcomers' relationship as the established group can communicate things that would not be possible by official British institutions or citizens.

It is valid to ask then—how widespread are these attitudes and is this the face of Polish 'community' in London—fiercely nationalistic, patriotic, and uninterested in those co-ethnics that do not make it? This would be oversimplistic as there is evidence of numerous counter-narratives questioning the dominant role of the established ethnic formal association. First of all, these organisations group a relatively small number of Polish immigrants and cannot be regarded as representing wide sections of their views. Many Poles interviewed during my numerous studies regarded entering formal ethnic associations as not something in which they are at all interested; in fact, small membership may be seen as a contestation of the very idea of the need for such groupings. This shows that ethnic associations are far from the only one able to organise migrants' collective actions and ideals. As Marzena, an activist of London Citizens says: *I am simply a Pole living in London, I don't identify myself with Polonia.* Thus, being civically active does not have to be informed mainly by ones' ethnic identity; in fact, ethnicity can be one of many, numerous ways with which migrants organise and express themselves—something that, as Glick Schiller reminds us, methodological nationalism, and subsequent use of 'ethnic lens' prevent us from realizing. As the recent research by Instytut Spraw Publicznych notes,[375] Poles in London are active in numerous movements, associations, groups, networks, and formal organisations that do not identify them as Polish. In fact, the numbers of Poles active in non-ethnic institutions—trade unions, sexual minorities organisations, religious, professional, human rights based, political parties, green politics, etc.—are in proportion probably higher than those in the *Polonian* ones.[376] In other words, *Polonia* is just one; among many ways, Poles can be active in London public space. However, by playing the ethnic card, they fit into the British multicultural dominant discourse that sees groups as homogeneous and hierarchically organised, thus gaining a prestigious voice in public domain. As the study by scholars from Instytut Zachodni note,[377] these formal ethnic associations are also treated generally by Poles with suspicion and reluctance to engage, seeing them as elitist and too close to the state. In that sense, many migrants retain a form of autonomy and resist dominant ethnic ascriptions by simply refusing to participate in public life 'as Poles'.The same study notes that Poles they interviewed stress the preference for informal way of association and action— something myself[378] and Małgorzata Irek notes, along with a study by Paulina Pustulka who depicts a rich social environment of informal associations among Polish migrants living in the UK[379]. Drawing on the myth of Polish conman argu-

[375] J. Kucharczyk. 2013. Nic o nas bez nas. [in]: W. Brytanii (red.) *Partycypacja obywatelska Polaków*. Warszawa: Instytut Spraw Publicznych.

[376] J. Kucharczyk. 2013. *Ibidem.*

[377] A. Fiń, A. Legut, K. Mazurek, W. Nowak, M. Nowosielski, K. Schöll-Mazurek. 2013. *Polityka polonijna w ocenie jej wykonawców i adresatów*. Poznań: Instytut Zachodni.

[378] M. Garapich. 2016. Breaking borders, changing structures—transnationalism of migrants from Poland as anti-state resistance. *Social Identities: Journal for the Study of Race, Nation and Culture* 22(1):95–111.

[379] M. Garapich. 2013. Pomijani multiuczestnicy? Polacy w inicjatywach nieformalnych w Wielkiej Brytanii' [Disregarded multi-participants? Polish migrants and informal social participation initiatives in Great Britain]. [in]: J. Kucharczyk (ed.) *Nic o nas bez nas. Partycypacja obywatelska Polaków w Wielkiej Brytanii*. Warszawa: Instytut Spraw Publicznych, pp. 105–132.; I. Fitzgerald, J. Hardy, M. Martinez Lucio. 2012. The internet, employment and Polish migrant

ment, I think both aspects need to be taken relationally, and the reluctance of Poles to engage and reproduce the nationalistic discourse, arises from its implicit exclusionist and class-related features. By framing ethnic identity in very rigid, dogmatic, and essentialistic frame, it removes itself from everyday experience of migrants who slowly, gradually learn to live within diverse setting of London, accepting its unwritten rules of living a plural life and subsequent complexity of individual identity. In other words, Polish migrants in general resist attempts of the elites—diasporic and state oriented—in order to maintain a degree of social and cultural autonomy to be free to define what being Polish means for them and be free to situationally adapt it to changing conditions. The plurality of counter-narratives woven around class ideas among trade unionists[380] religion[381] and gender[382] give quite a wide scope for not just contesation but keeping the identities of Poles fluid and open-ended enough to absorb new meanings and ideas of Polishness. The unequal power relation which of these is

---

workers: Communication, activism and competition in the new organisational spaces. *New Technology, Work and Employment* 27(2);93–105; I. Fitzgerald, J. Hardy. 2010. 'Thinking outside the box'? Trade union organising strategies and polish migrant workers in the United Kingdom. *British Journal of Industrial Relations* 48(1):131–150.

[380] See, for example: M. Garapich. 2013. Między apatią a aktywnością—partycypacja polityczna migrantów z Polski w Wielkiej Brytanii. [in]: J. Kucharczyk (red.) *Nic o nas bez nas. Partycypacja obywatelska Polaków w Wielkiej Brytanii*. Warszawa: Instytut Spraw Publicznych, pp 133–162; I. Fitzgerald, J. Hardy. 2010. 'Thinking outside the box'? Trade union organising strategies and polish migrant workers in the United Kingdom. *British Journal of Industrial Relations* 48(1):131–150.

[381] J. Krotofil. 2011. 'If I am to be a Muslim, I have to be a good one'. Polish migrant women embracing Islam and reconstructing identity in dialogue with self and others. [in]: K. Górak-Sosnowska (ed.) *Muslims in Poland and Eastern Europe. Widening the European Discourse on Islam.* Warsaw: University of Warsaw.

[382] See, for example: B. Siara. 2013. Construction of gender in the migration space: Polish women in the UK. *GENDER. Zeitschrift für Geschlecht, Kultur und Gesellschaft [GENDER. Journal of Gender, Culture and Society]* 1:105–120; E. Duda-Mikulin. 2013. Migration as opportunity? A case study of Polish women: migrants in the UK and returnees in Poland. *Problemy Polityki Społecznej [Social Policy Issues]* 23(4):105–121. http://www.problemyps.pl/

seen by the state and nationalist discourse as the 'right' and 'truly' Polish one, is the issue for researchers to explore further, but also civil society to question and adress. Polish historical experience, as we have seen, in particular its migration has been very often claimed solely by the nationalist discourse, hence it is not a surprise that the political right in Poland is keen to stress that todays' migrants in London are also 'victims' of foreign (usually Western) plots, corrupt elites and the like. This construction of migration as a 'passive' response to external forces is probably the most contested one, so— as we have seen—if there is something that link strongly Polish migrants, it is their powerful sense of individual capability, creativity, and freedom from state-imposed—including symbolic—constraints.

Chapter 8

Conclusions: power of the individual

In this book, I have explored the ways in which migration from Poland to London has developed over the last 15 years, how Polish migrants from various groups and social backgrounds have negotiated their place in their new environment of the global city, and how individual agency shapes the world they live in and links various locations in Poland with the British national capital — in short, how transnational social fields work and why people maintain them. The numerous meaning-making practices influence how people operate in a transnational social field, which links these two societies merging them and creating a functional, sustainable migration system. These practices build on meanings and symbols embedded in the rich and established culture of Polish migration, and they involve both the discursive practices of meaning making and the practical development of networks, chain migrations, settlement, formations of ethnic groups, and formal associations. As demonstrated, these often emerge in order to act on the public arena using forms of capital at their disposal — connections, reputation, historical references familiar to British society, public perceptions, as well as newly constructed 'whiteness', which for many is seen as an asset. Migrants from Poland clearly engage with dominant discourses concerning the economy, multicultural diversity, and migration that punctuate public debates in contemporary British society. As we have seen, through the merger of particular discourses of neo-liberal individuality, self-reliance, ethical value of work, and a nationalistic tendency to direct migrants' moral compass towards national community and the collective, Poles abroad in power positions in ethnic associations are able to position themselves in quite a privileged position, after all, not a lot of migrants receive a public endorsement as 'Britain's favourite migrants'.

The tendency to privilege ethnicity in migration studies, the 'ethnic lenses' as Glick Schiller calls it, have obscured discreet processes through which social class and hierarchy are produced and recreated in migration context as well as debates on multiculturalism. In fact, I would argue that it is false to contain social class in one national context only. The construction of transnational social fields shows how social class, as well as perceptions of the state, the group and community dynamics, take place across boundaries and borders, they are never empirically contained within one society or one state. The social life of Polish migrants, established groups, 'stayers', as well as 'storks' develop all the time with reference to national borders. 'Here' assumes a 'there', back 'home' assumes a 'here in London'. Transnational social fields are transnational precisely *because* they link two different places; places that need to be conceptually contained and made meaningful through boundary-making processes. In this context, even second-generation Poles are influenced by transnational fields – not only when a proverbial never-seen cousin knocks to one's door but when is confronted with one's own assumptions about Polishness, Polish history, and numerous contradictory meanings Polish culture brings this ultimately triggers an unresolvable conflict between egalitarian undertones of ethnicity and the reality of class stratification both in a post-socialist society as well as neo-liberal hypercapitalist global city.

For all arguments about the demise of the nation states, the major conclusion of this book is that from the perspective of social actors, this transnational reflexivity through physical and mental manoeuvring across borders and the complex reconstructions of social class and ethnicity combine ways of being and ways of belonging, which paradoxically reproduce national borders. This occurs despite the freedom of movement, which attended the eastwards expansion of the EU and which has been one of the most crucial aspects of weakening of the nation-state. So while migrants have flowed across borders in massive numbers, there has been a constant tendency for people to recreate them and re-define them, to ascribe new meanings to border crossing, shifting the boundaries from the domain of the physical, administrative obstacle, to symbolic, cultural tool of distinctions in a global city. As we have seen, migrants need borders to define themselves in terms of their cultural backgrounds, constructions of proximity to sources of power, social class position, status acquisition, and identity. In the Polish case, it has been impossible for dominant nationalist narratives to symbolise the national community with-out implicit or explicit references to border-crossing practices. National 'communities' are—or in this case always were—made through migration, hence their importance in contemporary de-bates in Poland as well as within transnational social fields in which migrants participate.

All this raises a crucial question about the limits of cosmo-politanism and postmodernity understood here as the process of emergence of increasingly fragmented, displaced, subjective and fluid identities, group formations, and individual loyalties. On the one hand, the lifestyles of many Polish migrants—many of whom are featured in this book—embody the dream of the cosmopolitan citizen, moving between nation-states freely, taking advantage of the best of both worlds, navigating through different cultures, social environments, and contexts, almost effortlessly responding to labour market gaps and new opportunities ahead. Most im-portantly, as seen by the transition from pre-EU enlargement mi-gration regimes to the world of free movement, social actors were in fact one of the driving forces of that structural changes, in a way through sheer volume of pre-enlargement migration law breaking, migrants from Poland created conditions that the British state had to accept. The power of the individual migrants *en masse* ought then to be celebrated as a victory of the small over the pow-erful.

For many commentators, politicians, and EU policy makers, these migrants effectively illustrate the desirable face of modernity—young, inspired individuals uprooting themselves, pursuing individual economic goals, and solving the problem of unemployment in Poland and skill shortages in the receiving societies. In many narratives—and migrants themselves are active producers of them—it is almost a story about neo-liberal pioneers, who pursue a specific version of the American Dream, albeit in the EU. In this view, primordial, traditional attachments fade and individualistic attitudes prevail and a new person is born—the true proof of the success of European integration from below.

A careful, more nuanced, and actor-oriented anthropological gaze, however, shows that, for many others, migration results in strengthening of a particular set of cultural meanings that are far from cosmopolitan and individualistic. These meanings reinforce nationalist and collective ideas, encourage new forms of racism, or support new class discrimination and social exclusion. We saw how many Polish nationals reposition themselves on a local geography of perceived hierarchy and emphasise new ways of belonging, which express essentialist attitudes towards 'culture' understood as whiteness, Europeanness, and proximity to the British 'middle class' or the 'English' embodied in a magical way in the persona of members of the royal family. We also saw how class identity and interest encourage many to question hegemonic ideologies of ethnicity and turn towards vaguer but still highly essentialist notions of race and 'whiteness'.

Transnational social fields thus have a dual potential. They can weaken the nation-state and its ability to influence people's minds and, consequently, behaviour. They can also encourage the very same state to strengthen and reaffirm traditional discourses of ethnic and national purity, solidarity, and notions of a metaphorical kinship bonded by moral ties. The significance of the nationalist dominant discourse in Polish culture has been further strengthened by the fact that, after the collapse of Communism, the state could do little to contain mass outflows of its citizens. Its use of symbolic tools is aimed at retaining at least some degree of control over peoples' understandings of mobility and the power to ascribe meanings to symbols and human actions. Thus, the Polish state and its elites attempt to portray the emigration as a 'problem' an 'evil' or 'bloodletting.' These symbols are carried along specific policy actions, which merge the Polish state and formal *Polonia* associations into one particular lobby whose goal is to control and dominate. The intention is to reproduce a particular set of meanings associated with Polishness — its historic role, which legitimises its place in Europe, together with a class consciousness, which plays on the role of intelligentsia as the bearer of national identity and 'carer' of the lower classes. As shown, Poland has a rich tradition of such de-territorialised politics and the notion of *Polonia* as the symbolic equivalent of the state abroad fulfils the task of social control and class reproduction abroad also today.

Social actors do not passively receive and accept these dominant narratives and their cultural understanding of these is far from uniform. Polish migrants employ various strategies to reformulate them, contest them, or — if it suits them — reproduce them. Cultural strategies, such as myth-making, transnational reflexivity, intentional unpredictibility, the perception of class as both fixed and changeable, strongly asserted individualism, the contestation of equation of ethnic ties with moral ones, among many others described in this book, seek to ease individual operations in the transnational social field by keeping the dominant narratives and systems of norms and values in line with their everyday applicability. Dominant narratives inescapably create tensions and contradictions. In the business of the everyday, norms can be crossed, values corrupted, and the 'ought' comes into conflict with 'is'. What people do and say is aimed at easing these tensions.

Perceiving and analysing social class as an aspect of transnational meaning-making practice helps us to grasp the limitations and political underpinnings of methodological nationalism. A prime example of methodological nationalism at work concerns the endless debates and questions about whether 'Polish migrants' are still in Britain or have already left. These often depict migrants as soulless subjects of economic conditions, moving around nation-states in search of work. However, the description of the self-perpetuating transnational social field—with its sub-fields of political and economic links connecting London and Poland—show that contemporary debates in the context of the economic crisis about whether Polish migrants will remain in the UK or will head home are misplaced, and simply wrong. Diverse migration strategies are strongly interdependent and can be activated into an accelerating migration chain whether conditions will require, such as a sudden downturn in Poland, a boom in the UK, or—the looming prospect of UK's exit from the EU. 'Stayers' can form the basis for successful short-term migratory trips for 'storks' or 'searchers', for instance. Even if some predictions are correct, and some Polish migrants have indeed returned over the last few years, people maintain ties that may be reused if economic climate changes again as these ties have a tremendous ability to endure. The endurance of these ties is sustained by the specific culture of migration Polish society has developed over generations.

The cultural significance of social mobility in modern Poland, connected to land tenure, educational aspirations, and ethos of 'making it' despite the odds, reinforced by strong anti-institutional attitudes, means that Britain, and more specifically London, will always remain an attractive option for short-term gain or a place where one can achieve social mobility in the eyes of its peers at home. In this, Polish migrants strongly resemble migrants who were moving to the USA at the beginning of the 20th century and created links and transnational fields spanning generations. This book shows both the complexity of these flows and the fascinating continuity in terms of cultural constructions and attitudes towards social class, ethnicity, and the nation. For Polish society, as a whole, this is simply another chapter in their deterritorialised nation-state development, albeit a chapter which involves a new phase of westwards migration as the EU moves eastwards. In this, it is both new and old: it offers both new opportunities but at the same time utilises and reproduces old symbolic structures which link long history of migration from Poland with contemporary debates over the future of Europe.

I began this book with a brief vignette of the referendum on Polish accession into the EU back in 2003. Who could have predicted that almost 15 years later, this referendum would be partially responsible for another one in the most popular country of destination for Polish migrants — the UK, and that this referendum in turn would be about the future of this country in the same supranational bloc. Without doubt, the political outcome of the massive human flow this book is about has been for British society to begin to question the whole idea of the EU and in particular one of its main pillars — the freedom of movement. Although potentially British exit could affect the future flows, as well as the social rights of those already here, this book proves that immigration restrictions and reconstructions of the East and West divisions in Europe are a futile attempt to restrict individual aspirations and abilities to bend and resist structures of domination. If there is one lesson that migrants from Poland teach us, it is that there are no structural boundaries that cannot be crossed and that European integration, the one forged from below, through actions of millions of mobile people is a process that cannot be curtailed easily, if at all.

Literature

Anderson, Benedict. 1991. *Imagined Communities: Reflections on the Origin and Spread of Nationalism*. London: Verso.

Anderson, Benedict. 1992. *Long-Distance Nationalism: World Capitalism and the Rise of Identity Politics*. Amsterdam: The Wertheim Lecture, Centre for Asian Studies.

Babiński, Grzegorz. 1992. Uwarunkowania przemian organizacji polonijnych w Europie i Ameryce. [in]: Szydłowska-Cegłowa Barbara (eds.) *Polonia w Europie*. Warsaw: Polska Akademia Nauk, pp. 77–90.

Barth, Frederic. 1999. A personal view of present tasks and priorities in cultural and social anthropology. [in]: Robert Borofsky (eds.) *Assesing Cultural Anthropology*. New York: McGraw-Hill, pp. 349–361.

Barth, Frederic. 1969. Introduction. [in]: Frederic Barth (eds.) *Ethnic Groups and Boundaries: The Social Organization of Cultural Difference*. London: George Allen and Unwin.

Basch, Linda, Nina Glick Schiller, Cristina Szanton Blanc. 1994. *Nations Unbound: Transnational Projects, Postcolonial Predicaments, and Deterritorialized Nation-States*. Langhorne: Gordon and Breach.

Bauman, Zygmunt. 1997. The making and unmaking of strangers. [in]: Pnina Werbner, Tariq Modood (eds.) *Debating Cultural Hybridity. Multicultural Identities and the Politics of Anti-Racism*. London/New Jersey: Zed Books, pp. 46–57.

Bauman, Zygmunt. 1994. After the patronage state: a model in search of class interests. [in]: Christopher G.A. Bryan, Edmund Mokrzycki (eds.) *The New Great Transformation? Change and Continuity in East-Central Europe*. London/New York: Routledge, p. 33.

Baumann, Gerd. 1996. *Contesting Culture. Discourses of Identity in Multi-Ethnic London*. Cambridge: Cambridge University Press.

Benedyktowicz, Zbigniew. 2000. *Portrety "Obcego."* Kraków: Wydawnictwo.

Berger, Peter, Thomas Luckman. 1967. *The Social Construction of Reality. A Treatise in the Sociology of Knowledge*. Harmondsworth: Penguin Books.

Berlin, Isaah. 1997. *Against the Current. Essays in the History of Ideas*. Pimlico: Random House.

Billing, Micheal. 1995. *Banal Nationalism*. London: Sage.

Blejwas, Stanislaus. 1981. Old and new Polonias: tension within an ethnic community. *Polish American Studies* 38(2): 55–83.

Borowik, I. 2003. *Blokowiska. Miejski habitat w oglądzie socjologicznym.* Wrocław: Oficyna Wydawnicza Arboretum.

Bourdieu, Pierre. 1985. The social space and the genesis of groups. *Social Science Information* 24(2):195–220.

Bottomley, Gillian. 1998. Anthropologists and the rhizomatic study of migration. *The Australian Journal of Anthropology* 9(1):31–44.

Bouvais, Daniel. 2005. Trójkąt ukraiński. Szlachta, carat i lud na Wołyniu, Podolu i Kijowszczyźnie. Kraków: Wydawnictwo UMCS.

Breton, Raymond. 1964. Institutional completeness of ethnic communities and the personal relations of immigrants. *American Journal of Sociology* 70(2):193–205.

Brettell, Caroline. 2002. *Anthropology and Migration; Essays on Transnationalism, Ethnicity, and Identity.* New York: Routledge.

Brubaker, Rogers. 1998. Immigration, citizenship, and the nation-state in France and Germany. [in]: Gershon Shafir (ed.) *The Citizenship Debates: A Reader.* Minneapolis: University of Minnesota Press, pp. 131–164.

Brubaker, Rogers. 1996. *Nationalism Reframed. Nationhood and the National Question in the New Europe.* Los Angeles: University of California, pp. 84–86.

Buchowski, Michał. 2006. The spectre of orientalism in Europe. From exotic other to stygmatised brother. *Anthropological Quarterly* 73(3):463–482.

Buchowski, Michal. 2004. Redefining work in a local community in Poland. Transformation and class, culture and work. [in]: Angela Procoli (ed.) *Workers and Narratives of Survival in Europe. The Management of Precariousness at the End of the Twentieth Century.* New York: State University of New York Press.

Buchowski, Michal, Edouard Conte, Carole Nagengast (eds.). 2001. *Poland Beyond Communism: "Transition" in Critical Perspective.* Fribourg: Fribourg University Press, pp. 259–279.

Bukowczyk, John J. 1996. *Polish Americans and their History Community, Culture and Politics.* Pittsburgh: University of Pittsburgh Press.

Burrell, Kathy. 2008. Time matters: temporal contexts of Polish transnationalism. [in]: Michael P. Smith and John Eade (eds.) *Transnational Ties: Cities, Migrations and Identities.* New Bunswick: Transaction Publishers.

Burell, Kathy. 2003. Small-scale transnationalism: homeland connections and the Polish 'community' in Leister. *International Journal of Population Geography* 9(4):323–335.

Burell, Kathy. 2004. Homeland Memories and the Polish Community in Leister. [in:] Peter D. Stachura (ed.) *The Poles in Britain 1940-2000*. London: Franck Cass, pp. 69–84.

Burrell, Kathy. 2006. *Moving Lives: Narratives of Nation and Migration Among Europeans in Post-War Britain*. London: Ashgate.

Burrell, Kathy 2009. Polish migration to the UK in the "new" European Union: after 2004. [in]: Kathy Burrell (ed.) *Studies in Migration and Diaspora*. Aldershot: Ashgate.

Burrell, Kathy. 2008. Male and female Polishness in post-war Leicester: gender and its intersections in a refugee community. [in]: Louise Ryan, Wendy Webster (eds.) *Gendering Migration: Masculinity, Femininity and Ethnicity in Post-War Britain*. Aldershot: Ashgate, pp. 71–87.

Castles, Stephen. 2010. Understanding global migration: a social transformation perspective. *Journal of Ethnic and Migration Studies* 36(10):1565–1586.

Centrum Badania Opinii Społecznej (CBOS). 2006. *Praca Polaków w krajach Unii Europejskiej*. Warszawa: Listopad.

Cenckiewicz, Stanisław. 2006. Polski Londyn na celowniku służb; Nowe aństwo nr 3/2006, pp. 62–64.

2002. Geneza Towarzystwa Łączności z Polonią Zagraniczną "Polonia." *Pamięć i Sprawiedlowość* 1(1):161–168.

Chałasiński, Józef. 1968. *Kultura i naród*. Warszawa: Ksiązka i Wiedza.

Chodakiewicz, Marek J. 2005. "Brytyjska Polonia," review of the book by Peter Stachura (red.) *The Poles in Britain, 1940-2000: From Betrayal to Assimilation*. London/Portland: Frank Cass, 2004. [in]: Glaukopis, 2–3 2005, p. 413.

Cohen, Anthony P. 1985. *The Symbolic Construction of Community*. London: Open University.

Cohen, Anthony P. 1994. *Self Consciousness. An Alternative Anthropology of Identity*. New York: Routledge.

Cohen, Anthony P. 1975. *The Management of Myths: The Politics of Legitimation in a Newfoundland Community*. St John's: Institute of Social and Economic Research, Memorial University.

Centrum Badania Opinii Społecznych. 2005. *Tożsamość narodowa Polaków oraz postrzeganie mniejszości narodowych i tnicznych w Polsce. Komunikat z badań*.

Cygan, Mary. 1998. Inventing Polonia: notions of Polish American identity, 1870-1990. *Prospects* 23:209–246.

Datta, A. 2009. "This is special humour": visual narratives of Polish masculinities on London's building sites. [in]: Kathy Burrell (ed.) *Polish Migration to the UK in the 'New' European Union*. London: Ashgate.

Domański, Henryk. 1995. Rekompozycja stratyfikacji społecznej i reorientacja wartości. [in]: Antoni Sułek, Józef Styk (eds.) *Ludzie i instytucje. Stawanie się ładu społecznego*. Lublin: Wyd UMCS.

Domański, Henryk. 2000. *On the Verge of Convergence: Social Stratification in Eastern Europe*. Budapest: CEU Press.

Domański, Henryk. 2002. *Ubóstwo w społeczeństwach postkomunistycznych*. Warszawa: Wyd. Instytut Spraw Publicznych.

Drinkwater, Stephen, Michal Garapich, John Eade. *International Migration* 47(1):161–190.

Driver, Stephen, Michal Garapich. 2012. 'Everyone for themselves'? Nonnational EU citizens from eastern and central Europe and the 2012 London elections. http://www.sociology.ox.ac.uk/documents/epop/papers/EPOP_article_garapichdriver_SEPTEMBER_07_mg.pdf

Drozdowski, Marian M. 1974. Ewolucja pojęcia "Polonia" w XIX-XX wieku. [in]: M.M. Drozdowski (ed.) *Dzieje Polonii w XIX i XX wieku*. Toruń, p. 5.

Dustmann, C. 2005. Immigrantsin the British labour market. *Fiscal Studies* 26:423–470; Gilpin, N., et al. 2006. *The impact of free movement of workers from Central and Eastern Europe on the UK labour market*. London: Department of Work and Pensions Working Paper No. 29.

Duvell, Franck. 2001. *Highly Skilled, Self-Employed and Illegal Immigrants from Poland in United Kingdom*. Warsaw: Working Papers, Centre for Migration Studies. http://www.migracje.uw.edu.pl/obm/pix/054.pdf

Duvell, Frank. 2006. Active Civic Participation of Immigrants in the United Kingdom. Country report: patrz. http://www.uni-oldenburg.de/politis-europe/

Dzialek, Jaroslaw. 2009. *Social Capital and Economic Growth in Polish Regions*. Germany: MPRA Paper 18287, University Library of Munich.

Eade, John, Michał Garapich, Stephen Drinkwater. 2006. *Class and Ethnicity: Polish Migrants in London*. Economic and Social Research Council End of Award Report, RES-000-22-1294. www.surrey.ac.uk/Arts/Cronem.

Elias, Nobert, John L. Scotson. 1994. *The Established and the Outsiders — A Sociological Enquiry into Community Problems*. London: Sage.

Erdmans, Mary Patrice. 1992a. The social construction of emigration as a moral issue. *Polish American Studies* 49(1):5–25.

Erdmans, Mary Patrice. 1992b. *Emigres and Ethnics: Patterns of Cooperation Between New and Established Organizations in Chicago's Polish Community*. PhD thesis. Evanston Illinois: Northwestern University.

Erdmans, Mary Patrice. 1995. Immigrants and ethnics: conflict and identity in Polish Chicago. *The Sociological Quarterly* 36(1):175–195.

Erdmans, Mary Patrice. 1998. *Opposite Poles. Immigrants and Ethnics in Polish Chicago, 1976–1990*. Philadelphia: The Pennsylvania State University Press.

Eriksen, Thomas H. 1993. *Us and Them in Modern Societies*. Oslo: Scandinavian University Press.

Eriksen, Thomas. 1993. *Ethnicity and Nationalism. Anthropological Perspectives*. London: Pluto Press.

Faist, Thomas. 2007. *Dual Citizenship in Europe: From Nationhood to Societal Integration*. Surray: Ashgate Publishing.

Favell, Adrian. 1998. *Philosophies of Integration: Immigration and the Idea of Citizenship in France and Britain*. London: Palgrave.

Favell, Adrian, Hansen Randall. 2002. Markets against politics: migration, EU enlargement and the idea of Europe. *Journal of Ethnic and Migration Studies* 28(4):581–601.

Favell, Adrian. 2008. The new face of east-west migration in Europe. *Journal of Ethnic and Migration Studies* 34(5):701.

Fiń, Anna, Agnieszka Legut, Witold Nowak, Michael Nowosielski, Kamilii Schöll-Mazurek. 2013. *Polityka polonijna w ocenie jej wykonawców i adresatów*. Poznań: Instytut Zachodni.

Fitzgerald, Ian, Jane Hardy, M. Martinez Lucio. 2012. The internet, employment and Polish migrant workers: Communication, activism and competition in the new organisational spaces. *New Technology, Work and Employment* 27(2):93–105

Fitzgerald, Ian, Jane Hardy. 2010. "Thinking outside the box"? Trade union organising strategies and Polish migrant workers in the United Kingdom. *British Journal of Industrial Relations* 48(1):131–150.

Foreman, Murray, Mark Anthony Neal (eds.). 2004. *That's the Joint! The Hip-Hop Studies Reader*. New York: Routledge.

Fotyga, B. 1999. *Dzicy z naszej ulicy: antropologia kultury młodzieżowej*. Warszawa: Ośrodek Badań Młodzieży.

Frieske, Kazimierz. 1997. *Ofiary sukcesu. Zjawiska marginalizacji społecznej w Polsce*. Warszawa: Instytut Socjologii UW.

Friszke, Andrzej. 1995. *Myśl polityczna na wygnaniu. Publicyści i politycy polskiej emigracji powojennej* (red.). Warszawa: ISP PAN.

Friszke, Andrzej. 1999. *Życie polityczne emigracji*. Warszawa: Więź.

Fukuyama, Francis. 1992. *The End of History and the Last Man*. London: Penguin.

Gabaccia, Donna R., Dirk Hoerder, Adam Walaszek. 2007. Immigration and nation building during the mass migration from Europe. [in]: Nancy L. Green, François Weil (eds.) *Citizenship and Those Who Leave: The Politics of Emigration and Expatriation*. Chicago: University of Illinois Press, p. 75.

Gadowska, Kaja. 2005. Clientelism in the Silesian Coal Mining Industry. [in]: *Political Corruption in Poland*. Arbeitspapiere und Materialien, Forschungsstelle Osteuropa Bremen, 65/2005, pp. 21–48.

Galasińska, Aleksandra, Olga Kozłowska. 2009. Discourses of "normal life" among post-acceession migrants from Poland to Britain. [in]: Kathy Burrell (ed.) *Polish Migration to the UK in the 'New' European Union*. Surray: Ashgate.

Galasiński, Dariusz, Aleksandra Galasińska. 2007. Lost in communism, lost in migration: narratives of post-1989 Polish migrant experience. *Journal of Multicultural Discourses* 2(1):47-62.

Galasińska, Aleksandra, Anna Horolets. 2012. The (pro)long(ed) life of a "grand narrative": the case of internet forum discussions on post-2004 Polish migration to the United Kingdom. *Text and Talk* 32(2):125–143.

Garapich, Michał. 2006a. My nie mamy z tym nic wspólnego. Polska diaspora w Wielkiej Brytanii na skrzyżowaniu między lokalizmem a globalizacją. *Przegląd Polonijny* 32[1(119)]:69–88.

Garapich, Michał. 2006b. Flexibel und individualistisch. Polnische Migranten zwischen den Welten. Osteuropa. 11/12 2006, pp. 191–204.

Garapich, Michal, Dorota Osipovic. 2007. Badanie sondażowe wśród obywateli polskich zamieszkałych w Wielkiej Brytanii i Irlandii. http://www.polishpsychologists.org/wp-content/uploads/2012/12/Raport_migpol.pdf

Garapich, Michał. 2008a. The migration industry and civil society: Polish immigrants in the United Kingdom before and after EU enlargement. *Journal of Ethnic and Migration Studies* 34(5):735–752.

Garapich, Michal. 2008b. Odyssean refugees, migrants and power: construction of the "other" within the Polish community in the United Kingdom. [In]: Deborah Reed-Danahay, Caroline Brettell (red.) *Citizenship, Political Engagement and Belonging. Immigrants in Europe and the United States*. New Brunswick/New Jersey/London: Rutgers University Press, pp. 124–144.

Garapich, Michal. 2009. [in]: Maciej Duszczyk, Magdalena Lesińska (eds.) *Współczesne migracje: dylematy Europy i Polski*. Publikacja z okazji 15-lecia Ośrodka Badań nad Migracjami UW. Warszawa: Wydawnictwo Petit.

Garapich, Michal. 2011. 'It's a jungle out there. You need to stick together": anti-institutionalism, alcohol and performed masculinities among Polish homeless men in London. *Liminalities: A Journal of Performance Studies* 7(3):Autumn 2011.

Garapich, Michal. 2012. Between cooperation and hostility – constructions of ethnicity and social class among Polish migrants in London. *Annales Universitatis Paedagogicae Cracoviensis; Studia Sociologica* 2:31–45.

Garapich, Michal. 2013. Między apatią a aktywnością – partycypacja polityczna migrantów z Polski w Wielkiej Brytanii. [in]: JacekKucharczyk (red.) *Nic o nas bez nas. Partycypacja obywatelska Polaków w Wielkiej Brytanii*. Warszawa: Instytut Spraw Publicznych, pp 133–162.

Garapich, Michal. 2014. Sprzątanie grobów, nacjonalizm diaspory i ciężka robota – tworzenie rytuałów cmentarnych wśród poakcesyjnej migracji w Wielkiej Brytanii. [in]: Dariusz Niedźwiedzki (ed.) *Kultura, tożsamość i integracja europejska. Księga jubileuszowa na 60-lecie urodzin Zdzisława Macha*. Kraków: NOMOS.

Garapich, Michal P., Stephen Drinkwater. 2015. Migration strategies of polish migrants: do they have any at all? *Journal of Ethnic and Migration Studies* 41(12):1909–1931.

Garapich, Michal P. 2016. Breaking borders, changing structures – transnationalism of migrants from Poland as anti-state resistance. *Social Identities: Journal for the Study of Race, Nation and Culture* 22(1):95–111.

Geertz, Clifford. 1973. *The Interpretation of Cultures*. New York: Basic Books.

Gellner, Ernest. 1983. *Nations and Nationalism*. Ithaca: Cornell University Press.

Giddens, Anthony. 1991. *Modernity and Self-Identity*. Cambridge: Polity Press.

Gilmore, David D. 1987. Honor, honesty, shame: male status in contemporary Andalusia. [in]: David D. Gilmore (ed.) *Honor and Shame and the Unity of the Mediterranean.* American Anthropological Association Special Publication 22. Washington: American Anthropological Association, pp. 90–103.

Glick Schiller, Nina. 1977. Ethnic groups are made not born. The Haitian immigrants and American politics. [in]: George Hicks, Philip Leis (red.), *Ethnic Encounters and Contexts.* North Scituate: Duxbury Press, pp. 23–35.

Glick Schiller Nina, Basch Linda, Cristina Szanton Blanc. 1995. From immigrant to transmigrant: theorising transnational migration. *Anthropological Quarterly* 68(1):48–63.

Glick Schiller, Nina, Andreas Wimmer. 2003. Methodological nationalism, the social science and the study of migration: an essay in historical epistemology. *International Migration Review* 37:576-610.

Górny, Agata, Dariusz Stola. 2001. Akumulacja i wykorzystanie migracyjnego kapitału społecznego. [in]: Ewa Jaźwińska, Marek Okólski (eds.) *Ludzie na huśtawce. Migracje między peryferiami Polski a Zachodu.* Warszawa: Scholar.

Górny, Agata, Dorota Osipowicz. 2005. Return migration of second generation British Poles. CMR Working Papers.

I. Grabowska. 2016. *Movers and Stayers: Sociaal Mobility, Migration and Skills.* Frankfurt Am Main: Peter Lang..

Green, Nancy L., Francois Weil (eds.). 2007. *Citizenship and Those Who Leave: The Politics of Emigration and Expatriation.* Chicaago: University of Illinois Press.

Grzymała-Kazlowska, Aleksandra. 2001. Dynamika sieci migranckich: Polacy w Brukseli. [in]: Ewa Jaźwinska, Marek Okólski (eds.) *Ludzie na hustawce. Migracje miedzy peryferiami Polski i Zachodu.* Warszawa: Wydawnictwo Naukowe Scholar, pp. 272–302.

Grzymala-Kazlowska, Anna. 2005. From ethnic cooperation to in-group competition: undocumented Polish workers in Brussels. *Journal of Ethnic and Migration Studies* 31(4):675–697.

Gupta, Akhil, James Ferguson. 1992. Beyond culture: space, identity and politics of difference. *Cultural Anthropology* 7(1):6–23.

Gupta, Akhil, James Ferguson. 1997. Culture, power, place. Ethnography at the end of an era. [in]: Akhil Gupta, James Ferguson (eds.) *Culture, Power, Place, Explorations in Critical Anthropology.* Durhm: Duke University Press.

Habielski, Rafal. 1999. *Życie społeczne i kulturalne emigracji.* Warszawa: Więź.

Literature   333

Hahn, Hans H. 1987. Kilka rozważań o rozwoju organizacyjnym Wielkiej Emigracji w pierwszych latach jej istnienia. [in]: *Losy Polaków w XIX wieku*. Warszawa: PWN.

Hann, Chris. 1996. Political society and civil anthropology. [in]: Chris Hann, Elisabeth Dunn (eds.) *Civil Society – Challenging Western Models*. London: Rutledge.

Hann, Chris. 1998. Post-socialist nationalism: rediscovering the past in southeast Poland. *Slavic Review* 57(4):840–863.

Hansen, Randall. 2000. *Citizenship and Immigration in Post-War Britain: The Institutional Origins of a Multicultural Nation*. Oxford: Oxford University Press.

Hansen, Randall. 2009. The poverty of postnationalism: citizenship, immigration, and the new Europe. *Theory and Society* 38(1):1–24.

Hartman, Andrew. 2004. The rise and fall of whiteness studies. *Race and Class* 46(2):22–38.

Hausner, Jersey, et al. 1999. J. *Trzy Polski. Potencjał i bariery integracji z Unią Europejską*. EU-Monitoring. Warszawa: Fundacja Ericha Brosta.

Held, David, Anthony McGrew, David Goldblatt, Jonathan Perraton. 1999. *Global Transformations: Politics, Economics and Culture*. Palo Alto: Stanford University Press.

Hirschman, Albert O. 1970. *Exit, Voice, and Loyalty: Responses to Decline in Firms, Organizations, and States*. Cambridge: Harvard University Press.

Hładkiewicz, Wiesław. 1997. Bilans i perspektywy emigracji polskiej w Wielkiej Brytanii. *Przegląd Polonijny* 23(2):53–68.

Hobsbawm, Eric J. 1983. Introduction: invented tradition. [in]: Eric Hobsbawn, Tom Ranger (red.) *The Invention of Tradition*. Cambridge: Cambridge University Press.

Home Office. 2002. Secure Borders, Safe Haven. Integration with Diversity in Modern Britain. http://www.archive2.official-documents.co.uk/document/cm53/5387/cm5387.pdf

Home Office. 2003. Control of Immigration Statistics. http://www.homeoffice.gov.uk/rds/pdfs04/hosb1204.pdf

Home Office. Accession Monitoring Report, May 2004–September 2007. http://www.ind.homeoffice.gov.uk/sitecontent/documents/aboutus/accession_monitoring_report/

Home Office. 2010. *Control of Immigration: Quarterly Statistical Summary*.

Irek, Malgorzata. 2011. The myth of 'weak ties'. [in]: Bohdan Jałowiecki, Marek Szczepański (eds.). 2008. *Dziedzictwo polskich regionów. Jedna*

Polska? Dawne i nowe zróżnicowania społeczne. PAN 2007. Wroclaw: Wydawnictwo WAM.

Jaźwińska, Ewa, Okólski Marek (eds.). 2001. *Ludzie na huśtawce. Migracje między peryferiami Polski a Zachodu.* Warszawa: Scholar.

Jenkins, Richard. 1997. *Rethinking Ethnicity. Arguments and Explorations.* London: Sage Publications.

Joppke, Christian. 2003. Citizenship between de- and re-ethnicization. *European Journal of Sociology* 44:429–458.

Joly, Daniele. 2002. Odyssean and Rubicon refugees: towards a typology of refugees in the land of exile. *International Migration Review* 40(6):3–23.

Jordan, Bill, Frank Duvell. 1999. Undocumented Migrants in London. Full Research Report; Economic and Social Research Council R000236838. http://www.esrcsocietytoday.ac.uk/esrcinfocentre/viewawardpage.aspx?awardnumber=R000236838

Jordan, Bill. 2002. Migrant Polish workers in London. Mobility, Labour Markets and Prospects for Democratic Development. Paper given during conference: *Beyond Transition, Development Perspectives and Dilemmas,* Warsaw, 12/13 April.

Jordan, Bill, Franck Düvell. 2002. *Irregular Migration. The Dilemmas of Transnational Mobility.* Cheltenham: Edward Elgar.

Kaczmarczyk, Pawel, Marek Okólski. 2008. Demographic and labour market impacts of migration on Poland. *Oxford Review of Economic Policy* 24(3):600.

Kamiński, Antoni. 1988. The privatization of the state. Trends in the evolution of "real" socialist political systems. *The Asian Journal of Public Administration* 10(1):27–47.

Kantor, Ryszard. 1990. *Między zaborowem a Chicago; kulturowe konsekwencje isnienia zbiorowości imigrantow z parafii zaborowskiej w Chicago i jej kontaktów z rodzinnymi wsiami.* Warszawa: Zakład Narodowy Imienia Ossolinskich.

Kempny, Marta. 2010. *Polish Migrants in Belfast: border crossing and identity construction.* Newcastle upon Tyne: Cambridge Scholars Press.

Kicinger, Marta. 2005. Polityka emigracyjna II Rzeczypospolitej; CEFMR Working Paper, 4/2005. http://www.cefmr.pan.pl/docs/cefmr_wp_2005-04.pdf

Kieniewicz, Stefan. 1969. *The Emancipation of the Polish Peasantry.* Chicago: University of Chicago Press.

Koralewicz, Jadwiga, Marek Ziółkowski. 2003. *Mentalność Polaków. Sposoby myślenia o polityce, gospodarce i życiu społecznym 1988-2000*. Warszawa: Scholar.

Koslowski, Ronald. Migration and the democratic context. [in]: Ermek Ucarer, Donald Puchala (eds.) *Immigration into Western Societies*. London: Pinter, p. 80.

Kozłowski, Jerzy. 1992. Znaczenie emigracji politycznej dla narodu polskiego w dobie zaborów. [in]: Barbara Szydłowska-Ceglowa (red.) *Polonia w Europie*. Warszawa: PWN.

Kozek, Wiesława. 1995. Tradycje i wartości związane z pracą a przemiany rynkowe w ostatnich latach. [in]: Antoni Sułek, Józef Styk (eds.) *Ludzie i instytucje. Stawanie się ładu społecznego*. Lublin: Wyd. U MCS, pp. 187–200.

Krotofil, Joanna. 2011. 'If I am to be a Muslim, I have to be a good one'. Polish migrant women embracing Islam and reconstructing identity in dialogue with self and others. [in]: Katarzyna Górak-Sosnowska (ed.) *Muslims in Poland and Eastern Europe. Widening the European Discourse on Islam*. Warszawa: University of Warsaw.

Kucharczyk, Jacek (red). 2013. *Nic o nas bez nas. Partycypacja obywatelska Polaków w Wielkiej Brytanii*. Warszawa: Instytut Spraw Publicznych.

Kula, Marcin. 1999. Polonia to najpierw ludzie a dopiero potem Polonia. *Przegląd Polonijny* 25(1):11–23.

Lemos, Sara, Jonathan Portes. 2008. The impact of migration from the new European Union Member States on native workers. Department for Work and Pensions. June, 2008. http://www.dwp.gov.uk/asd/asd5/wp52.pdf

Lencznarowicz, Jan. 2000. Wyobraźnia polityczna polskiej emigracji niepodległościowej po II wojnie światowej. Zarys tematu. [in]: Jan E. Zamojski (ed.) *Migracje polityczne XX wieku. Migracje i społeczeństwo 4*. Warszawa: Neriton, pp. 65–85.

Lencznarowicz, Jan. 2005. Postać Stanisława Mikołajczyka w mitologii politycznej polskiej emigracji pojałtańskiej. [in]: Adam Walaszek, Krzysztof Zamorski (eds.) *Historyk i historia. Studia dedykowane pamięci Prof. Mirosława Francicia*. Krakow: Historia Iagiellonica, pp. 237–259.

Lévi-Strauss, Claude. 1967. The story of Asdiwal. [in]: Edmund Leach (ed.) *The Structural Study of Myth and Totemism*. London: Tavistock Publications Limited, pp. 1–47.

Lévi-Strauss, Claude. 1963. The structural study of myth. [in]: Claire Jacobson, Brooke Grundfest Schoepf (trans.) *Structural Anthropology*. London: Basic Books, Inc., p. 229.

Levitt, Peggy. 2001. Transnational migration: taking stock and future directions. *Global Networks* 1(3):195–216.

Levitt, Peggy, N. Glick Schiller. 2004. Conceptualizing simultaneity: a transnational social field perspective on society. *International Migration Review* 38(3):1009.

Lewicki, Stanisław. 1960. Polityczna czy zarobkowa. Orzeł Biały nr 43.

Lopez, Rodriguez Maria. 2010. Migration and a quest for 'normalcy'. Polish migrant mothers and the capitalization of meritocratic opportunities in the UK. *Social Identities: Journal for the Study of Race, Nation and Culture*. 16(3):339–358.

Los, Maria, Andrzej Zybertowicz. 2000. *Privatizing the Police-State: The Case of Poland*. London: Palgrave; Zybertowicz, Andrzej. 2002. Demokracja jako fasada: przypadek III RP. [in]: Edmund Mokrzycki, Andrzej Rychard, Andrzej Zybertowicz (eds.) *Utracona dynamika? O niedojrzałości polskiej demokracji*. Warszawa: Wydawn.

Mach, Zdzisław. 1993. *Symbols, Conflict and Identity*. Albany: SUNY Press; Mach, Zdzisław. 1998. *Niechciane miasta. Migracja i tożsamość społeczna*. Kraków: Universitas.

Mach, Zdzisław. 2005. Polish diaspora. [in]: Matthew J. Gibney, Randall Hansen (eds.) *Immigration and Asylum. From 1900 to the Present*. Santa Barbara: ABC Clio.

Malkki, Liisa H. 1997. National geographic: the rooting of peoples and the territorialization of national identity among scholars and refugees. [in]: Akhil Gupta, James Ferguson (red.) *Culture, Power, Place. Explorations in Critical Anthropology*. Durham/London: Duke University Press.

Mandelbaum, David. 1965. Alcohol and Culture. *Current Anthropology* 6(3):281–293.

Martiniello, Marco. 1993. Ethnic leadership, ethnic communities' political powerless and the state in Belgium. *Ethnic and Racial Studies* 16(2):236–255.

McGhee, Derek, Sue Heath, Paulina Trevena. 2012. Dignity, happiness and being able to live a 'normal life' in the UK—an examination of post-accession Polish migrants' transnational autobiographical fields. *Social Identities* 18(6):711–727.

Micińska, Magdalena. 2004. Zdrada, dezercja czy jedyna szansa? Dyskusje wokół tzw. emigracji talentów z ziem polskich w drugiej połowie XIX wieku i na początku XX w. [in]: Jan E. Zamojski (red.) *Migracje i Społeczeństwo t.* Warszawa: IH PAN, MWSH-P, Wydawnictwo Neriton, pp. 91–109.

Millard, Frances. 1994. Nationalism in Poland. [in] Paul Latawski (ed.), *Contemporary Nationalism in East Central Europe.* London: Macmillan.

Miller, Mark, Stephen Castles. 1993. *The Age of Migrations. International Population Movements in the Contemporary World.* London: Macmillan.

Morawska, Ewa. 1978. Motyw awansu w systemie wartości polskich imigrantów w Stanach Zjednoczonych na przełomie wieków. O potrzebie relatywizmu kulturowego w badaniach historycznych. *Przegląd Polonijny* 4(1):1978.

Morawska, Ewa. 1985. *For Bread with Butter: The Life-Worlds of East Central Europeans in Johnston, Pennsylvania 1890-1940.* Cambridge: Cambridge University Press.

Morawska, Ewa. 1998. *The Malleable Homo Sovieticus: Transnational Entrepreneurs in Post-Communist East Europe.* EUI Working Papers. RSC No 98/53. Badia Fiesolana, San Domenico 1998.

Morawska, Ewa. 2001. The new-old transmigrants, their transnational lives and ethnicization: a comparison of 19th/20th situations. [in]: W. John Mollenkopf, Gery Gerstle (red.) *Immigrants, Civic Culture and Modes of Political Incorporation.* New York: Sage and Social Science Council, pp. 175–211.

Morawska, Ewa 2001. Structuring migration: the case of Polish income-seeking travelers to the west. *Theory and Society* 30(1):47–80.

Morawska, Ewa. 2002. Transnational Migration in the Enlarged European Union: a perspective from the East and Central Europe. [in]: Jan Zielonka (ed.). *Europe Unbound.* Oxford: Oxford University Press.

Mostwin, Danuta. 1981. *The Transplanted Family: A Study of Social Adjustment of the Polish Immigrant Family to the United States After the Second World War.* North Stratford: Ayer Co Pub.

Mostwin, Danuta. 1986. Emigrant polski w Stanach Zjednoczonych 1974-1984. [in]: Mieczyslawa Paszkiewicz, Prace Kongresu Kultury (eds.) *Polskie więzi kulturowe na obczyźnie.* Londyn: Polskiej na Obczyźnie, vol. 8.

Nagengast, Carole. 1991. *Reluctant Socialists, Rural entrepreneurs: Class, Culture and the Polish State.* Boulder/San Francisco/Oxford: Westview Press.

Nicholas, R. 1966. Segmentary factional political systems. [in]: Marc J. Swartz, Victor Turner, Arthur Tuden (eds.) *Political Anthropology.* Chicago: Aldine.

Nowicka, Ewa. 1999. *U nas dole i niedole – sytuacja Romów w Polsce.* Wyd; Andrzej Mirga, Nicolae Gheorghe. 1999. *Romowie w XXI wieku: studium polityczne.* Kraków: Universitas.

Okólski, Marek. 2003. The effects of political and economic transition on international migration in Central and Eastern Europe. [in]: J. Edward Taylor, Douglas S. Massey (eds.) *International Migration. Prospects and Policies.* Oxford: Oxford University Press, pp. 35–58.

Okólski, Marek. 2004. Migration trends in Central and Eastern Europe on the eve of the European Union enlargament: an overview. [in]: Agata Górny, Paolo Ruspini (eds.) *Migration in the New Europe: East-West Revisited.* Houndmills/Basingstoke/Hampshire: Palgrave Macmillan, pp. 23–48.

Okólski, Marek. 2001. The transformation of spatial mobility and new forms of international population movements: incomplete migration in central and eastern Europe. [in]: Janina W. Dacyl (ed.) *Challenges of Cultural Diversity in Europe.* Stockholm: CEIFO, pp. 57–109.

Okólski, Marek. 2006. Costs and benefits of migration for Central European countries. Center of Migration Research Working Papers. http://www.migracje.uw.edu.pl/site_media/files/007_65.pdf

Okólski, Marek, J. Salt. 2014. Polish Emigration to the UK after 2004; Why Did So Many Come? *Central and Eastern Migration Review*, December 2014, pp. 1–27.

Osumare, Halifu. 2007. *The Africanist Aesthetic in Global Hip-Hop: Power Moves.* New York: Palgrave Macmillan.

Paluch, Andrzej K. 1976. Inkluzywne i ekskluzywne rozumienie terminu "Polonia." *Przegląd Polonijny* 2(22):37–48.

Patterson, Sheila. 1964. Polish London. [in]: Ruth Glass (ed.) *London: Aspects of Change.* London: University College.

Patterson, Sheila. 1968. *Immigrants in Industry.* London: Oxford University Press for Institute of Race Relations.

Patterson, Sheila. 1977. The poles: an exile community in Britain. [in]: James L. Watson (red.) *Between Two Cultures.* Oxford: Blackwell.

Pawlak, Renata. 2004. *Polska kultura hip-hopowa.* Poznań: Wyd. Kagra; Andrzej Buda. 2012. *Historia kultury hip-hop w Polsce 1977-2013.* wyd. Niezależne.

Pilch, Andrzej (eds.). 1984. *Emigracja z ziem polskich w czasach nowożytnych i najnowszych (XVIII–XX w.).* Warszawa: Państwowe Wydawnictwo Naukowe.

Pollard, Naomi, Maria Latorre, Danny Sriskandarajah. 2008. Floodgates or turnstiles Post-EU enlargement migration flows to (and from) the UK. IPPR. http://www.ippr.org/files/images/media/files/publication/2011/0 5/floodgates_or_turnstiles_1637.pdf?noredirect=1

Portes, Jonathan, Simon French. 2005. The impact of free movement of workers from central and eastern Europe on the UK labour market: early evidence. Department of Work and Pensions report.

Praszałowicz, Dorota. 1999. Wokół mechanizmów migracji łańcuchowych. *Przegląd Polonijny* 28(4):9–40.

Rabikowska, Marta. 2010. *Social Identities: Journal for the Study of Race, Nation and Culture* 16(3):285–296.

Rabikowska, Marta. 2016. A Pole Like a Wolf to Another Pole': Class (Im)mobility and Group Resentment among Polish Immigrants in London. *International Journal of Politics, Culture and Society.*

Radzik, Tadeusz, Wiesław Śladkowski. 1996. Mit polskich wychodźców. [in]: Wojciecha Wrzesińskiego (ed.) *Polskie mity polityczne XIX i XX wieku.* Wrocław.

Radzik, Tadeusz, Władysław Śladkowski. Diaspora polska a niepodległość ojczyzny. [in]: Wojciecha Wrzesiński (ed.) Między irredentą, lojalnością a kolaboracją. O suwerenność państwową i niezależność narodową (1795–1989). Toruń 2001.

Rakowski, Marek. 2009. *Łowcy, zbieracze, praktycy niemocy.* Warszawa: Słowo/obraz/terytoria.

Reay, Diane. 1998. Rethinking social class: Qualitative perspectives on gender and social class. *Sociology* 32:259–275.

Romaniszyn, Krystyna. 1996. The invisible community: undocumented Polish workers in Athens. *New Communities* 22(2):321–333.

Romejko, Adam. 2000. Rola duszpasterstwa w kształtowaniu tożsamości polonijnej w Wielkiej Brytanii. Gdańsk: Wydawnictwo Uniwersytetu Gdańskiego.

Rutter, J. 2007. Britain's immigrants: an economic profile. IPPR. http://www.ippr.org.uk/research/teams/?id=3571&tID=3571

Ryan, Louise, Rosemary A. Sales, Mary Tilki. 2009. Recent Polish migrants in London: accessing and participating in social networks across borders. [in]: Kathy Burrell (ed.) *Polish Migration to the UK in the 'New' European Union.* Aldershot: Ashgate.

Ryan, Louise. 2010. Becoming Polish in London: negotiating ethnicity through migration. *Social Identities: Journal for the Study of Race, Nation and Culture* 16(3):359–376.

Ryan, Louise, Rosemary A. Sales, Mary Tilki, Bernadetta Siara. 2009. Family strategies and transnational migration: recent Polish migrants in London. *Journal of Ethnic and Migration Studies* 35(1):61–77.

Ryan, Louise, Alessio D'Angelo. 2011. Sites of socialisation — Polish parents and children in London schools. *Przegląd Polonijny* XXXVII(1):237–258.

Sassen, Sakia. 1991. *The Global City: New York, London, Tokyo*. Princeton: Princeton University Press.

Schneider, Jo Anne. 1990. Defining boundaries, creating contacts: Puerto Rican and Polish presentation of group identity through ethnic parades. *Journal of Ethnic Studies* 18(1):33–57.

Schwander-Sievers, Stephanie (eds). 2002. Albanian Identities. Myth, Narratives and Politics. London: C Hurst & Co Publishers Ltd.

Scott, James C. 1990. *Domination and the Art of Resistance: Hidden Transcripts*. New Haven: Yale University Press.

Siara, Bernadetta. 2013. Construction of gender in the migration space: Polish women in the UK. *GENDER. Zeitschrift für Geschlecht, Kultur und Gesellschaft [GENDER. Journal of Gender, Culture and Society]* 1:105–120.

Siara, Bernadetta. 2011. Body, gender and sexuality in recent migration of Poles to the United Kingdom. *Migration Studies: Polish Review* 1:111–128.

Smith, Anthony D. 1999. *Myths and Memories of the Nation*. Oxford: Oxford University Press.

Smith, Anthony D. 1998. *Nationalism and Modernism. A Critical Survey of Recent Theories of Nations and Nationalism*. London: Routledge.

Smith, Michael P. 2001. *Transnational Urbanism: Locating Globalization*. Oxford: Blackwell.

Smith, William E. 2005. *Hip Hop as Performance and Ritual*. Washington: CLS publications.

Soysal, Y. 1994. *The Limits of Citizenship*. Chicago: University of Chicago Press.

Spivak, Gayatri C. 1996 [1985]. Subaltern Studies. Deconstructing Historiography. [in]: Gayatri Spivak, Donna Landry, Gerald MacLean. 1996. *The Spivak Reader*. London: Routledge.

Stachura, Peter. 2000. *The Poles in Britain 1940-2000*. London: Franck Cass.

Staniewicz, Teresa. 2011. Negotiating space and contesting boundaries: the case of Polish Roma and Polish migrants. *Przegląd Polonijny* 2011(1):259–290.

Staniszkis, Jadwiga. 1991. *The Dynamics of the Breakthrough in Eastern Europe: The Polish Experience (Society and Culture in East-Central Europe)*. Los Angeles: University of California Press.

Staniszkis, J. 1998. Polityka postkomunistycznej instytucjonalizacji w perspektywie historycznej. *Studia Polityczne* 4(5):39–60.

Stenning, Alison. 2005. Where is the post-socialist working class? Working-class lives in the spaces of (post-)socialism. *Sociology* 39(5):983–999.

Stola, Dariusz. 2001. Międzynarodowa mobilność w PRL. [in:] Ewa Jaźwińska, Marek Okólski (eds.) *Ludzie na huśtawce*. Scholar: Warszawa, pp. 62–97.

Stolcke, V. 1995. Talking culture. New boundaries. New rhetorics of exclusion in Europe. *Current Anthropology* 36(1):1–24.

Stomma, Ludwik. 1986. *Antropologia wsi polskiej XIX wieku*. Warszawa: Instytut Wydawniczy Pax.

Sulima, Roch. 2000. Antropologia libacji alkoholowej. [in]: *Antropologia codzienności*. Warszawa: Wydawnictwo UJ.

Sumption Madeleine. 2009. *Social Networks and Polish Immigration to the UK*. Economics of Migration Working Paper 5 Institute_for_Public_Policy_Research.
http://www.ippr.org.uk/members/download.asp?f=%2Fecomm%2F files%2Fsocial%5Fnetworks%5Fpolish%5Fimmigration%2Epdf

Sword, Keith. 1986. Problemy adaptacji i duszpasterstwo Polaków w Wielkiej Brytanii. *Studia Polonijne* 10:270–286.

Sword, Keith. 1996. *Identity in Flux. The Polish Community in Great Britain*. London: SSEES UCL.

Szacki, Jerzy. 1987. Naród w socjologii Floriana Znanieckiego. *Przegląd Polonijny* 3:7–28.

Szacki, Jerzy. 2007. O wieczności pytań typu: "Jedna Polska?". [in]: Andrzeja Kojder (ed.) *Jedna Polska? Dawne i nowe zróżnicowania społeczne*. Kraków: WAM, Polska Akademia Nauk, pp. 31–46.

Sztompka, Piotr. 2005. *Socjologia zmian społecznych*. Kraków: Znak.

Sztompka, Piotr. 1999. *Trust: A Sociological Theory*. Cambridge: Cambridge University Press.

Sztompka, Piotr. 1993. Civilizational incompetence: the trap of post-communist societies. *Zeitschrift fur Soziologie* 22:85–95.

Szydłowska-Cegłowa, Barbara. 1992. Wstęp. [in]: Barbara Szydłowska-Cegłowa (ed.) *Polonia w Europie.* Warszawa: Polska Akademia Nauk.

Śladkowski, Wiesław. 1996. Wychodźstwo polskie—narodziny mitu. *Przegląd Humanistyczny* 1(334):201–208.

Świde-Ziemba, Hanna. 1994. Mentalność postkomunistyczna. *Kultura i Społeczeństwo* 1(3):35–50.

Svasek, Maruska. 2009. Shared history? Polish migrant experiences and the politics of display in Northern Ireland. [in]: Kathy Burrell (ed.) *Polish Migration to the UK in the 'New' European Union.* Aldershot: Ashgate.

Temple, Bogusia. 1994. *Polish Identity and Community.* Manchester: University of Manchester Occasional Papers in Sociology no 38.

Topolska, Maria B. 1999. Wprowadzenie i głos w dyskusji: bilans i perspektywy emigracji polskiej w Wielkiej Brytanii. *Przegląd Polonijny* 1:71–72.

Toruńczyk-Ruiz, Sabina. 2008. Being together or apart? Social networks and notions of belonging among recent Polish migrants in the Netherlands. CMR Working Papers. No 40/98.

Trevena, Paulina. 2011. Divided by class, connected by work. Class divisions among the new wave of Polish migrants in the UK. *Przegląd Polonijny.* 1(139):71–96.

Triandafyllidou, Anna. 2000. The political discourse on immigration in southern Europe: a critical analysis. *Journal of Community and Applied Social Psychology* 10(5):373–389.

Triandafyllidou, Anna (ed.). 2006. *Contemporary Polish Migration in Europe. Complex Patterns of Movement and Settlement.* Lewiston: Edwin Mellen Press.

Turner, Victor. 1995. *The Ritual Process: Structure and Anti-Structure.* New York: Hawthorne.

Turner, Victor, Edith Turner. 1978. *Image and Pilgrimage in Christian Culture.* New York: Columbia University Press.

Walaszek, Adam 1988. *Robotnicy polscy, praca i związki zawodowe w Stanach Zjednoczonych Ameryki 1880-1922.* Wrocław: Ossolineum.

Walaszek, Adam. 2001. Polska diaspora. [in]: Jan E. Zamojski (ed.) *Diaspory. Migracje i społeczeństwo,* vol. 6.

Walaszek, Adam. 2003. Migracje w historii Europy: kilka uwag niekoniecznie nowych. *Przegląd Polonijny* 29(3):4–35.

Werbner, Pnina, Muhammad Anwar. 1991. *Black and Ethnic Leaderships in Britain. The Cultural Dimension of Political Action.* London: Routledge.

Weber Eugen, Joseph. 1976. *Peasants into Frenchmen: The Modernization of Rural France, 1880–1914*. Stanford: Stanford University Press.

Wciórka, Bogdan. 2008. Społeczeństwo obywatelskie 1998-2008 (Civil society 1988-2008). "Opinie i diagnozy" ("Opinions and diagnoses") no 8. Warszawa.

Wedel, Janine. 1986. *The Private Poland: An Anthropological Look at Everyday Life*. New York: Columbia University Press.

White, Anne. 2011a. *Polish Families and Migration since EU Accession*. Bristol: Policy Press, University of Bristol.

White, Anne. 2011b. The mobility of Polish families in the West of England. Translocalism and attitudes to return. *Przegląd Polonijny*. 1:11–32.

Vertovec, Stephen. 1999. Conceiving and researching transnationalism. *Ethnic and Racial Studies* 22(2):447–462.

Vertovec, Stephen. 2007. The Emergence of Superdiversity in Britain. New Yorkshire: COMPAS; Super-diversity and its implications. *Ethnic and Racial Studies* 30(6):1024–1054.

Vertovec, Stephen. *Transnationalism*. London: Taylor & Francis.

Zbyszewski, Wacław. 1949. Bilans emigracji w Anglii. *Kultura* 4(12):201.

Znaniecka, Lopata Helena. 1976. *Polish Americans: Status Competition in an Ethnic Community*. New York: Prentice Hall.

Znaniecki, Florian. 1931. Studia nad antagonizmem do obcych. *Kwartalnik Socjologiczny* 1930/31 nr. 2-4 Poznań.

Znaniecki, Florian, William I. Thomas. 1976. *Chłop polski w Ameryce*. Warszawa: PWN.

Zubrzycki, Jerzy. 1956. *Polish Immigrant in Britain. A Study of Adjustment*. Oxford: Oxford University.

Zubrzycki, Jerzy. 1988. *Soldiers and Peasants. The Sociology of Polish Migration*. The Second M.B. Grabowski Memorial Lecture. London: Orbis Books.

Zubrzycki, Genevieve. 2006. *The Crosses of Auschwitz. Nationalism and Religion in Post-Communist Poland*. Chicago/London: The University of Chicago Press, pp. 44–45.

Zieliński, Andrzej. 1994. Polish culture — wet or dry? *Contemporary Drug Problems* 21:329–340.

Ziólkowski, Maciej. 2001. Changes of interests and values of polish society. [in]: Michal Buchowski, Edouard Conte, Carole Nagengast (eds.) *Poland Beyond Communism. "Transition" in Critical Perspective*. Fribourg: Fribourg University Press, pp. 161–179 (169).

ibidem-Verlag / *ibidem* Press
Melchiorstr. 15
70439 Stuttgart
Germany

ibidem@ibidem.eu
ibidem.eu